THE ROMA
A MINORITY IN EUROPE

THE ROMA
A MINORITY IN EUROPE

HISTORICAL, POLITICAL AND
SOCIAL PERSPECTIVES

Edited by
Roni Stauber and Raphael Vago

C E U PRESS

Central European University Press
Budapest • New York

Associate Editor: Beryl Belsky

Published in 2007 by

Central European University Press
An imprint of the
Central European University Share Company
Nádor utca 11, H-1051 Budapest, Hungary
Tel: +36-1-327-3138 or 327-3000
Fax: +36-1-327-3183
E-mail: ceupress@ceu.hu
Website: www.ceupress.com

400 West 59th Street, New York NY 10019, USA
Tel: +1-212-547-6932
Fax: +1-646-557-2416
E-mail: mgreenwald@sorosny.org

ISBN 978-963-7326-86-8 cloth
ISBN 978-963-386-760-0 paperback

Library of Congress Cataloging-in-Publication Data

The Roma : a minority in Europe : historical, political and social perspectives / edited by
Roni Stauber and Raphael Vago.
    p. cm.
Papers from a conference held in Dec. 2002 at Tel Aviv University.
Includes bibliographical references and index.
ISBN 978-9637326868 (cloth)
1. Romanies–Europe–History. 2. Europe–Ethnic relations. 3. Romanies–Nazi persecution. I.
Stauber, Roni. II. Vago, Raphael. III. Title.

DX145.R586 2007
305.891'49704–dc22

2007001304

CONTENTS

ACKNOWLEDGMENTS

Throughout the planning and editing of this volume we were fortunate in having the help and counsel of our colleagues from the Stephen Roth Institute, Tel Aviv University. Prof. Dina Porat, head of the Institute, supported the project from the outset and we are indebted to her for her advice and encouragement. Beryl Belsky, assisted by Yocheved Welber, did an excellent job of preparing the book and bringing it to publication.

We wish to express our gratitude to the Friedrich Naumann Foundation, Jerusalem, which supported us in organizing both the conference and publishing the book. Thanks go especially to Dr. Burckhard Blanke, resident representative of the foundation at the time the conference was being prepared, his successor Dr. René Klaff, and the current project director Dr. Hans-Georg Fleck, as well as to our dear friends Bettina Malka-Igelbusch, head of the Israel Desk, and Anne Köhler.

Many thanks to Ambassador Avi Primor, formerly vice president of Tel Aviv University and currently head of European Studies at Herzliya's Interdisciplinary Center, who encouraged our efforts to organize the conference on the Roma and the visit of Roma camp survivors to Israel.

Finally, we would like to express our appreciation to the staff of CEU Press, and particularly Assistant Editor Linda Kunos, who coordinated publication of the volume, and Copy Editor Michael Blumenthal.

FOREWORD

The genocide of the Roma (Gypsies) at the hands of Nazi Germany and some of its allies, known in Romani as the *Porrajmos* (catastrophe, very much parallel to the Hebrew term *Shoah*), has still not been properly and exhaustively researched. Indeed, some historians even deny that it was a genocide. However, if one takes seriously the definition of genocide in the 1948 Convention on the Crime of Genocide, there should be little doubt on that point. The definition speaks of an intent to destroy an ethnic, national or racial group as such, in part or completely. If there is anything one can learn from the historical work done until now (2005), it can be stated as a fact that there was a Nazi intent to annihilate the Gypsies as a separate ethnicity, in part. Nazi allies, such as the Arrow Cross regime in Hungary (the Nyilas), and the Antonescu dictatorship in Romania, as well as the Slovak puppet regime, joined this policy, in the main. Clearly, it was a genocide.

The present volume, the result of a conference held at Tel Aviv University, is yet another important attempt to explore this issue. There is, of course, a continuous effort by some historians, as well as representatives of the Roma themselves, to include their suffering with that of the Jews by using the term Holocaust (together with *Porrajmos*) in relation to the genocide of the Roma. In my view, this is a basic error: every genocidal act is specific and directed toward a certain group, and throwing them together is a disservice to the memory of the victims. In this case, the Roma were not Jews, and they were not destined to be treated like the Jews. There was a distinction between nomadic and settled Roma, as clearly stated in German documents, although in practice this was not always followed. Nomadic Roma were to be treated like Jews, that is, murdered, while settled Roma were to be dealt with like the local population. One can see this not only in Poland and the occupied Soviet Union, but, as shown in this volume, in the Romanian case. The fact that the murderers of the Roma and the Jews were usually the same individuals, and that in many cases the Germans placed Polish and Austrian Roma together with the Jews, should not mislead us. Soviet POWs were also sometimes murdered together with Roma and Jews. They were among the total number of Soviet POW victims (some 3.2 million, according to some historians). In fact, one can say that Nazi Germany was responsible for three genocides: of the Poles, the Roma, and the Jews—for different reasons, often but not always by different means, and with different results, and by the same people, at the same time. What unites these three genocides is not only National Socialist policy but also, and most importantly, the suffering of the victims—and one must emphasize, that the suffering was the same. Jews did not suffer more, or less, than Roma, Russians, Poles, or anyone else who was subject to torture and murder. Nor is it a matter of statistics. Historians differ as to the number of Roma killed, directly or indirectly, in Nazi-controlled Europe. Some tend to think that about 90,000, out of an estimated one million Roma in Nazi-controlled Europe, died. I would put the number much higher, at about 150,000, or 15 percent of the total number of Roma. However, such numbers hide, rather than illuminate, the tragedy of individuals, families and communities. The present volume directs our attention not only to the overall picture in the different countries, but also to individual stories, to the fate of families and communities, and to the destruction of traditions and ways of life.

There is yet another difference between the Jews and the Roma: the Jews rebuilt their communities, established an independent state, and received partial restitution of their properties. The Roma did not; they never had anything of great material value that could be restituted. They are still discriminated against, persecuted, disregarded and denied equality, not everywhere but in many places in Europe. Their case should be defended, not out of pity but because they are human beings who should be equal to everyone else, and because they have the same inalienable rights as the rest of us.

Genocide, or genocidal massacre, has been a part of humanity since time immemorial and it is still with us today. Only by convincing large numbers of people in democratic countries that such acts should be prevented can we raise our heads. The genocide of the Roma, an ancient people with a unique cultural heritage, is a tragedy for all mankind. The present volume deals with parts of that tragedy; it is hoped that other institutions and countries will follow this example. The fact that the conference took place in Israel, at a major academic venue, is a positive sign: Jews and their state have an obligation to remember, not only their own tragedy but that of others as well.

Yehuda Bauer
Yad Vashem
November 2005

INTRODUCTION

This volume stems from a conference organized by the Stephen Roth Institute in December 2002 at Tel Aviv University and was the first international conference held in Israel on the Roma. Participants held in-depth discussions on various aspects relating to the history and current situation of the Roma in Europe. Prior to the conference, the editors of this volume, with the support of the German foundation Remembrance, Responsibility and Future, initiated a visit to Israel by a group of ten Romani Nazi camp survivors from Hungary, accompanied by representatives of the second generation. The group, which was organized and escorted by Dr. Katalin Katz, met with high school students and educators and visited Yad Vashem as well as other memorial institutes and sites. In addition, they participated in a conference session dedicated to testimonies of Roma camp survivors.

The term Roma appearing in the title of this volume refers to people generally known as Gypsies. The term only became common in recent decades, as part of the continuing democratic and liberal process that Europe has been undergoing. The word 'gypsy,' or *Zigeuner*, is associated with negative stereotypes rooted in European culture; hence its use in public discourse and in the media has ceased, although it is still employed frequently in daily life. The term Roma is also linked to the struggle for the acceptance of Gypsies as equal citizens in Europe with a unique ethnic identity. Nevertheless, since 'Roma' became more prevalent only after World War II, some authors dealing with Gipsy history before and during that period, including several of those included here, prefer to use the term 'Gipsy.'

It should also be noted that the questions of who is a Roma and the relationship between the various Gypsy groups are part of an ongoing debate about the ethnic definition and ethnic boundaries of the 'Gypsies,' themes widely discussed in this volume.

The essays included here present some of the main issues resulting from the encounter between the Roma and the surrounding European society, from the time of their arrival in Medieval Europe until today. The history of their persecution, and in particular, their genocide during the Nazi era, occupies a central place in this volume. Significantly, some authors did not limit themselves to one historical period, but sought to emphasize the continual history of prejudice and persecution, which reached a peak during the Nazi era and did not cease with the end of the war.

Shulamith Shahar's article focuses on the perception of the Gypsies in Early Modern Europe. She shows how the discourse even at that time exhibited prejudices and deep dislike of the Gypsies, who were widely perceived as an integral part of the vagrant criminal underworld and classified as a 'rabble' because of their unacceptable way of life. Shahar's chapter can perhaps serve as a road map to the emergence of modern 'Gypsy' (Roma) stereotypes, providing a better understanding of negative attitudes toward them in the modern era. It traces two distinct perceptions dating back to Early Modern Europe: their image as a distinct ethnic group, and their representation as a mob of mixed origins. Shahar demonstrates that these views largely fashioned the attitude of the surrounding European society toward the Gypsies and to a certain degree determined their fate.

Peter Widmann discusses the influence of criminal biology theories which emerged at the end of 19th century on Nazi theoreticians, and consequently on the persecution of the Roma. Focusing on Germany, he shows how in the 1920s the concept of 'born criminal' was fused with social stigmatization of the Roma as criminals. Following dissemination of the concept that the roots of crime lay in heredity, a 'restless way of life' also viewed as an inborn characteristic, came to be associated with criminality. This approach, claims Widmann, undermined the traditional policy which sought to force the Roma and other 'travelers' to abandon their nomadism and opened the way for much more drastic means, such as sterilization and murder. It was, however, the encounter of criminal biology with other ideas absorbed by the Nazis, such as racial theory and social Darwinism, which paved the way to the genocide of the Roma, Sinti and other 'travelers.'

Indeed, the depiction of Gypsies, Roma and Sinti as well as other travelers in Germany as criminals in the first years of the Nazi regime actually furthered a perception held by German bureaucrats prior to 1933. As shown by Michael Zimmermann, measures against Roma, Sinti and other 'travelers' in Germany escalated in the first years of the Nazi regime. In a comparative study, Zimmermann analyzes similarities and differences between the 'Final

Solution' of the Jews in Europe, the policy of annihilating the Gypsies and the murder of millions of Soviet prisoners. A central question in his essay is whether the Nazi 'Gypsy policy' might be considered 'genocide.' Zimmermann relates to issues such as ideology and perceptions, mental predisposition in favor of mass extermination and the intensity of persecution. While he reveals a number of similarities between the Nazi policies of destruction of these three groups, he also discerns significant differences that stem from the varying patterns of hostility toward Russians, Jews and Gypsies and in the severity of their persecution. Relating to the 1948 UN definition of genocide, Zimmerman characterizes the annihilation of the Jews and the Gypsies, but not the death of millions of Russian war prisoners, as genocide. Nonetheless he points out a major distinction between Nazi attitudes toward the Jews and the Gypsies, which affected implementation of their destruction.

Zimmermann notes that the Nazi policy of persecution of the Gypsies in Europe was inconsistent, influenced by factors such as differing racial theories toward various segments of the Gypsy population, their categorization as travelers versus sedentary people, and the degree of fanaticism of Nazi bureaucrats in the various parts of Europe, as well as the level of hatred of local bureaucrats who exploited the war to get rid of Gypsies and other vagabonds.

Zimmermann's analysis of Nazi policy toward the Gypsies in Europe is followed by case studies of their persecution in Austria, Hungary and Romania. The role of local bureaucrats in intensifying the hounding of Roma and Sinti is revealed in Erika Thurner's essay about their fate in Austria. Nazi measures against the Roma and Sinti after the *Anschluss* had already been formulated as ideas prior to 1938, claims Thurner. This was a result of deep animosity toward the Gypsies, which had become entrenched among Austrians over the centuries. After the *Anschluss* the local Nazi administration imposed even harsher measures on the Roma and Sinti in Austria, and in the Burgenland in particular, than those implemented initially in Germany. The local authorities, the police and other law enforcement agencies carried out internment, as well as deportation to the east, with the assistance of health, welfare and labor bureaus. Fewer than one-third of Austrian Gypsies survived the war. Nevertheless, discrimination against them, and even persecution, has continued. Not only were the perpetrators not punished, but the Gypsies' suffering during the war was not officially recognized and in order to avoid paying them compensation the authorities frequently portrayed them as swindlers. This attitude has hardly changed and awareness in Austria of the Nazi policy of genocide of the Roma and Sinti remains slight.

xvi

In Hungary, too, the Nyilas (Arrow Cross), the local Nazi collaborator, played a major role in the internment, deportation, and murder of Hungarian Roma in the last months of the war, while the surrounding society remained indifferent. Katalin Katz focuses on the Komárom camp, the main site in Hungary for the concentration of Roma in the last stages of the war. The author based her study on a series of interviews with 57 survivors, which exposes the suffering of the Roma in Hungary, as well as in the concentration camps of Germany, during this period. Persecution of Hungarian Roma continued after the liberation when they returned to their devastated villages. Using various theories and methodologies, Katz seeks to trace the construction of historical memory among the Roma. Collective memory was absent, denied due to the attitude of both the authorities and society since the war, as well as to Romani cultural codes relating to memory of suffering and persecution. By letting the victims speak and by combining fragments of memory, Katz contributes to a reconstruction of the collective memory of suffering among the Roma in Hungary.

The deportation of Romanian Roma to Transnistria and the death of some 25,000 of them was a lacuna in Romanian historiography, which Viorel Achim fills in his study. The author, one of the few academics in post-1989 Romania studying the fate of the Roma during World War II, was a member of the International Commission of Historians on the Holocaust in Romania. As such, he represents a growing awareness among the Romanian public of the cruelty displayed by the Antonescu regime toward the Roma and their fate, a topic that was taboo for generations. Achim's approach is to examine the attitude of Romanian society to the persecutions, and ultimately the deportation of some 45,000 Romanian Roma to Transnistria, known until now only as the killing fields of a significant part of Romanian Jewry. As source material, the author brings numerous appeals from various segments of the Romanian population against the anti-Gypsy policies of the Antonescu regime. While he leaves moral judgment to the reader, he demonstrates that Romanian society, especially in the small towns and villages, exhibited humanitarianism, though perhaps for utilitarian reasons, toward a certain type of Roma—those who had settled and were known individually to the local people as an integral part of the local economy or entertainment scene. This was in contrast to their attitude toward migrant Roma, who remained a faceless rabble onto which classical stereotypes of the Gypsy were projected.

Questions of ethnic definition and the construction of ethnic-national identity constitute principal issues of this volume. Involving complex subjects, such as collective memory, myth making and social constructionism, they have triggered intense debate among researchers dealing with Romani studies. As noted above in Shahar's article, the question of whether the Gypsies were an ethnic group or a motley group of individuals from various nations was raised as early as the Middle Ages and in Early Modern Europe, thereafter affecting their fate. Gilad Margalit and Yaron Matras focus on identity, ethnicity and nationalism among Romani speakers in Germany. They analyze the dichotomy between two distinct self-images: those who perceive themselves part of a dispersed transnational ethnic minority; and those who, despite their cultural distinction, view themselves as Germans and reject the idea of a non-territorial collective identity. The authors discuss the efforts of the Sinti, Lovara and Roma each to define a distinct ethnic identity and its boundaries in relation to the surrounding population. As always in a discourse about ethnicity and nationalism, myths of origin, traditions of wandering and migratory waves play a major role in defining the limits of their ethnic identity and bonds with Gypsy groups in neighboring countries, as well as with other Gypsy groups in Germany. A particularly controversial issue in the polemic over ethnic identity today is the question of assimilation versus integration of the Roma into the majority of the nation state while preserving cultural distinctiveness.

The history of persecution, and especially the mass murder and destruction of communities during the Nazi era, is a major component of Romani ethnic identity and of their relations with European nations. Significant similarities exist between Jews and Roma. Roni Stauber and Raphael Vago discuss the impact of the history of persecution on the ethnic identity of Jews and Roma and its role in the process of nation building. Persecution in both cases affects the defining of symbolic ethnic boundaries. However, like Jewish national writers and political leaders in the past, Romani leaders and intellectuals understand well that basing national identity solely on traumatic events could be counterproductive to the efforts to strengthen national self-esteem and establish relations with the surrounding nations. Thus, alongside commemoration of their persecution, they stress legends that highlight the notion of bravery as part of the myths of origin and exodus. The relationship between commemoration of the Holocaust and commemoration of the *Porrajmos* (the genocide of Roma, Sinti and other 'travelers' during the Nazi era) is complex. The well-established Jewish commemoration of the Shoah has had a clear impact on Romani efforts to institute an official memory of their destruction and arouse worldwide attention to their suffering. However, Romani intellectuals and scholars reject the distinction accepted by some leading scholars of the Nazi extinction policy, between the selective murder of Gypsies in different parts of Europe and the Nazi plan to exterminate the entire Jewish people. The polemic has gone beyond historical evidence to include questions relating to morality, hierarchy of the 'victims,' 'Jewish exclusivity' and discrimination. As in the case of the Jews, remembrance of the Romani tragedy during the war has important implications for their present place in Europe and for their future. The search for identity runs through a definition of origins and historical destiny to forms of modern political activism.

Discrimination and persecution of the Roma persisted in the postwar era. During the communist period, violence against them was not a widespread phenomenon, but discrimination against them continued. Following the collapse of the communist regimes, violence against the Roma increased, as did explicit racist and discriminatory action, both official and unofficial. Together, Romani representatives and human rights activists began a struggle to improve their socio-economic and civic status. Two chapters are devoted to the post-communist realities in Central and Eastern Europe: Eva Sobotka in the context of human rights and Roma policy formulation, and Pál Tamás in Central European policy toward the Roma. The bitter legacy of the communist regimes' treatment of the Roma, a topic that has come under scrutiny in the past few years, constitutes a starting point for a discussion of post-1989 developments. Both studies emphasize the linkage between changing patterns of European integration—expansion of the EU and efforts of cooperation and integration of other bodies—and their influence on Romani self-perceptions and political and social activism. Focusing on the Czech Republic, Slovakia and Poland, Sobotka distinguishes between 'human rights policy' and 'human rights politics,' analyzing the influence of international politics on changes in policy making at the state level. She outlines the development of Roma representation on the national level, a growing trend since 1989, based on the emergence of civil society in the respective countries, and the new legal structures related to ethnic and minority representation. Tamás deals with the growing public debate in Central Europe over the status of the Roma in light of the integration of these states into the EU. Using a sociological approach, he analyzes the attitude of various elite groups toward the Roma and explains how Central European Romani NGOs, supported by Western organizations, monitored Western government attitudes and adjusted their demands accordingly. Thus, the Romani insistence on adhering to a 'common European standard'—a perception that developed over the 1990s—ensured that their plight appeared on the agenda of the committees of the Council of Europe and the European Parliament. Nevertheless, he points out that since accession to the EU the ability to impose changes from outside has weakened and it is not yet clear through which channels and tools pressure can be exerted with the intensity observed in the debates prior to integration.

The editors trust that this volume, like the conference preceding it, will contribute to greater awareness and knowledge of the unique history, culture and identity, as well as the current circumstances, of the Roma in Europe.

Roni Stauber and Raphael Vago
Stephen Roth Institute
Tel Aviv University
November 2005

Postscript

Shortly before publication of this volume, we learned that Michael Zimmerman had passed away. Professor Zimmerman was a leading expert on the fate of the Roma during World War II. His untimely death is a great loss to academic research in this field.

RELIGIOUS MINORITIES, VAGABONDS AND GYPSIES IN EARLY MODERN EUROPE

SHULAMITH SHAHAR

INTRODUCTION

Western Europe was made up of diverse tribes and ethnic groups, which set-tled there at different times.[1] Historians generally concur that nationalist ide-ology came into being in Europe only in the 18th century, but they disagree over when national consciousness arose. Many historians of the Middle Ages maintain that it appeared quite early. Marc Bloch suggested there was na-tional consciousness in England, France and Germany as early as 1100. Ac-cording to others (Johan Huizinga, George Coulton), it had existed since the 14th century in Germany, France and England, as well as in Spain, Hungary, Scotland and the Italian states. Some historians of the Reformation in Ger-many emphasize the role of national consciousness in the acceptance of the Reformation in Germany, although Germany was made up of many separate political entities—i.e., in the sense that Germanism stood up to the exploita-tive papacy.[2]

Other historians categorically reject the idea that national consciousness emerged before the 18th century. A few even deny the existence of nations before that time, claiming there were only ethnic communities. Some main-tain that even in the 18th century national consciousness was limited to the educated elite and reached wider social strata only in the 19th century. Eugene Webber's study of French nationality perceives the emergence among the peasantry of a national identity and a consciousness of belonging to the French nation only during World War I, and stresses the physical, political and cultural isolation of the typical French village.[3]

The question of the rise of national consciousness, however, lies be-yond the parameters of the present discussion. The issue to be addressed when considering the Gypsies as a group is, on the one hand, the demands made by the ruling power on different ethnic groups, as well as the relations between them and the group that emerged in the course of history as the dominant ethnic community and, on the other hand, the attitude toward 'strangers' regarded as members of a different nationality or ethnic group. This essay will discuss the role of ethnicity *vis-à-vis* religion in creating barriers and hostility between distinct groups in Early Modern Europe. In this context, it will further seek to analyze various European perceptions of the Gypsies as a distinct group, their depiction as an ethnic group as opposed to denial of their ethnicity, and attitudes considering them a rabble of mixed national origins.

ETHNICITY, RELIGIOUS CONFLICTS AND XENOPHOBIA

During the Middle Ages and the Early Modern period, some ethnic groups continued to speak their own languages without hindrance, and to maintain their distinct traditions. In France—regarded as the prime example by proponents of the rise of national consciousness in the late Middle Ages—people in the Early Modern period still spoke, in addition to French, the official language, Flemish, Breton, Gascon and Basque, as well as various regional dialects. (Provencal had lost its status as an official language and declined even as a literary language in the 16th century.) In Alsace and Lorraine, which until 1648 acknowledged the sovereignty of the German emperor, the population spoke various French dialects. Albanians who settled in the kingdom of Naples in the late 15th century went on speaking Albanian. During the Reformation, Huguenots who had left France and settled in East Prussia continued to speak French and kept up some of their traditions. The Hutterites (an Anabaptist sect), who had migrated to Moravia, persisted in speaking German.

Thus, the Gypsies were by no means the only group to speak their own language. As Robert Bartlett has shown, the language question and ethnic tensions arose on the frontiers of Latin Europe, in the territories that had been conquered during the High Middle Ages. The appointment of a foreign clergyman who did not speak the local language annoyed the populace. This happened, for example, when a parish priest who knew no Welsh was posted to Wales, or to Ireland, where he spoke no Gaelic, or to East Germany, where he was unfamiliar with the local Slavic language, or to Bohemia, where he spoke no Czech. (Similar tensions, tinged with xenophobia, between the local populace and the conquerors or new settlers also arose in eastern and central Europe.)

These frictions increased in the 14th century, manifested by discrimination against the local populace within the municipal administration, and, at times, in admission to guilds. Municipal councils in the cities of Prussia issued orders restricting positions in the town councils to men of Germanic descent. Such statutes, known as the 'Deutschtum paragraph,' persisted in Prussia till the 17th century. In certain cities some guilds refused to accept apprentices of Slavic origin, in addition to illegitimate offspring, children of shepherds and others. In certain cities of Ireland and Wales, the local population was barred, not only from municipal posts and membership in the guilds, but even from citizenship. At the same time statutes were issued to prevent English settlers assimilating with the Irish. The so-called Statutes of Kilkenny of 1366 prohibited marriage between English settlers and Irish persons; the settlers were commanded to speak English, to ride on saddles unlike the Irish, to dress like Englishmen and to give their children English names. Moreover, within the Pale, no Irish person could hold church property or join a monastery.[4]

Spain was also a frontier region of Latin Europe. Its re-conquest from the Muslims and subsequent colonization went on for some five hundred years, ending in 1492 with Spain adjoining Muslim Africa. Discrimination against Jews and Muslims who had converted to Catholicism, and whose exclusion was part of the official ideology, was considerably more severe than discrimination against the local population in other frontier regions, and converted Muslims were eventually expelled. By and large, however, except in border regions, ethnic and language differences did not make for barriers between inhabitants of diverse local identities, who were all subjects of the same sovereign, although an inhabitant of one region might feel strange in another region of the same realm. Thus, in 1608, when Pierre de Lancre was sent by the *parlement* of Bordeaux to France's Basque region to investigate residents' complaints against local witches, the place and the inhabitants struck him as savage and alien, as strange as foreign countries.[5] Yet the local population's legal position as French subjects was no different from that of the inhabitants of the Île-de-France. Differences in social status, privileges and duties were based on people's class and/or corporation, as well as gender, but not on ethnic identity.

The 16th and 17th centuries saw large-scale migrations. Protestants driven from Catholic cities in Germany, or from entire regions (such as the Tyrol), or who chose to leave a place where they were subject to restrictions, migrated mainly to Protestant cities. But there was also migration from one country to another. Protestants from the southern Low Countries moved to the United Provinces of Holland, to England or to the Protestant regions of Germany.

Anabaptists emigrated from Germany to Bohemia and Moravia, Huguenots from France to Prussia and other Protestant countries. If newcomers were subjected to restrictions in their new countries, or were expelled from them at a later stage, it was due to their affiliation with a different church, not to their ethnic 'otherness.' When Mary the Catholic came to the throne, Calvinists who had come to England were compelled to leave. They moved on to Lutheran Sweden and Denmark, where they were accepted, though not without restrictions.[6] When the Anabaptists were expelled from England in 1527 during the reign of Elizabeth, and from Bohemia and Moravia in 1622, on orders from the Hapsburg emperors, it was on account of their Anabaptist faith, not their ethnic foreignness.[7]

There was also a migration of merchants (who decided to stay in a country), of skilled craftsmen, whose specialty was in demand in the country in which they settled, and of suppliers, bankers, physicians and scholars, who clustered around the rulers' courts, where some of them became advisors and office holders. Some became 'citizens,' and were thus exempt from the restrictions placed on strangers (mainly the right to bequeath and inherit property). Yet even they were distinguished, at least for the first generation, from the native population. Public attitudes toward them changed according to the circumstances—political and socio-economic—and did not always match the official position. Xenophobic expression proliferated both in scholarly discourse and in popular opinion in times of economic hardship, or of fear of enemies, when strangers were suspected of being spies since some of them had actually come from enemy countries (e.g., Protestants who immigrated to England from France and Spain).

In England the central government on the whole supported foreigners who were useful to it, while the local authorities sought to restrict or even to expel them. In 1567 the city of Norwich sought to expel foreigners who had settled there, as did the city of Colchester in 1580, but the queen did not permit it.[8] In 16th century France there were immigrants from Scotland, Lorraine and Italy, with the latter especially acquiring key positions in the king's service. The Italians enjoyed the government's patronage, while the general population regarded them with fascination and admiration, on the one hand, and hostility and envy, on the other.

Concurrent with their cultural influence, an anti-Italian discourse and a negative stereotype prevailed, leading to anti-Italian riots and petitions to the Estates General to exclude them from holding government positions.[9] After the St Bartholomew's Eve massacre (1572), a group consisting of Huguenots and Catholics demanded that Italians be barred from political life and influence at court and even driven from the kingdom.[10] However, they were not expelled, nor were they driven from England where corporations sought to deport foreign merchants and craftsmen. This was in spite of the fact that the number of foreign immigrants in various countries rose steeply during the 16th and 17th centuries, arousing local national consciousness and feeling in response. As a historian of the Italian presence in France put it: "Italian immigrants accelerated the development of national feeling in its Galician, monarchist and xenophobic form."[11]

In Spain, as noted above, the course of events was different. The Jews who became Christian, some voluntarily and some under coercion, were called *Conversos,* or 'New Christians.' Muslims who had been forced to convert were known as *Moriscos.* Once they became Christian, they could no longer be regarded as religious minorities. But in Spain in the Early Modern period, unlike in the Middle Ages, it was no longer sufficient to be baptized in order to belong to the dominant community. Unified Spain, which was striving to achieve a homogenous and monolithic society, insisted on the 'purity of blood' (*limpieza de sangre*), and the blood of *Conversos* and *Moriscos* was not 'pure.' The baptismal font could not wash away the taint of their origin, and they remained 'others.'

THE GYPSIES—ETHNIC GROUP OR RABBLE OF VARIOUS NATIONS

Whereas the *Conversos* and *Moriscos* had clearly been viewed as distinct ethnic groups—whether or not it had been their ethnic 'otherness' that principally led to their persecution and expulsion—the position was not so clear-cut with regard to the Gypsies.

The definition of the Gypsies, both in learned discourse and in official statutes, had changed over the centuries and was sometimes contradictory even in the same period. In some of the first texts that described their appearance in western Europe in the early decades of the 15th century they were left unclassified. Writers referred to them as 'people,' or 'creatures,' who had turned up in the country;[12] or "a large crowd of alien vagabonds first showed up;"[13] or "there appeared ugly people whose skin was burnt black by the sun, wearing filthy clothes... The commonality calls them Tartars."[14] Other observers spoke of a 'nation' (*natio* or *gens,* in the Latin texts), or a 'people' (*Volk,* in the Germanic texts). In the first half of the 15th century the priest Andreas of Regensburg spoke of "the nation of Gypsies (*Ciganorum*), called *Cigawnar* in the vernacular."[15] Others denoted the Gypsies as "a miserable people;"[16] or "a useless people known as Gypsies."[17] In the first half of the 17th century some authors still referred to the 'people' or 'nation' of Gypsies. The German historian, geographer and chronicler of Hessen wrote of the "disorderly Gypsy nation of thieves, sorcerers and beggars,"[18] while the Swiss Johannes Guler, like his predecessors in the 15th century, described them as "a people—a wondrous and strange people."[19]

While the Gypsies were still referred to as a people or nation (often qualified as worthless), a different depiction gradually emerged in the latter half of the 16th century and eventually became dominant. Though the term 'a people' was still occasionally used, it no longer designated an ethnic group but rather a mixed rabble of individuals from various nations: "a thievish treacherous licentious people, consisting of an assembly of diverse felons."[20] Their ability to speak several languages was no longer seen as a talent, but was due to their being a gang of people of various native languages (which made them all the more dangerous).[21] It was said that they had no language of their own. They spoke an argot of swindlers and thieves; alternatively, they spoke the Wendish language.[22]

It was also suggested that there had originally been a nation of Gypsies, but that the current lot (i.e., in the 16th and 17th centuries) were not descendants of the original Gypsies who had come to western Europe in the early 15th century—those genuine Gypsies had returned to their homeland, and all that was left was a rabble of thieves.[23] The statement that this 'rabble' was composed of peoples "who are not far from us," or "are living among us"[24] (the 'genuine' ones having gone back to their homeland), meant a denial of the Gypsies' entire past, as well as all their cultural characteristics. In time, all mention of the 'genuine' Gypsies who had returned to their native land was also abandoned, and the Gypsies were depicted as an assortment of the lowest members of all nations. As the Bavarian chronicler Aventinus put it, "It is a species of the biggest thieves, the filth and refuse of various nations."[25]

Early descriptions of the Gypsies upon their appearance in western Europe emphasized their black skin as a characteristic of their ethnic identity; this feature could not be ignored even when it became commonplace to deny that they were a distinct ethnic group. The solution was to assert that their distinctive skin color was not natural. According to the Dutch Calvinist pastor Gisbert Voetius, their children were light-skinned at birth, but as they grew older they rubbed their skin with black coloring, or became sunburned[26]—that is, they were pretending to be an ethnic group with distinctive physical features. According to the 17th century English author Thomas Dekker (1570-

1632), their dirty skin color was not inborn, nor was it the result of sunburn, but was due to the fact that they painted their faces. "No red-ochre man carries a face of a more filthy complexion. Yet they are not born so, neither has the sun burnt them so, but they are painted so; yet they are not good painters either, for they do not make faces but mar faces."[27] He was quoted by his contemporary Samuel Rid.[28] Scholars concurred with this view.

In a work published in 1646, the English scientist Thomas Browne discussed at length the complexion of the Africans. He rejected the explanations put forward by his predecessors and contemporaries, arguing that the Africans' coloring, having been acquired in the distant past, had become immutable. By contrast, he described the Gypsies as 'artificial Negroes' and 'counterfeit Moors,' who 'acquire their complexion by anointing their bodies with bacon and fat substances and so exposing them to the sun." Browne criticized the various theories concerning their origin, expressing the opinion that they probably came from nearby countries, such as Wallachia, Bulgaria and Hungary. He concluded by stating that it mattered not what nation they had sprung from, since by this time they were a mixture of all nations, having taken on members in all the countries where they wandered.[29]

Browne was not the only one who was preoccupied with the Africans' black complexion. The 16th century saw the start of English colonialism: commerce with Africa was a stage in the transit of Mediterranean trade to the Atlantic, and representations of Africa and its black inhabitants made their appearance. It was an accepted fact, rooted in both the classical and biblical traditions, that the African's black coloring was immutable, and that the notion of lightening it was a metaphor for the impossible.[30] The novelty lay in the discourse about the color's origin. Among the various explanations proposed in the 16th and 17th centuries were cosmetics, God's curse on Noah's son Ham, and exposure to the fierce sun—all of which were discarded by Browne and gradually by others.

The view that became widespread and was never rejected was that the Africans had acquired their dark coloring in the distant past, and that it had become permanently fixed since then. Christian culture regarded the black color not only as ugly but as symbolizing the forces of evil (darkness), sin and death. (In Spain, Christians who sought to vilify Muslims described them as black as pitch.[31]) In the 16th century this association sharpened the distinction between 'us'(we) who are white, fair and Christian, as opposed to the 'other' who is black, ugly, evil and pagan. Black and white became typical of binary contrasts and hierarchical definitions, if not of race (modern racial theory was yet to be born), certainly of ethnicity and culture.[32]

Needless to say, the description of the Gypsies as a rabble of various nationalities pretending to be an ethnic group was hardly complimentary, yet those who denied them their ethnicity and their naturally dark complexion unwittingly weakened the contrast between them and white European nations.

The opinion which became accepted in the scholarly discourse—that the Gypsies were not an ethnic group but a rabble of vagabonds, beggars and criminals of diverse nationalities—was also expressed in the statutes of the Spanish government, although these tended to be contradictory. Some referred to an ethnic group of Gypsies which other people joined, while others did not—leaving their identity unclassified. A statute issued by Carlos II in 1685 stated: "Lest there be any doubt who may be deemed a Gypsy, we declare that any man or woman caught wearing the dress that hitherto this category of people have been known to wear, or who speaks the Jerigonza language, will be deemed a Gypsy."[33]

The inner contradiction was even more evident in the record of the debate that followed the roundup in 1749 in Spain, which led to the confinement of 9,000–10,000 Gypsies. Shortly after the operation a discussion arose about the need to free those of the detainees who possessed documents from the state authorities or the local councils where they lived, showing that they were permanent inhabitants, made their living by honest work, and were law-abiding, tax-paying and legally married. These, it was said, were 'good Gypsies,' or 'non Gypsies' (*de-noser Gitanos*). Only the bad ones, vagabonds, beggars and the like, should be kept in detention. These were labeled in the statutes as "a multitude of infamous and harmful people," or "the disreputable caste (*mala casta*) of Gypsies by birth, or a malicious usurpation of this name."[34]

King Carlos III, who in 1783 ordered the release of Gypsies still in detention, and issued the 'pragmatic sanction' intended to advance their integration in a more humane manner, was also more consistent than the authors of those statutes. He repeatedly asserted that the Gypsies were not a nation, but did not describe them as a rabble of base rogues: "I declare that those called or calling themselves Gypsies are not so by origin or nature, and that they come from no unwholesome root."[35] That is to say, they were a people following a way of life that had to be eradicated, but this was not an inborn defect of an ethnic group, and could be changed and corrected.

Did the view that the Gypsies were not a distinct ethnic group produce a change in attitude and policies toward them? As we have seen, belonging to a different ethnic group, as opposed to a different religious or Christian denomination, did not necessarily lead to restrictions and persecution. Hostility and controls occurred in particular circumstances, as for example on the frontiers of Latin Europe, or when a group competed with one of the economic sectors, or when it acquired what seemed to be excessive power (like the Italians who settled in France). The rulers did not always accede to the demands made by this or that element to restrict the foreigners, and the latter could also become subjects of the realm and thus be freed from the few and well defined restrictions placed on foreigners as such. Nevertheless, in times of economic hardship or fear of enemies, foreigners could become popular scapegoats, although they were less likely to be victimized than were socially marginal people, such as lepers (in the late Middle Ages), prostitutes, and, in times of religious fervor, homosexuals. They were certainly less liable to become scapegoats than were the Jews.

The Gypsies were an ethnic group whose appearance was strikingly different, and whose way of life resembled that of vagrants—a persecuted marginal group. Their distinct ethnicity was a feature of their image as much as were their questionable Christianity and objectionable way of life. Yet denial of their ethnicity, which was taking shape just when policies toward vagrants were becoming tougher, did not change the Gypsies' image, nor the attitude toward them. Nor was it a factor in the transition from a policy of expulsion to one of integration, even in Spain. Integration was adopted because the expulsions had failed. In all countries it also formed part of the general trend of growing governmental intervention into the lives of subjects of all classes.

Denial of the Gypsies' ethnicity and their depiction as a rabble of mixed national origins were insults added to the long-established litany of their supposed bad qualities. But it did not put an end to their perception as a different human group, even among other vagrants and beggars. The English writer Thomas Dekker, mentioned above, wrote in his pamphlet "Lanthorne and Candle Light" that the Gypsies darkened their faces with paint—that is, they pretended to be a group with distinct physical attributes. At the same time, he declared, "Look at the difference there is between a civil citizen of Dublin and a wild Irish kern, so much difference there is between one of these counterfeit Egyptians and a true English beggar."[36]

The Spaniard Cristobal Perez de Herrera was a royal physician who headed the medical services in the Spanish navy in the first two decades of the 17th century. He wrote a pamphlet in installments, advocating changes in the organization of assistance for the poor, similar to reforms instituted in other countries. Before the expulsion of the *Moriscos*, he expressed concern with the growing numbers and high birth rate of *Moriscos* and Gypsies, while "our numbers are diminishing on account of the wars."[37] He regarded the Gypsies, like the *Moriscos*, as differing from the Spanish 'us.' Similarly, Edward Hext, who served as justice of the peace in Somerset, England, wrote a report in 1596 about vagabonds and beggars in his county, referring to the Gypsies as a separate group with customs unlike those of others.[38] William Harrison (1535–93) wrote of "the English scoundrels" that "in counterfeiting the Egyptian rogues, they have devised a language among themselves which they name 'canting.'"[39]

Throughout western Europe there were people who joined the Gypsies, if only for a time—young persons who fell out with their families, deserters from various armies, adventurers and criminals on the run. There is no telling how many such cases there were. Historians differ on the subject, and it is doubtful that the sources are of much use in determining the extent of the phenomenon. It is also difficult to assess the frequency of mixed marriages, given that the Gypsies on the whole tended to keep apart from the *gadjo* (external, non-Gypsy) world, and that their purity laws greatly restricted their contacts with non-Gypsies. Denunciation of bogus Gypsies or those who joined them in the 16th–17th centuries came at a time when anger regarding beggars and vagrants, as well as legislation against them, was increasing. It seems that the denunciations indicate less the large numbers of Gypsy impostors than anxiety about the spread of 'Gypsyness'—i.e., a way of life characterized by vagrancy, no fixed abode and lack of regular work in the service of a master.

In 2002 the historian Brian Reynolds published research that integrated a study of the Gypsies in Early Modem England with one of the criminal world. He argued that the actual number of Gypsies in England was quite small and that they were wholly assimilated into the criminal world, its language and way of life. English vagrants and criminals had heard about the Gypsies of Continental Europe, and sought to imitate them rather than the few Gypsies in England.[40] According to this contention, the Gypsies did not wander or live apart from the rest of the population, and moreover, did not form groups that non-Gypsies joined. They were simply an undistinguishable part of the world of criminals and vagrants. The theory, however, fails to convince, since it ignores all the distinctions made in contemporary sources between Gypsies and other vagabonds, and the fact that even on the Continent—where, as the author states, there was a greater number of Gypsies—some sources mention non-Gypsies who joined them and pretended to be Gypsies.

Romanticized depictions of Gypsies had already appeared in various literary genres in the Early Modern period. These often described a non-Gypsy joining their bands and seeking to be one of them. But it is doubtful whether these stories tell us much about the realities of the time—the notion that many beggars and vagrants joined the Gypsies, when joining them or pretending to belong among them could serve no useful purpose. The fate of Gypsies who were arrested was hardly an inducement. But whether or not there were significant numbers who joined the Gypsies, the assumption that their bands were swelled by non-Gypsy vagrants and dangerous types from the lowest strata of society merged with the denial of Gypsy ethnicity. We can only speculate whether denial of Gypsy ethnicity strengthened the view that they were joined by others or that Gypsy bands included many non-Gypsies, supported the opinion that they were not an ethnic group. Either way, the two theories became fused.

In many countries, in addition to statutes against non-Gypsy vagrants, against both Gypsy and other vagrants or specifically against Gypsy vagrants, there were laws against both Gypsies and those who joined them, wandered with them, and pretended to be Gypsies by dressing like them. Such, for example, were the decrees issued by Queen Elizabeth of England in 1597,[41] and by the Prince Elector of Saxony in 1652, which declared the Gypsies outlaws, and specifically included demobilized soldiers who joined them and dressed like them.[42] This phenomenon was depicted as an undesirable one-way trend—non-Gypsies adopting the Gypsy way of life. The statutes do not tell us how widespread this tendency actually was, but they certainly indicate the extent of anxiety regarding vagrancy. In the final analysis, denial of their ethnicity neither improved nor worsened the lot of the Gypsies. It might even have encouraged some circles to believe that they could be made to assimilate. This is implied in the proclamation of Carlos III, noted above, which stated that the Gypsies' way of life did not derive from an "unwholesome root," while not disparaging them as a rabble of base rogues.

Ironically, it was in the late 18th century when Gypsy ethnicity was being denied, when the policy of forced assimilation was most intense, when Carlos III issued his 'pragmatic sanction' and when Maria Theresa and Joseph II issued their decrees, that early study of the Gypsies' language gave rise to the view that they were an ethnic group originating in India. Not uncommonly, similar theories, definitions and categorizations can lead to different conclusions. The assertion that the Gypsies were not an ethnic group reinforced Carlos III's belief that they could be 'reformed.' Yet the definition labeling them as a racial group in the 19th century did not discourage the missionaries of the evangelical movements from seeking to eradicate their paganism and to reform them morally, maintaining that only their physical characteristics were inherited and were therefore unchangeable.[43]

There were several incidents in France in which Gypsy groups detained by the authorities benefited from denial of their ethnicity. In 1626 the chief prosecutor of the Parlement of Paris, Molé, informed the minister of justice that some vagrant Gypsies in the Île de-France were French families, who simply had to return to their village of origin and settle down.[44] In 1727 an official of the crown instructed the town council of Saint-Jean-de-Luz in southwestern France about a detained Gypsy band, stating that it was not birth that made a person a Gypsy (*Bohême*), but vagabondage. Therefore, if these people were permanent residents they should be freed;[45] that is to say, if they were not vagabonds they were not Gypsies. The Gypsies sometimes identified themselves as such, while others denied the fact in the hope of evading punishment, and on occasion identified themselves in a subtler way in keeping with the contemporary discourse about them among non-Gypsies. One band member, arrested in 1667, argued that while they were commonly called *Bohêmes*, in reality he had never been to Egypt. Another argued that though his parents had been Gypsies, he himself was born in France. But the judge did not take any interest in their origins, and though they argued that they were honestly employed, he decided that they were vagabonds and sent them to prison, from where they would have been sent to the galleys. Luckily for them, they escaped.[46]

In the second half of the 19th century, recognition of Gypsy ethnicity gave rise both to racist anti-Gypsy attitudes that justified their continuing persecution and discrimination, and to a romanticized view of them. The latter notion vindicated the nomadic existence of some Gypsies, since it was believed to be genetically predetermined. Romantic racism was especially widespread in England. The Gypsies were depicted as the oldest members of the Aryan race who spoke an Aryan language. It was in this spirit that an organization was formed in 1888, entitled the Gypsy Lore Society, which still exists. Prior to World War II, most of the articles in its periodical dealt with Gypsy language and folklore. Both the hostile racist and the romanticized view of the Gypsy race recapitulated in modern terms the attitudes of the Early Modern period, when Gypsies were still viewed as an ethnic group and referred to as a nation or a people. The 16th century distinction between 'genuine' and 'false' Gypsies was also revived. In the 16th century it was said that the 'genuine' ones had returned to their homeland, and in the 19th it was argued that most of the 'genuine' Gypsies had disappeared due to persecution and mixed marriages. Only those classified as 'genuine' Gypsies were entitled to continue traveling. It was mainly writers and folklorists who adopted the romanticized view. By contrast, most social reformers, local officialdom, philanthropists and missionaries, attacked the Gypsies as parasites and vagrants who needed to be reformed at any cost.[47]

The Nazis applied their own rationalization to the racial definitions that had prevailed in the 16th-17th centuries—the Gypsies were not a nation (in Nazi terms a pure race) any more than the Jews were one. Both were 'bastardly people' (a bastardized people—*Bastard-völk*), a filthy rabble defiling the pure Germanic blood. The imagery and stereotypes that had taken root through the centuries were explained on the basis of a racial theory that led to a policy of repression and extermination. Gypsies were sterilized—like the mentally retarded, the mentally ill and 'asocial' cases. They were confined in concentration camps and eventually transported from Germany and Nazi-occupied countries to the death camps. Many of them died of hunger and disease in the camps, many others were put to death in the camps in Germany, and in the occupied countries by the local population, whose conduct was legitimized by Nazi policy.[48] They were murdered without any provocation, without having sought to break away from Germany or the occupied countries in order to set up their own state, and without having collaborated with the enemy.

A small minority survived, thanks to romantic racism. Though more widespread in England than in Germany, it was accepted in certain Nazi circles, represented, notably, by Himmler. They revived the distinction between 'impure' rabble and 'pure,' noble Aryans, speakers of an Indo-European language. Thanks to Himmler, a minority of the Sinti tribe in Germany was classified as 'pure' and hence was saved. There was a further continuity in policy toward Gypsies: as in the Early Modern period Gypsies were conscripted, despite their bad reputation, by the various national armies. Thus in the 20th century hundreds of Gypsies were forcibly recruited by Nazi Germany and served in the Wehrmacht in 1942-43. In the final stages of the war hundreds of Gypsies of the Sinti tribe were taken from the concentration camps and sent to the Russian front to fight for Germany alongside other 'asocial' cases and convicted criminals.[49]

EPILOGUE

After the end of World War II, the debate about the Gypsies reappeared among both scholars and policy makers. Whether or not they are an ethnic group continues to be discussed. A number of historians argue that philologists who studied the Gypsy language and concluded that they were an ethnic

group were responsible for creating a fictitious Gypsy identity that ultimately led to anti-Gypsy racism and its horrendous outcome.[50] In 1998 a
collection of articles by Lucassen and others emphatically denied Gypsy
ethnicity. Refuting any basis for such a definition, the authors assert that
defining the Gypsies as an ethnic entity opens the door to racist hostility
toward them. They argue that it ignores the changes that have taken place
over time in their way of life, differences in tribal customs, the lack of proof
that they have a common past, the extent of intermarriage, and the fact that
other wanderers have been dubbed Gypsies. They contend that stigmatization has influenced the Gypsies' group formation, and with it their ethnic
consciousness, to a large degree.[51]

However, the authors signally failed to prove their case, just as Brian
Reynolds has failed to show that the Gypsies did not constitute a distinct
group during the Early Modern period. (Among other flaws, there is no
basis to the claim that since the Gypsy way of life changed over the years
they are not an ethnic group.) Those who argue against the Gypsies' ethnicity resemble those who reviled them in the 16th and 17th centuries, denying
them both a history and cultural characteristics. Those who regard the Gypsies as an ethnic group, or, rather, stress their common origins and distinctive culture, maintain that rejecting those roots, and thus the identity and
culture of the Gypsies, turns them into a 'social problem,' the solution to
which is coerced adaptation. Once defined as targets for assimilation, they
are perceived as misfits, a view that has become part of their image in non-
Gypsy eyes.[52]

Official policies toward the Gypsies continue to vary. The Soviet Union
recognized the Gypsies as a national minority in 1925, and Gypsies who
wished to could be so classified in their 'internal passports.' Later the same
principle was applied in communist Yugoslavia. In Britain, the Gypsies were
recognized as an ethnic minority in 1976, after considerable hesitation and
debate, and thus protected from discrimination by the Race Relations Act.[53]
In communist Czechoslovakia, on the other hand, the Gypsies were not recognized as an ethnic group, or one with its own language and culture, but
defined as people following an unwholesome way of life that needed to be
corrected by any means. In the post-communist period the Gypsy situation
there has worsened, as it has in Hungary and Romania.[54]

Many Gypsies have emigrated from Eastern Europe to the West, where
their situation is improved, and many more wish to do so. In Germany, the
Gypsies themselves are divided—some seek to stress their ethnic and cultural
distinction, others their identification with German society. In population

censuses held in Hungary (1990) and in Slovakia (2001), only a small percentage of Gypsies considered themselves members of the Gypsy national minority.[55]

NOTES

1. This article is based on a chapter from my book in publication, *Others and Other 'Others': Gypsies, Marginal Groups and Minorities in Western Europe in the Early Modern Period*. The study is intended to free the Gypsies from their isolation in historical research by comparing their image and status to that of other marginal and minority groups, and locating their story in the history of Western Europe in the Early Modern period.
2. C. S. Dixon, *The Reformation in Germany* (Oxford, 2002), pp. 14-15, 31-2.
3. For a survey of views on this question, see H. A. Winkler, "Nationalism and the Nation-State in Germany," in M. Teich and R. Porter (eds.), *The National Question in Europe in Historical Context* (Cambridge, 1993), pp. 182-95; W. Connor, *Ethnonationalism. The Quest for Understanding* (Princeton, 1994), Ch. 9; see also A. D. Smith, "The Problem of National Identity: Ancient, Medieval and Modern," *Ethnic and Racial Studies* 173 (1994), pp. 275-99.
4. R. Bartlett, *The Making of Europe: Conquest, Colonization and Cultural Change, 950-1350* (Penguin Books, 1994), pp. 197-242. The author also discusses ethnic-language tensions in international religious orders.
5. J. Céard, "La Sorcière, l'étrangere: Le voyage de Pierre de Lancre en sorcierie," in M. T. Jones Davies, *L'Étranger: identié et altcrité au temps de la renaissance* (Paris, 1996), pp. 79-100.
6. O. P. Grell, "Exile and Toleration," in O. P. Grell and B. Scribner (eds.), *Tolerance and Intolerance in the European Reformation* (Cambridge, 1996), pp. 164-81.
7. J. Panek, "The Question of Tolerance in Bohemia and Moravia in the Age of the Reformation," in Grell and Scribner, *Tolerance and Intolerance*, pp. 231-48.
8. L. Hunt Yungblut, *Strangers Settled Here among Us: Politics, Perceptions and Presence of Aliens in Elizabethan England* (London, 1996), pp. 40-51.
9. J. F. Dubost, *La France italienne XVe-XVIIe siècles* (Paris, 1997), pp. 307-87.
10. M. Plaisance, "Les florentins en France sous le regard de l'autre," in J. Dufournet, A. C. Fiorato and A. Redondo (eds.), *L'image de l'autre Européen XVe-XVIe siècles* (Paris, 1992), pp. 147-57.
11. Dubost, *La France italienne*, p. 387; Hunt Yungblut, *Strangers Settled Here among Us*, p. 46.
12. A. Tuetcy (ed.), *Journal d'un Bourgeois de Paris, 1405-1499* (Paris, 1881; reprint, Geneva, 1975). pp. 219-21.
13. "Quaedem extranea et praevie non visa vagabundaque multitudo huminum," Herman Cornerus, *Chronicon*, in R. Gronemeyer (ed.), *Zigeuner in Spiegel Frueher Chroniken und Abhandlungen. quellen von 15 bis zum 18 Jahrhundert* (Giesen, 1987), p. 15.

14. "... homines nigredine informes ex cocti sole, immundi veste... Tartaros vulgus appellat...." Albertus Krantzius, *Saxonia*, in Gronemeyer, *Zigeuner in Spiegel*, p. 25. Describing their arrival in Bologna, the author writes about the duke "... who came with women, children and companions from his country [*de suo paese*]." A. Sorbelli (ed.), *Corpus Chronicorum Boloniensium*, in *Rerum Italicarum Scriptores*, ed. A. L. Muratori, Vol. 18 (Citta di Castello, 1900), p. 568.

15. "Gens Ciganorum volgariter Cigawnar vocitata," Andreas, *Diarum Sexennale,* in Gronemeyer, *Zigeuner in Spiegel*, p. 19.

16. "elend volck," Sebastian Muenster, *Cosmographei*, in Gronemeyer, *Zigeuner in Spiegel*, p. 34.

17. "unnutz volck," Christian Wursitisen, *Bassler Chronick*, in Gronemeyer, *Zigeuner in Spiegel*, p. 39.

18. "... das diebrisch unartig und zaubersich bettelvolck die Zigeuner," in Gronemeyer, *Zigeuner in Spiegel*, p. 44.

19. "... fromd wunder selzam volck," Johannes Guler, *Ractia,* in Gronemeyer, *Zigeuner in Spiegel*, p. 45.

20. "Ein loses Diebische untreuwes Volck von allerley verlauuffenen bosen Buben Zusamen Gerottet," Cyriacus Spangenberg, *Sachsische Chronica*, in Gronemeyer, *Zigeuner in Spiegel*, p. 38.

21. Crusius, *Amales Suevici,* in Gronemeyer, *Zigeuner in Spiegel*, p. 40.

22. Johannes B. Goropius Becanus, *Hermathena,* in Gronemeyer, *Zigeuner in Spiegel*, p. 77.

23. Johannes Stumpf, *Schweytzer Chronik*, in Gronemeyer, *Zigeuner in Spiegel*, p. 32; Sprecher von Berneck, *Pallas Rhaetica*, in Gronemeyer, *Zigeuner in Spiegel*, p. 48.

24. "... ex variis nationibus non ita remotis," Christoph Besold, *Thesaurus Practicus,* in Gronemeyer, *Zigeuner in Spiegel*, p. 102; "ex variis nationibus etiam inter nos considentibus, collectam," Johann Limmaus, *De jure publico Imperii Romano Germanic*, in Gronemeyer, *Zigeuner in Spiegel*, p. 105.

25. "... furacissimam illud gens hominum, colluvies atque sentina variorum gentium," *Annales Boiorum*, in Gronemeyer, *Zigeuner in Spiegel*, p. 28; see also Martin Anton Delrio, *Disquisitiorum magicarum*, in Gronemeyer, *Zigeuner in Spiegel*, p. 79.

26. Gisbert Voetius, *De gentilismo et vocatione gentium*, in *Selectarum disputationum theologicarum*, pars. II (Utrecht, 1655), p. 656.

27. Thomas Dekker, "Lanthorne and Candle-Light," in A. F. Kinney (ed.), *Rogues, Vagabonds and Sturdy Beggars* (University of Massachusetts Press, 1973; reprint, 1990), p. 243.

28. Samuel Rid, "The Art of Juggling or Legerdemain," in Kinney, *Rogues, Vagabonds and Sturdy Beggars*, p. 266.

29. Thomas Browne, *Pseudodoxia Epidemica, or Enquiries into Very Many Received Tenets and Commonly Presumed Truths*, ed. G. Keynes (University of Chicago Press, 1964), Vol. II, Chs. X–XIII, pp. 467, 481–2.

30. "Can the Ethiopian change his skin...? (Jeremiah 13:23); likewise the Roman satirist Lucian coined the phrase, "Washing the Ethiopian to make him white," quoted in F. M. Snowden, jr., *Black in Antiquity: Ethiopians in the Greco-Roman Experience* (Cambridge, MA, 1970), p. 50 and note 36.

31. On this subject, see E. Lourie, "Black Women Warriors in the Muslim Army Besieging Valencia and the Cid's Victory: A Problem of Interpretation," *Traditio* 55 (2000), p. 19.

32. For a thorough discussion of this subject, see K. Hall, *Things of Darkness: Economies of Race and Gender in Early Modern England* (Cornell Univ. Press, 1995).

33. The documents discussed appear in translation in J. P. Ligeois, *Gypsies: An Illustrated History*, trans. T. Berrett (London, 1986), pp. 105-7.

34. The documents, some in the original and translation and some only in translation, appear in A. G. Alfaro, *The Great Gypsy Round-Up: The General Imprisonment of Gypsies in 1749*, trans. T. W. Roberts (Madrid, 1993), pp. 78-82.

35. Liegeois, *Gypsies*, p. 106.

36. Dekker, "Lanthorne and Candle-Light," p. 243. In the Early Modern period, Gypsies were thought to have come from Egypt.

37. The pamphlet, entitled "Discorsos del amparo de los legitimos nobres y reducion de fingidos," is discussed in B. Geremek, *Les fils de Cain: Pauvres et vagabonds dans la literature europeenne (XVe-XVIIIe siècles)* (Paris, 1991), pp. 293-6.

38. The report appears in full in F. A. Aydelotte, *Elizabethan Rogues and Vagabonds* (London, 1913; reprint 1967), Appendix A14.

39. William Harrison, G. Edelen (ed.), *The Description of England* (Cornell Univ. Press, 1968), p. 184.

40. B. Reynolds, *Becoming Criminal. Transversal, Performance and Cultural Dissidence in Early Modern England* (John Hopkins Univ. Press, 2002), pp. 28-44. The number of imposters listed is very small, and it is not certain they were imposters. Thomas Fricke estimates that there were only sporadic and brief cases of cooperation between Gypsies and non-Gypsies, and few cases of intermarriage. T. Fricke, *Ziguener im Zeitalter des Absoluismus* (Pfaffenweiler, 1996), pp. 390, 398.

41. A. Luders, T. E. Tomlins and J. Raithby (eds.), *The Statutes of the Realm* (London, 1810-25; reprint 1963), Vol. 41, p, 448; see also A. L. Beier, *Masterless Men: The Vagrancy Problem in England, 1560-1640* (London, 1985), pp. 61-2.

42. A. Fraser, *The Gypsies* (Oxford, 1992), p. 150; one of the early texts which stated that the Gypsies accepted indiscriminately any men and women who wished to join them dates back to 1520: "Recipiunt passim et viros et foeminas volentes in cunctis provinces, qui se illorum moscent contubernio," Krantzius, *Saxonia*, p. 25; see also statement of Delrio at the end of the 16th century, in Gronemeyer, *Zigeuner in Spiegel*, p. 80.

43. D. Mayall, *Gypsy Travellers in 19th Century Society* (Cambridge, 1988), p. 29.

44. H. Asséo, *Le traitement administratif des Bohémiens* (Problèmes socio-culturels en France au XVIIe siècle) (Paris, 1974), p. 43.

45. F. de Vaux de Loletier, *Les Tsiganes dans l'ancienne France* (Paris, 1961), p. 203.

46. Ibid., pp. 104-5.

47. On this issue, see B. Vesey-Fitzgerald, *Gypsies in Britain: An Introduction to Their History* (Devon, 1973), p. 208; L. Lucassen, W. Willems and A. Cottar, *Gypsies and Other Itinerant Groups: A Socio-Historical Approach* (London/New York,

1998), pp. 25, 31-2; D. Mayall, "Lorist, Reformist and Romanticist: The Nine-teenth Century Response to Gypsy Travellers," *Immigrants and Minorities* 43 (1985), pp. 53-67; Mayall, *Gypsy Travellers*, pp. 29-33.

48. On this issue, see Lucassen *et al.*, *Gypsies and Other Iterant Groups*, pp. 26-9, 89-93; G. Margalit, "Racist Occupation in Germany with the Gypsies from the Late 19th Century until 1945," *Historia* 1 (1998; Hebrew), pp. 105-19. There is no question that a genocide of Gypsies took place, but scholars are divided on the question of whether the Nazis intended to exterminate all the Gypsies in the world, as they did the Jews, or whether the Gypsy problem was more marginal in Nazi policy. There is also a dispute over the number of Gypsies who per-ished, whether murdered or starved to death. Estimates vary between 200,000 and one million and a half, as claimed by Gypsy activists: R. Vago, "The Roma in Central and Eastern Europe: The Plight of a Stateless Minority," in *An-tisemitism Worldwide 2000/1* (Tel Aviv University, 2002), pp. 26-9; M. Zimmer-mann, *Rassenutopie und Genozid* (Hamburg, 1996).

49. Margalit, "Racist Occupation in Germany," pp. 117-18.

50. On this issue, see Y. Matras, book review of J. Gierke (ed.), *Die Gesellschaftliche Knostruktion des Zigeuners zur Gense eines Vortweils* (Frankfurt am Main, 1991), in *Journal of the Gypsy Lore Society*, Series 58 (1998), pp. 67-70. Groellmann, one of the first to study the Gypsy language, regarded them as an ethnic group originating in India, opposed their expulsion and favored missionary work among them in order to 'reform' them. But he also copied earlier texts and helped to entrench negative stereotypes. Though he acknowledged their ethnic-ity, it did not prevent him from repeating his predecessors' argument that their dark complexion was not natural. He maintained that it was caused by their way of life—in the summer they were exposed to the sun, and in winter they stayed in a smoky hut. It was also because the mothers rubbed their children with a dark ointment, or placed them in the sun or near the fireplace. He argued that the proof of this assertion was that Gypsies serving in the imperial army in Hungary and Gypsy musicians, who kept themselves cleaner, had a lighter skin. H. M. G. Grellmann, *Dissertation on the Gypsies*, trans. M. Raper (London, 1787), p. 10.

51. "Stigmatization has influenced group formation and along with it ethnic con-sciousness to a large degree": Lucassen *et al.*, *Gypsies and Other Itinerant Groups*, p. 6, also pp. 7-9, 20-4.

52. Liegeois, *Gypsies*, pp. 181, 193.

53. J. O'Connell, "Ethnicity and Irish Travellers," in M. McCann, S. Ó Síocháin and J. Ruane, *Irish Travellers: Culture and Ethnicity* (Belfast, 1994), p. 119; Vago, "Roma in Central and Eastern Europe," pp. 21-2.

54. Liegeois, *Gypsies*, p. 111; I. Hancock, *The Pariah Syndrome: An Account of Gypsy Slavery and Persecution* (Ann Arbor, 1987), pp. 126-7.

55. On this issue, see G. Margalit, "Identity and National Consciousness among German Sinti and Roma (Gypsies)," in S. Volkov (ed.), *Being Different: Minori-ties, Aliens and Outsiders in History* (Jerusalem, 2000; in Hebrew); Vago, "Roma in Central and Eastern Europe," p. 26.

THE CAMPAIGN AGAINST THE RESTLESS: CRIMINAL BIOLOGY AND THE STIGMATIZATION OF THE GYPSIES, 1890-1960

PETER WIDMANN

THE GYPSIES AND THE ROOTS OF CRIMINAL BIOLOGY

In a book much discussed at the end of the 19th century, the Italian psychiatrist Cesare Lombroso, regarded as the founder of criminal biology, mentioned an alleged superstition held by the Gypsies. If a Gypsy commits a murder, claimed Lombroso, he subjects himself to a special ritual of atonement: "The Gypsies believe that God will be merciful if they wear for a year the same shirt they had on when they committed the murder."[1]

This description may be found in the chapter entitled "The Religion of the Criminals" in Lombroso's main work, which was destined to become a classic. The first edition of the German translation was published in 1887 under the title *Der Verbrecher* (Homo delinquens) *in anthropologischer, ärztlicher und juristischer Beziehung* (The Criminal [*Homo delinquens*] in Anthropological, Medical and Legal Relations). Lombroso had published the original Italian version eleven years earlier, in 1876. Using the Latin term *homo delinquens* he sought to introduce a new generic biological concept. The 'born criminal,' stated Lombroso, is a unique kind of person, an anthropological type who stands out biologically from the normal population. One recognizes this type by specific 'signs of degeneration.' He believed, for instance, that skull sclerosis or an asymmetrical head was more frequent amongst criminals than amongst other people. Thieves, he maintained, can be identified by a sloping forehead and large eye sockets, murderers by powerful lower jaws.[2]

In his book Lombroso showed little interest in the Gypsies. He mentioned them five times in the five hundred pages of the first volume of his work; nowhere did he deal with them systematically. They were referred to alongside many other groups, which he used as evidence to prove his hypothesis that the 'born criminal' exists. Lombroso saw Gypsies as a criminal entity, but not necessarily as a race; his writings do not evince a clear conception of the term 'race.' He concentrates on individual hereditary criminality and only occasionally mentions groups like the Gypsies. Nevertheless, his book can be viewed as the beginning of an explicitly biological criminalization of a minority. From then on, Gypsies in Germany belonged routinely to those groups targeted by the science of criminal biology. The theories arising from this focus were one of the prerequisites for the National Socialist genocide of the Sinti and Roma.

Considering the Gypsies as criminal was a widespread attitude at the end of the 19th century. Police and bureaucrats in the local administrations of the German Reich held this view. They spoke of a 'Gypsy plague' and expended considerable time and energy in expelling Gypsies and other groups traveling through their respective districts, or at least in having them accompanied by police officers. In pursuing this practice, they were adhering to a common assumption requiring no scientific findings.[3]

Some criminologists prior to Lombroso assumed that crime was a part of the 'Gypsy nature.' In 1863 Richard Liebich described Gypsies as an unchangeable people of morally inferior thieves and frauds.[4] Lombroso differed from his contemporaries in that he held biological factors responsible for the alleged criminal tendency. In his opinion, the Gypsies were descended from the Indian untouchables. The ancestors of the Gypsies, the pariahs, he claimed, had "the largest eye sockets of all races" and thus bore the characteristic typical of thieves. Elsewhere he characterized the Gypsies as "born criminals and villains." He ascribed to them a disinclination for work typical of criminals: "The Gypsies certainly follow a trade, but they only work as much as is necessary in order not to die of hunger, and that is why they remain so poor." In a passage on recidivistic offenders, Lombroso reported on a Gypsy family he knew who had been convicted 16 times for vagrancy. He claimed that they had repeatedly had themselves arrested in winter so as to receive bread and clothing.[5]

THE BIRTH OF AN IDEA

The discussion of Lombroso's theory exerted a formative influence on the origins of criminology in Germany. Besides the debate on the reform of criminal law, the argument over whether criminality was genetic or not was one of the reasons why criminology came to be established as an autonomous scientific area in Germany. In the 1890s many experts, such as Abraham Baer, Paul Näcke, Hans Kurella and Julius Koch, responded to Lombroso's propositions with their own books. Psychiatrists discussed Lombroso's theories, as did jurists, anthropologists, prison doctors, psychologists and journalists.[6]

In fact, Lombroso found only a few followers who endorsed his ideas completely. But the belief in the born criminal spread nevertheless. Emil Kraepelin, one of the most influential psychiatrists of his time, as well as others, was convinced that the born criminal existed, even if the signs of degeneration were not visible physically. After World War I the influence of criminal biology increased. Psychiatric research of the 1920s looked mainly into causes of crime which were regarded as inherited and less into those ascribable to the environment of the perpetrator.[7]

In 1923 criminal biology theory was put into practice in Bavaria when the Bavarian Ministry of Justice ordered a biological examination of prison inmates. Prison doctors were asked to distinguish between those capable of being reformed and those whose tendency toward crime was regarded as innate and hence unchangeable. This was done by a criminal biological analysis of individual physical and biographical data and by examining the family history of the prison inmate. Two years earlier, in 1921, the Bavarian government had introduced a graded penal system, separating habitual criminals from petty ones. Hence, the justice authorities hoped to increase the chances of rehabilitating a suitable portion of the prisoners. They believed that with the help of criminal biology they could scientifically identify prisoners who could be returned to society.[8]

A collection point was set up in a detention center at Straubing in Lower Bavaria where Bavarian prisons sent their criminal biology reports. Theodor Viernstein, a doctor who was appointed director, eventually came to be regarded as the eminent authority on practical criminal biology in the German Reich. Ernst Rüdin, a leading German eugenicist, had suggested to Viernstein that he investigate issues of genetics. The Bavarian collection point became a model for other German states. For instance, in 1930 Prussia introduced criminal biology examinations for prison inmates.[9]

TARGETING THE 'TRAVELING PEOPLE'

The examination reports on the individual prisoners are informative as a historical source. They suggest that the history of the persecution of the Sinti and Roma needs to be placed in a larger framework. The Gypsies were regarded as only one component of a group generally viewed as suspicious and having a restless way of life, characterized as 'traveling people,' 'vagabonds' or 'tramps.' In addition to 'Gypsies,' such groups as 'vagrants,' 'persons roving around like Gypsies,' 'hobos' and 'beggars' were also included in these categories, which personified the restless because they were 'wanderers' or were generally regarded as such. That begging and vagrancy were punishable offenses made collective criminalization easier. Under the label of criminal biology, doctors and jurists undertook a campaign against sections of the underclass. The examination reports of the criminal biology collection point in Berlin mirror the thrust of the direction taken: most of those examined were simple skilled or unskilled manual workers, and almost none were members of educated circles.[10] The examinations were similar to those carried out in Bavaria and included anthropometrical measurements and an analysis of the biography and family history of the individual.

In compliance with instructions issued by the Bavarian Ministry of Justice in 1923, prison doctors had to ask examinees if they followed a traveling way of life or went begging. As director of the Bavarian criminal biology collection point, Theodor Viernstein applied the restless category regularly in his examination reports. A July 1931 report on prisoner W., characterized as a 'Gypsy,' who was serving a sentence for horse thieving and attempted murder, reads:

> Both offenses typically express the gypsy nature. As a Gypsy, W. has the unbound life form of his nomadic blood. The capacity for empathy with the conditions of social life... of our culture is thus low... Given the entire development of W.'s life, it is in the nature of things that the social prognosis is unfavorable.[11]

Viernstein's diagnoses of restlessness were not limited to this group, however; he also formulated similar judgments concerning prisoners not considered 'Gypsies.' In April 1928 he wrote of a prisoner sentenced on counts of begging and theft:

> Not only through his last, thoroughly restless journey throughout the whole of Germany has the subject documented a constant need for change, but also already through earlier similar wanderings at the age of sixteen he had displayed this need which appears to be very similar to the instability of a psychopath... Such a disposition should be viewed mainly as an expression of a crisis of dissatisfaction which at times overcomes certain psychopaths amongst criminals and determines their actions in such a way that they wander from place to place without being able to summon up the will for a settled form of existence and regular work.[12]

Viernstein therefore wanted to see the prisoner placed under strict control: "In terms of racial biology, the viewpoint of safeguarding society should take priority." In April 1928 Viernstein characterized a prisoner convicted of begging, vagrancy and theft as suffering from 'dromomania,' and noted: "Already as a child he had once, as his mother later told him, roamed around aimlessly in the woods without being aware of it, and he could not say why. So he became a tramp and sank into the criminality characteristic of this brotherhood."[13]

Criminal biologists also believed that crime and epilepsy were connected—Lombroso had already attempted to prove this assumption. Viernstein made the connection between epilepsy and restlessness in 1928: "In any event, it is an empirical fact that a considerable number of such epileptics are concealed amongst vagabonds and roamers, the people of the country roads."[14] The affliction became visible, said Viernstein, in the unruliness they displayed when confronted by an official of the state. He explained this further in a report:

> The assumption that we are dealing with epilepsy becomes even more convincing due to the fact that the subject is an immensely irritable, stubborn and obviously extremely independent person who, according to his own confession, behaves in a fundamentally fractious and contrary manner toward organs of the rural police authorities... His criminality, practiced for decades... appears to be a form of parasitical, uprooted existence typical of the traveling people and more annoying than dangerous. The social prognosis is, of course, extremely poor.

Viernstein recommended permanent incarceration in an institution.[15]

SCIENCE AND THE FEAR OF CRIMINALITY

One can interpret criminal biology as an attempt to rationalize the anxiety manifested among sections of the bourgeoisie caused by some of the consequences of modernization and urbanization. Poverty, criminality and alcoholism demanded an explanation. Criminal biologists appeared to offer one. They swam with a tide that had its source in social Darwinism and was the confluence of many contemporary currents: eugenics, heredity and degeneration theories. Fear of the restless also mirrored the concern that even more of the old order might be lost than that which had already been destroyed in World War I.

Many contemporaries hoped to find answers to epochal questions in the biology of heredity. One group espousing this idea was the medical elite. In a report from December 1924, the members of the Bavarian chief medical committee expressed the conviction that the roots of crime were to be found in heredity. The more science deals in detail with heredity, says the report, the more clearly does its "powerful importance" emerge. Character and will are already established as basic characteristics at birth:

> This innate nature is in turn only to a limited degree caused by the favorable or unfavorable living conditions in the mother's womb; rather to a far greater extent it is acquired and may be traced back to the composition of the cell material out of whose union the individual originates.[16]

Just how much the popularity of criminal biology was due to the widespread anxiety of particular social groups is revealed in definitions of the healthy and the sick. Criminal biologists regarded disrespect for state authority as a sign of sickness. Their examination categories included concepts such as 'social discipline,' 'position in social order,' 'political attitudes' and 'religious values.' The prisoner was also asked in the examination such questions as what newspaper he read. Thus, criminal biologists passed off social judgments as scientific findings.[17]

Theodor Viernstein interwove the political, social and religious attitudes of prisoners expertly into his diagnoses. In May 1928 he wrote the following of a prison inmate: "He showed himself to be an unruly, uncivilized person who was mischievous, a rabble-rouser against religion and someone who expressed spiteful communist views."[18] Only discipline, principally military discipline, could alleviate this, claimed Viernstein. In January 1928 Viernstein reported on a prisoner whose offenses included vagrancy and begging: "From March 1914 till June 1919 there was a pause in his criminal activities, evidence that the subject was capable of keeping discipline in a soldier's uniform and under a strict hand."[19]

EFFECTS

Criminal biology had an impact first and foremost on prison inmates. If a prison doctor assigned a prisoner to the 'traveling people,' on the basis of his examination report, the latter was threatened with more severe penal conditions than other prisoners who were convicted of the same offense. Diagnoses based on criminal biology could also influence the trial. The courts could refer to the reports if they considered this necessary. In an annual report from October 1928, Viernstein asserted that the state prosecutor's office had requested the reports compiled by the Bavarian collection point in 120 cases. In addition, the examinations provided a basis for many criminal biology studies. The Bavarian collection point also made their material available to researchers.

In contrast, during the period of the Second Reich and of the Weimar Republic criminal biology had no influence at first on the conduct of the police, local administrative bodies and the *Länder* interior authorities. Certainly, the race concept was used in individual documents dealing with 'combating' the Gypsy plague, for example, in the decree implementing the Bavarian Gypsy and work-shy legislation of 1926. In everyday practice, however, the ideas of eugenics and criminal biology scarcely played a role. Police and bureaucrats were oriented mainly toward a sociological concept of the 'Gypsy.' This understanding covered people who, as stated, "roamed around in the Gypsy way," without reference to ethnic descent or hereditary line.[20]

PRECURSORS

In the long term, however, the consequences of criminal biology hypotheses were grave. Scientific works, both academic and popular, supported the prejudices in circulation and lent them the dignity of learned insight. Thus, they also undermined the basis of traditional policy toward Gypsies, which had lain in the assumption that one could change the Gypsies once their restless life was expunged from them by necessarily severe means. However, those who believed that the roots of Gypsy restlessness lay in their hereditary make-up had ultimately to dismiss an enforced settled form of existence as a goal. Elements of the biological image of the Gypsy filtered slowly into the scientific and public debate. The precondition for the transition from traditional to National Socialist Gypsy policy, introduced by the German criminal police in the late 1930s, was thus created.

Ideas developed by criminal biologists in the 1920s were adopted over a decade later by racial hygienist Robert Ritter, the leading Gypsy expert of the National Socialist regime. Besides registering all so-called Gypsies and 'Gypsy half-castes,' Ritter planned to record all those sections of the population that, in his opinion, tended toward criminality due to their hereditary make-up. In 1927 Theodor Viernstein had suggested to the scientific advisory committee of the criminal biology collection points that the scope of research on heredity be extended beyond the prisoners. He wanted to record in index files all sectors of the population he viewed as potentially criminal—irrespective of whether criminal offenses could be proven or not. In June 1933 Viernstein named the groups that he wanted to see registered in terms of their hereditary composition: "orphans and welfare children, drinkers, those vocationally impoverished for inherent reasons, the feeble-minded, certain groups of psychopaths, specific forms of epileptics, the mentally ill and deaf-mutes."[21] It was this utopian goal that Robert Ritter sought to implement several years later.

Viernstein also proved himself to be a precursor in political objectives. In 1933 he demanded the detention and sterilization of 'incorrigible criminals' in order to "liberate society in the future from the recognized permanent damage they cause and to relieve the burden of cost incurred by the state through their eternal demands on the courts." "A 'people in distress,'" he asserted, "has other tasks than to breed inferior beings and those with a strange nature."[22]

From the outset, ideas of internment and prevention of procreation were a part of the criminal biology discussion. In his main work Lombroso had already proposed that born criminals be locked up for life. He also wanted to influence reproduction: "The only means of preventing the unfortunate creatures, which criminals are, from seeing the light of the world, would perhaps be to prevent alcoholics and criminals from marrying."[23]

It should be emphasized that some roots of the criminal biology thesis supported by 'Gypsy experts' of the National Socialist state lay outside both Nazi ideology and *Völkisch* racial theory. Lombroso, for instance, was a socialist whose writings did not include the notions of ethnic cleansing and genocide. In a tract on anti-Semitism, he attributed hate between peoples to the "most repugnant secretions of man." "The European nations," claimed Lombroso, were a "mosaic of various races," and the mixing of races was one of the most important factors in progress. In contrast, anti-Semitism was atavistic.

Viernstein was also not a National Socialist but a faithful Catholic and German nationalist, whose thinking was conservative. In the first years of the National Socialist dictatorship, however, he welcomed the new regime. His authoritarian ideas of state and society doubtlessly made this easier for him. The initial impetus for his proposals lay in what he believed to be the exigencies of the state. The dignity and civil rights of the individual were to him hurdles to redressing the problems. In a memorandum from June 1933 he stated his opinion that "the interests of the general public and the state [should] take priority over those of the culprit's personality."[24]

Without necessarily thinking in National Socialist or *völkish*-racist terms, criminal biologists since the 1890s had prepared the ground upon which

Robert Ritter would later move. Genocide, however, cannot be solely explained by ideas of criminal biology.[25] It was only after the encounter with other concepts, such as racism and Social Darwinism, and the centralization of the criminal police from 1936 onwards that the specific fatal dynamic was created of which Sinti and Roma in Germany and in many other European countries were to become the victims.[26]

THE AFTERLIFE OF AN IDEA

Besides its role as a forerunner of National Socialist Gypsy policy, criminal biology had a further impact. Its assumptions were incorporated into textbooks for training jurists and police officers. Even after the collapse of the National Socialist regime, the ideas of criminal biology circulated in this area in particular. The work of Franz Exner, one of Germany's leading criminologists, is one example. His textbook, over three hundred pages long, was published in three editions, 1939, 1944 and 1949. While Exner published both books from the Nazi period under the title *Criminal Biology*, he had the postwar one published under the more harmless title, *Criminology*. The third edition of Exner's work was the first important criminology textbook published in West Germany after the war.

In both the 1939 and the 1944 editions Exner treated the criminality of the Jews and the Gypsies. In 1939 Exner wrote of the Jews that their criminality corresponded in its "basic features to the Jewish essence." He continued: "In the social as in the antisocial he [the Jew] is driven by the most powerful striving for profit and pursues his material interests often unhesitatingly and inconsiderately."[27]

After the war Exner removed the passages on the Jews; he discussed, however, the alleged criminal tendency of the Yenish, a group of travelers living in the south of Germany, who were generally characterized as 'white Gypsies,' 'vagrants' or as 'persons who roam around in the gypsy way.' Exner summarized the results as follows: "Mostly they wander around as good-fornothings and vagabonds and even when their blood is mixed they are incapable of denying their 'type' and its asocial ways." Further, he says: "One confirmation of the durability of such blood elements is the experience gained in education institutions and workhouses, where the descendants of these groups mostly prove to be completely resistant to change."[28]

As evidence for this thesis Exner cites the work of Robert Ritter. The phrase, "From what Ritter told me," suggests that Exner had personal contact with the leading 'Gypsy specialist' of the National Socialist regime. Exner was not alone: various authors were still referring to Ritter's research into the 1960s. Nobody found this contentious—German society ignored the genocide of the Sinti and Roma until the 1970s. Within criminology itself, criminal biology began to lose its influence in the course of the 1960s when a younger generation of criminologists turned their attention to the sociological causes of crime.

CONCLUSIONS

The development of criminal biology suggests that the persecution of Sinti and Roma needs to be viewed against the broader backdrop of social history. The fear of specific sections of the underclass that had gripped the bourgeoisie must find a more analytical focus than has been the case till now; likewise, the attempts made to discipline such groups. The demands arising from criminal biology were directed against groups that followed a traveling way of life, or were purported not to lead settled lives. This connection became clear during National Socialism: the same authorities that persecuted 'asocials' also had Sinti and Roma sent to the concentration camps. The thinking that nurtured this persecution may be observed from the late 19th century.

NOTES

1. Cesare Lombroso, *Der Verbrecher* (Homo Delinquens) *in anthropologischer, ärztlicher und juristischer Beziehung*, Vol. 1 (Hamburg, 1894), p. 362.
2. Ibid., 170f.
3. Rainer Hehemann, *Die "Bekämpfung des Zigeunerunwesens" im Wilhelminischen Deutschland und der Weimarer Republik, 1871-1933* (Frankfurt am Main, 1987).
4. Richard Liebich, *Die Zigeuner in ihrem Wesen und in ihrer Sprache. Nach eigenen Beobachtungen dargestellt* (Leipzig, 1863).
5. Cesare Lombroso, *Der Verbrecher*, pp. 179, 316, 338, 368.
6. Richard F. Wetzell, *Inventing the Criminal: A History of German Criminology, 1880-1945*, (Chapel Hill/London, 2000) pp. 15, 46.
7. Ibid., p. 120.
8. Bayerisches Staatsministerium der Justiz (ed.), *Der Stufenstrafvollzug und die kriminalbiologische Untersuchung der Gefangenen*, Vol. 1 (Munich, 1926).
9. Ferdinand von Neureiter, *Kriminalbiologie* (Berlin, 1940), p. 8.
10. Files, "Kriminalbiologische Sammelstellen," Landesarchiv Berlin, A Rep. 380.

11. *Kriminalbiologische Sammelstelle*, Nr. 534, Hauptstaatsarchiv München.

12. Gutachten für Josef V., 5.4.1928, Hauptstaatsarchiv München, M Ju 22512.

13. Gutachten für Bernhard H., 7.4.28, loc. cit.

14. Ibid.

15. Ibid.

16. Gutachten des Obermedizinalausschusses, 19.12.1924, 4, Hauptstaatsarchiv München, M Ju 22511.

17. Letter of the Ministry of Justice to higher courts and public prosecutors, 11 Oct. 1926, including a list of examination categories, Hauptstaatsarchiv München, M Ju 22515.

18. Gutachten über Ludwig G, 2.5.1928, Hauptstaatsarchiv München, M Ju 22512.

19. Gutachten für Gregor G., 27.1.1928, loc. cit.

20. Martin Luchterhandt, *Der Weg nach Birkenau: Entstehung und Verlauf der nationalsozialistischen Verfolgung der 'Zigeuner'* (Lübeck, 2000), pp. 9–59.

21. Theodor Viernstein, "Kriminalbiologie und Erneuerung der Rechtsordnung" (June 1933) p. 66, Landesarchiv Berlin, A Rep. 180, No. 154.

22. Ibid., pp. 69–71.

23. Lombroso, *Der Verbrecher*, p. 135.

24. Theodor Viernstein, "Denkschrift 'Kriminalbiologie und Erneuerung der Rechtsordnung,'" p. 64, Landesarchiv Berlin, A Rep. 180, No. 154; Wolfgang Burgmair, "Nikolaus Wachsmann und Matthias M. Weber, 'Die soziale Prognose wird damit sehr trübe...': Theodor Viernstein und die Kriminalbiologische Sammelstelle, in Bayern," in Michael Farin (ed.), *Polizeireport München, 1799–1999* (Munich, 1999), pp. 250–87.

25. See Michael Zimmermann in this volume.

26. Michael Zimmermann, *Rassenutopie und Genozid. Die nationalsozialistische 'Lösung der Zigeunerfrage'* (Hamburg, 1996), pp. 106–11.

27. Franz Exner, *Kriminalbiologie in ihren Grundzügen* (Hamburg, 1939), p. 70.

28. Franz Exner, *Kriminologie* (Berlin/Göttingen/Heidelberg, 1949), p. 115; Volker Berbüsse, "Das Bild 'der Zigeuner' in deutschsprachigen kriminologischen Lehrbüchern seit 1949," *Jahrbuch für Antisemitismusforschung* 1 (1992), pp. 117–51.

JEWS, GYPSIES AND SOVIET PRISONERS OF WAR: COMPARING NAZI PERSECUTIONS*

MICHAEL ZIMMERMANN

The explicit or implicit focus of most published studies dealing with the image of the Gypsy, or with policies toward Gypsies in Germany, is the Nazi policy of extermination. Avoiding the horror at its center, historians have approached this mass murder, too, with synoptic accounts, research on particular aspects of the Nazi persecution of the Gypsies, and attempts to measure the policy of annihilating the Gypsies against crimes perpetrated against other groups, primarily the Jews, who stand out among Nazi victims in terms of the extent and consistency, as well as the comprehensiveness, of annihilationist intent against them. A further question concerns how far the persecution of the Gypsies can be characterized as 'genocide.'

The political and racial reordering of Europe envisioned by the Nazis involved not only the persecution of Jews and Gypsies, but also the repression of ideological non-conformists and other groups stigmatized as 'racially inferior' or 'alien to the community.' Communists, socialists and other political opponents were the first to be sent to concentration camps. Then, during the 1930s, persecution was increasingly directed at social outsiders. Homosexuals were harassed by the police and often arrested. Those labeled 'asocial' or 'born criminals' suffered a similar fate. People considered 'congenitally diseased' were subjected to compulsory sterilization and, from the outset of the war, were killed as 'lives not worthy of living.'[1]

Moreover, during World War II, the non-Jewish and non-Romany populations of Poland and the Soviet Union suffered massively. This affected not only the leadership groups of those countries, but also hundreds of thousands of ordinary people—Byelorussian peasants in areas where the partisans were

* Translated from the German by Dr. Eve Rosenhaft (University of Liverpool).

active, non-Jewish residents of Warsaw at the time of the 1944 uprising, and many others—who were shot to death by SS, police and Wehrmacht units. Above all, however, we need to take into account the millions of Soviet prisoners of war who died in German custody.[2]

These victims, in particular, have received too little attention in comparative research on the crimes of the Third Reich, in spite of the enormous numbers who perished. Another reason to consider them is that they might add a new dimension to the comparison between the Nazi persecution of the Jews and that of the Gypsies.

This essay therefore begins with an outline of Nazi policies toward Jews, Gypsies and Soviet prisoners of war, and then goes on to address the following questions, with particular reference to those persecuted as 'Gypsies': What common elements and differences can be identified between the active persecution of Jews and Gypsies and the policy of tolerating and facilitating the large-scale death of Soviet prisoners of war? To what extent can the term 'genocide' be applied to these three mass crimes?

NATIONAL SOCIALIST POLICIES TOWARD JEWS

Based on numerous studies of the destruction of European Jewry, the escalation of the Nazi regime's anti-Jewish policy[3] can be described as follows: Once deportation had been used as an instrument of Nazi Jewish policy for the first time, with the expulsion of 17,000 Polish Jews from the Reich in October 1938, the tool of forced emigration, favored by the SS Security Service and the Gestapo since the mid-1930s, was extended from newly-annexed Austria to the *Altreich*. Measures for the economic and social marginalization of the Jews were simultaneously intensified.

Since the war made forced emigration more difficult, while at the same time the number of Jews under German control increased considerably, the next step was to attempt their forcible resettlement. As the war situation developed, the Polish territories around Krakow and Lublin were initially considered as possible 'reservations' for Jews. When it became clear that this was not viable and, moreover, that France had fallen, attention was turned to the more unrealistic project of deportation to Madagascar; the likelihood that this process would involve a large death toll was viewed with complacency.[4]

In parallel, the problems generated by the idea of forced emigration—with the expansion of the German sphere of domination to include millions of

Jews and the 'return' of German-speaking minorities from eastern and south-eastern Europe concluded between the Reich and the Soviet Union—fuelled the notion of creating a balance by forcing Jews and Poles to settle outside the Reich. Moreover, the concept of forced resettlement inspired the *Gauleiter* in Vienna, Berlin and other urban centers to call for the removal of Jews from their cities, blaming Jewish landlords for the housing shortage or stigmatizing the Jews as 'social ballast.'

The aims of the leadership, which now became explicit under the rubrics 'comprehensive measures' (*Gesamtmaßnahmen*), 'final objective' (*Endziel*) and 'final solution' (*Endlösung*), found expression in continuously improvised short-term and interim plans for concentrating more and more Jews in the parts of Poland occupied and annexed by Germany. However, this turned out to be impracticable due to the huge scale of the plan. At the same time, the promise of a definitive 'solution to the Jewish question' by forced resettlement led to a heightened expectation of, and pressure for, anti-Jewish measures.

Thus, even the German occupying authorities in Poland regarded the requirement of taking in Jews and creating ghettos for them as a short-term measure, especially since Hitler had also agreed to 'remove' Jews from the *Generalgouvernement* in early 1941. These authorities assumed that, since it was agreed that this would be a temporary phase, it was unnecessary to make more long-term arrangements to ensure the survival of the Jews. Such provisions would even be counterproductive, since the 'intolerable condition' of the Jewish settlements and ghettos was a guarantee that they would soon be cleared out. Linked to the construct of 'intolerable condition' was the distinction between Jews who were capable of work and those who were not. This division became the formula for later selections in the extermination camps and ghettos.

Behind Hitler's 1941 promise to remove the Jews from Poland lay German plans to attack the Soviet Union, which, simultaneously, would remove obstacles to population transfers to the East and satisfy the pressures of anti-Jewish expectations. At the same time, these plans envisaged a much more extensive 'final solution to the Jewish question' for German-dominated Europe, which it was assumed could be easily achieved after the predicted lightning-swift victory over Russia. In a vision analogous to the Madagascar project, the death of masses of Jewish victims was built into the planning, particularly since the war plans against the USSR anticipated the 'resettlement' of millions of Soviet citizens in Siberia or on the shores of the Arctic Ocean.[5]

Alongside other SS formations, *Ordungspolizei* ('order police') and army units, the death squads—Einsatzgruppen—of the SS Security Service, above all, took the step that led from approving mass death to active mass murder. Beginning with the invasion of the USSR in the name of the struggle against the imagined 'Jewish-Bolshevik arch-enemy,' these mass shootings many times exceeded the murders of members of Polish leadership groups carried out in 1939. From the late summer of 1941 on, women and children were also targeted. Soon this mass murder ceased to be limited to the USSR. When, in the autumn of 1941, the rapid defeat of the Soviet Union turned out to be a chimera, it also meant that the Nazi leadership had failed to acquire the space in which their racial utopia was to be realized, the territory for the 'territorial final solution' of the 'Jewish question.' At the same time, the Nazi leadership had agreed with the German authorities in the East that the territories under their jurisdiction would function only as 'transit camps' for Jews already there and for those who would be deported there. It was this constellation that paved the way for *Aktion Reinhard* against the Polish Jews and the mass extermination of the rest of European Jewry. Moreover, the decision in the autumn of 1941 to use the labor of Soviet POWs and civilians undermined economic arguments against the murder of the Jews.[6]

NATIONAL SOCIALIST POLICIES
TOWARD SOVIET POWS

Despite their deployment as forced labor, a means used extensively from 1942 onwards, Soviet prisoners of war (POWs) made up the second largest group of victims of Nazi extermination policies after the Jews. All together some 5.7 million Soviet soldiers fell into German hands between the middle of 1941 and the end of the war. Of these, 930,000 were still in POW camps in January 1945. About a million had been released from the camps and transferred to the Wehrmacht's armed forces for subordinate tasks. Another 500,000 had escaped or been liberated by the Soviet army. The remaining 3.3 million or so (57.5 percent) had died in German hands.[7] There were four main reasons, apart from brutal mass executions, for the massive death toll: hunger, the way in which prisoners were transported, inadequate housing, and the systematic murder of specific categories of prisoners.

A central German war aim in the East was the control and exploitation of food resources. It was clear to the men who planned the plunder of Russia and the Ukraine that as a result "millions of people would undoubtedly starve to death."[8] "Many tens of millions" in these territories would either "die or have to emigrate to Siberia."[9] Soviet POWs were the first victims of this policy. As a result, over a million people died of hunger in the first months of imprisonment.[10]

Tens of thousands of Soviet POWs also died on their way to the camps. Many had to march for hundreds of kilometers behind the front. Wehrmacht guards shot those who became exhausted along the way. Where the prisoners were transported by rail, the Wehrmacht permitted only the use of open freight cars. The cold Russian winter and denial of food, often for days at a time, led to enormous losses.

Scarcely any preparations had been made for housing the POWs because it had been presumed that the Soviet Union would collapse within several weeks. For the areas intended as camps, nothing more than barbed wire had been provided. The prisoners, worn out by the march and weakened by malnutrition, had few resources with which to counter the cold, contagion and hunger-related diseases in the temporary camps.

Moreover, in mid-July 1941, Reinhard Heydrich, on behalf of the Security Police, and General Hermann Reinecke, the Wehrmacht officer responsible for POWs, had agreed that the SS-Einsatzgruppen should identify and shoot all "politically and racially unacceptable elements" among the Soviet prisoners. These included "all significant functionaries of the state and the Party," "members of the intelligentsia," "all fanatical Communists" and "all Jews."[11] The number of victims of these murders was between 140,000 and 150,000. The number of Jewish Red Army soldiers taken prisoner alone is estimated at some 85,000. Without exception, any identified as Jews were killed. The same treatment was meted out to thousands of non-Jewish prisoners who—like the circumcised Muslims—were taken to be Jews in disguise or classified as 'racially inferior Asiatics.'

The fact that the mortality rate declined noticeably in 1942 had nothing to do with considerations of humanity or the rules of war, but was due to recognition by leaders of the regime and the Wehrmacht that German armaments production depended on the labor of those POWs. It had become clear that the Soviet Union would not be as easily beaten as the Germans had hoped. In view of a threatening labor shortage, the German mining industry in particular became the leading advocate of the use of Soviet labor, but the SS and the party leadership rejected this out of hand. A compromise was reached: Soviet POWs and civilians would be used, but under conditions that included maximum exploitation, strict isolation from the German population, miserable treatment and provisioning, and imposition of the death penalty for even minor infractions.[12]

NATIONAL SOCIALIST POLICIES
TOWARD GYPSIES[13]

After 1933, the police and the ministerial bureaucracy of the Third Reich maintained a Gypsy policy that alternated between the goals of 'expulsion' and 'settlement' (*Sesshaftmachung*). Yet the discrimination against and oppression of Gypsies that characterized the first years of National Socialist rule were not merely a continuation of traditional Gypsy policy. In the *Länder* (states), laws and regulations against Gypsies were often toughened. While some municipalities and lower police authorities used traditional methods such as high rents, substandard living conditions, sudden foreclosures or even the destruction of camping areas, as well as harassing police checks, to control Gypsy groups, others forced the Gypsies into centralized, sometimes fenced and even guarded camps. Moreover, these efforts to move the Gypsies from open sites or private quarters to local camps must be seen in relation to the overall camp system created under the Third Reich almost as soon as the NSDAP came to power. Between 1933 and 1939, it became virtually a trivial matter for mayors, police chiefs, district administrators, and other officials to demand that Gypsies be "admitted to a concentration camp," that "a general camp be erected," that they be "concentrated in labor camps" or be "forcibly put in a closed camp."[14]

Oppression of Gypsies intensified on the national level as well. Anti-Gypsy agitation grew in the press and in professional journals, while, as of 1934, some 500 Gypsies were sterilized under the Law to Prevent Genetically Deficient Offspring. They also came under the Law for the Protection of German Blood and German Honor and the ban on marriage between 'Aryans' and 'members of alien (*artfremden*) races,' as well as under the 1935 Marital Health Law, which forbade marriage to allegedly 'inferior' individuals.

The unambiguously racist attitude to the 'Gypsy question' in German policy after 1933 was linked to the concept of police intervention in society developed in 1937 by the Reich Criminal Police Office, Germany's central authority for the policing of crime. According to this notion, crime prevention should have the same status as detection. Crime was explained in terms of the antisocial behavior of certain segments of society—the term used was *Gemeinschaftsschädlich*, or damaging to the community—and this behavior in turn was explained by hereditary factors. It was thus imagined that it was possible to achieve a crime- and criminal-free *Volksgemeinschaft* (racial/national community) by applying scientific methods. Among other means, over 2,000

Gypsies, branded 'asocial,' were sent to concentration camps in the course of this racially motivated 'preventive crime-fighting' from 1938 onwards.

Himmler signed a decree at the end of 1938 calling for a "resolution of the Gypsy question appropriate to the character of this race." This marked the transition from a Gypsy policy conceived as part of a program to remove 'aliens' from the community to one of persecution in its own right. Once the war had begun, this persecution underwent further sharp radicalization. In parallel with the expulsions of Poles and Jews motivated by a Germanizing population policy, policy makers now looked to resettle the Gypsies in occupied Poland. The first to be affected were 2,800 people from the western territories of the Reich. In a second step, 5,000 Roma from the Austrian Burgenland were deported in fall 1941.

The grounds for persecuting the latter group dated back to the extraordinarily fervent local and regional witch-hunts against the Burgenland Roma that had been going on since 1938. Thus, when Himmler, Heydrich, and the criminal police saw an opportunity to deport these Gypsies, and despite the protests of the ghetto administration and the mayor of Lodz, who predicted overcrowding, food shortages and epidemics, they sent the Burgenland Roma to the Lodz ghetto. Shortly after the transports arrived, the housing and food situation indeed became ever more unbearable and epidemics spread. The German officials who had predicted the catastrophe had arranged conditions so that this would actually occur. In the end, those confined to Lodz were so malnourished and sick that the Germans responsible pronounced them 'subhumans' who must be eliminated. The Burgenland Gypsies, like the Jews, were suffocated in gas vans in Kulmhof.[15]

These murders were linked to the elimination of Jews, which the Nazi regime had set in motion after the attack on the Soviet Union. Along with Jews, functionaries of the CPSU, partisans and other 'undesirable elements,' Gypsies were indeed among the victims of the Einsatzgruppen and other SS and police units on Soviet soil.[16] The activity of the Einsatzgruppen was based on a hierarchically articulated image of the enemy. At its apex were Jews and Communists and their phantasmal conjunction in the form of a 'Jewish-Bolshevik world conspiracy.' Gypsies occupied a subordinate, though not insignificant, rung on this ideological pyramid. They figured as 'racially inferior' and purportedly 'asocial,' and as 'partisans,' 'spies,' and 'agents' of the imaginary 'Jewish world enemy.'

The Einsatzgruppen, which viewed them as fifth-column informers in the service of 'Jewish bolshevism,' targeted traveling Roma in particular whenever the killing units learned of their existence. Regarded only as auxiliaries of the 'world enemy,' their liquidation was not given first priority. The Einsatzgruppen murdered the Gypsies who fell into their hands, but did not search for them with the zeal employed in ferreting out Jews and Communists.[17] But when the killing units lingered for long in an area, as in the case of Einsatzgruppe D in the Crimea, they also began systematic liquidation of the Gypsy population. As a result of the myth of 'racially inferior'/'spying Gypsies,' Wehrmacht units also handed Roma over to the Einsatzgruppen or shot them themselves.

In the *Generalgouvernement*, as in the USSR, more Gypsies were shot by German Security Police (*Sicherheitspolizei*) and *Ordungspolizei* than were killed in concentration camps. Based on eyewitness testimony and extensive court investigations, it has often been claimed that the Gypsies were shot in rural police raids that were typically directed against partisans or the Jewish underground. Yet in the *Generalgouvernement*, Gypsies also risked death when they remained hidden in a village. Moreover, the German police shot many Gypsies—along with Poles, Jews, and Soviet prisoners of war—in retribution for partisan attacks that they had not carried out.[18]

Himmler himself tried to confine the extermination policy to traveling Polish Gypsies, since he imagined their 'spying' to constitute a special danger to the German occupying force. According to a model of persecution instituted by Wehrmacht units in the USSR and the German occupation administration in Latvia in 1941,[19] he ordered police in the *Generalgouvernement* in August 1942 not to proceed against sedentary Gypsies as a rule, meaning as long as they were not criminals or did not collaborate with the partisans.[20] Since the local police authorities could interpret this instruction as they saw fit, the conditions for murder remained relatively unchanged.

An uprising of communist partisans erupted in German-occupied Serbia[21] in July of 1941, surprising the Wehrmacht by its magnitude. From the outset, the tactics employed to defeat the partisans included 'reprisal executions.' For every German or 'ethnic German' soldier killed, 100 hostages would be shot; for every German or 'ethnic German' soldier wounded, 50 hostages were to be executed. The designated victims were males aged between 14 and 70. Since the Wehrmacht had too small a reservoir of victims for its 'reprisal executions,' the Einsatzgruppe stationed in Belgrade was asked to provide the requisite number of hostages. During summer 1941, the Einsatzgruppe forced the Jews of Belgrade and the Banat into a 'transit camp' and placed a large group of Jewish refugees in the overcrowded Sabac concentration camp, where Gypsies were also being held. The commander of the Einsatzgruppe decided on the 'removal' of 1,295 Jews from Belgrade, and 805

Jews and Gypsies from the Sabac camp, for the reprisal executions. Thus, Serbian Roma found themselves among the victims of the German 'retaliation' measures.

At the same time, the German authorities were faced with a new question: what was to be done with Jewish women, children and the elderly and Roma women and children whose husbands and fathers had been shot? At the end of October 1941, they decided on a temporary solution: the construction of a camp in Semlin (Zemun) on the bank of the Sava River opposite Belgrade. On 8 December 1941, the Jews, and most probably the Gypsies as well, were transported to Semlin, now under the command of the German Security Police. Yugoslav historians have estimated the number of Jews incarcerated there at 7,500, along with 292 Roma women and children.[22]

In the spring of 1942, the Jewish prisoners were gassed in an extermination van brought in especially from Germany for that purpose.[23] By contrast, the Roma women and children were released from Semlin. The exact date of their release remains unclear. In his 1967 trial, former Semlin commandant Herbert Andorfer recalled that the Roma were released immediately prior to the commencement of the murder of Jewish women and children, hence in March 1942.[24] However, since memory can often be deceptive when it comes to time, it is also conceivable that the decision to spare Roma women and children was linked to a discussion between Himmler and Heydrich held on 20 April 1942 and recorded in Himmler's service diary as: "No extermination of the Gypsies."[25]

This entry by the Reichsführer-SS could help to explain the release of Roma from Semlin, an action whose motives have remained to date obscure. In 1942, Himmler had begun to develop an interest in the Indian origin of the Gypsies. This led him to the notion that among the Roma were a small group of 'racially pure' Gypsies who, because they had originated in India, were bona fide 'Aryans.'[26] Although Himmler's diary entry does not have the force of a basic policy decision,[27] seen from this vantage point, his brief note points to differences in the SS leadership regarding extermination policy *vis-à-vis* Jews and Gypsies.

At the end of 1942 a further order signed by Himmler brought a degree of coherence into the diffuse and unsystematic persecution of the Gypsies. This order and the subsidiary decrees that followed it provided for the deportation of Gypsies from Germany, Austria, the Protectorate of Bohemia and Moravia, the Netherlands, Belgium and northern France to Auschwitz-Birkenau. Later, they were also deported from Poland, Russia and Lithuania. The guidelines for deportation, which were progressively radicalized in practice, established a hierarchy of three groups, defined in racial terms. Of these, only the first small group—the 'pure blooded' and '*Mischlinge* [mongrels], who were good by Gypsy standards'—were to be permitted to reproduce themselves. The second group of 'socially integrated Gypsy *Mischlinge*' were to be forcibly sterilized. Those deported to Auschwitz-Birkenau counted as the third group, at the bottom of the list in terms of their purported 'inferiority.' These 'Gypsy *Mischlinge*,' branded as 'socially not integrated' were never to be released from the camp system. This was a death sentence—but one that was never made explicit and which allowed the responsible authorities to maintain the pretence that, since in Auschwitz the camp commandant was in charge, they were not answerable for the predictable death of the Gypsies.

Over 19,300 of the roughly 22,600 Gypsies crammed together in Auschwitz-Birkenau died there. The great majority of them—like the Soviet POWs—perished of hunger, sickness and epidemic diseases. In order to make space for the Jews from Hungary and other countries whom the SS did not immediately murder on arrival, the Gypsy camp was liquidated at the beginning of August 1944. The Gypsies who were still there were gassed. Not all of those who came out of Birkenau alive survived the end of Nazi Germany. Transported to other camps before the summer of 1944, many died as a result of forced labor or horrific sterilization experiments. Others died on the death marches in the closing weeks of the war, in Bergen-Belsen or as suicide commandos in the SS Dirlewanger Brigade. As late as the spring of 1945, that unit was still sending Gypsies to the front line of fire in the fight against the Red Army. Meanwhile, in Germany the practice of compulsory sterilization of Gypsies was stepped up and systematized from 1943 on.

SIMILARITIES IN TREATMENT

The murder of Jews and Gypsies and the mass death of Soviet POWs had the following in common: They were directed at groups of people whom the Nazis characterized as racial entities, or more generally as sub-humans, but some of whom regarded themselves neither as a unified ethnic group nor as a nation in the modern sense of the word. This is self-evident in the case of the ethnically and nationally heterogeneous POWs from the Soviet Union, colonized by the tsarist empire and incorporated into a homogeneous 'Soviet people' solely by Stalinist fiat. But for parts of European Jewry, too, there was no necessary congruence between national, religious and cultural identity in the first half of the twentieth century. In Germany, to take but one example, Jews formed a highly differentiated group with strong ties to the majority population; the leading Jewish organization bore the telling name Central Association of German Citizens of the Jewish Faith (Centralverein deutscher Staatsbürger jüdischen Glaubens), and Zionism was a minority movement by comparison. In the case of those persecuted as 'Gypsies,' the notion of a unified identity is equally inappropriate, since at that time the concept of a common nation or nationality was meaningful only for a tiny fraction of them.[28]

But National Socialist racism also identified 'Gypsy blood' in and attached the label of 'Gypsy *Mischlinge*' to people who were completely integrated into the majority population and did not regard themselves as 'Sinti,' 'Roma' or 'Gypsies' at all. Here there was a parallel to the anti-Jewish Nuremberg Laws. While the definition of 'Jews' used there referred back to the identifiable confessional affiliation of an individual's grandparents, it was also applied in practice to people who were themselves indifferent to the Jewish tradition, had converted to Christianity, or were atheists. Granted, the *Mischlinge* played a different role in the categorization of Jews than that of Gypsies. In both cases, though, what was decisive for the racial labeling of an individual as 'Jew' or 'Gypsy' was not their own self-image, but an image imposed on them from outside.

Several other common features of Nazi extermination policies can be identified:

• dictatorship and war as fundamental determinants: All opposition on the basis of democratic and human rights principles was suppressed in Germany; the vast majority of members of German society who were not subject to persecution on the grounds of being 'racially inferior' or 'alien to the community' saw themselves as part of a *Volksgemeinschaft* that had to pull together in the face of Germany's wartime enemies, especially the Soviet Union.

• institutional preconditions comprising a bureaucracy, military and police machinery able to impose a grip on its targets, both on its own territory and in the occupied lands, and which, if not completely comprehensive, were nonetheless fairly systematic.

• a mental predisposition in favor of mass extermination provided by a racist approach to social questions and not confined to the ideological elites of the regime, and which, by deploying concepts such as 'final objective' and 'final solution,' opened the way for biological 'solutions' up to and including letting victims die, compulsory sterilization, and systematic murder.

• a policy of mass killing that was not planned in advance in 1933 or even in 1939, but only crystallized under wartime conditions in the interaction between regional initiatives and central decisions, and rapidly escalated to murder in the context of frictions and failures in Nazi policy; here, the attack on the Soviet Union as a 'Jewish-Bolshevik' power and its lack of rapid success played a key role.

• a regime and a population complicit in treating murder and the acceptance of mass death as taboo subjects, so that both verbally and through everyday behavior awareness of the crimes was glossed over.

• a dictator who was indispensable to the legitimation of mass extermination and condoned it, but who was only one of a number of factors in its execution—one whose specific importance has declined in the historiography as the radicalizing influence of other central and regional agencies has become clearer. Particularly in the case of persecution of the Gypsies, it is plain that the instrument of an order issuing from Hitler himself played nothing like the role that older accounts of Nazi extermination policy attributed to it. On the contrary, in this case the initiative often came from institutions such as the Reich Criminal Police Office and from regional policymakers.

Moreover, there was an important common element in the psychological strategies deployed, both in denying and in legitimating mass murder—though this is relatively under-researched in studies of the treatment of Soviet POWs. Murdering people, or letting them die, involved a division of labor. The resulting division of responsibility, the military chain of command, the conventions of civil administration that dictated that instructions from superiors both compelled action and relieved individuals of responsibility, and the tendency of bureaucratic processes to be seen as a legitimate end in themselves all contributed to the numbing of conscience and denial of personal responsibility. In the case of the Jews and Gypsies, the police and bureaucracy veiled the deportations in the language of 'evacuation' (*Evakuierung*), 'resettlement' (*Aussiedlung*) and 'relocation' (*Umsiedlung*); or 'transports' (*Transport*); or—in the case of the Gypsies—even of 'travel' (*Reise*). Like the terms 'final solution' (*Endlösung*) or 'ultimate solution' (*endgültige Lösung*), which were not originally meant to imply extermination, these phrases obscured the steps to murder by the very fact of being open to many interpretations.

There were other common patterns as well: people claimed they were only following orders, or that other institutions had played an even bigger part in the killing or had borne more responsibility. Furthermore, in the case of mass killings that a person had witnessed or known about, they could imagine (or claim) that these must have been isolated incidents or excesses, carried out without the knowledge or approval of the leadership under pressure of war. Another mechanism that had the consequence of easing the psychological burden was the effort to dehumanize the victims. The Soviet POWs, crammed together under horrific conditions like the Jews and Gypsies who were held in ghettos and extermination camps, rapidly became so ill and weak that the people who had created these conditions could see them as 'subhuman.' Then the fiction that elimination of the victims through mass murder could even be an act of mercy came into play. Indeed, the participants tried to legitimate these murders with the claim that killing was a much 'more humane solution' than a slow death from hunger and disease—a way out that would have the advantage of preventing the spread of epidemics and thus save the lives of POWs, Jews and Gypsies who were not already doomed.

In the case of members of the SS, police and military who were directly involved in shooting the victims, the constellation was again different. For them, the commandment "Thou shalt not kill" was canceled out, not only by ideological motivations, but also by a form of group pressure that dictated that each man should take part actively in a murder at least once. Careerism, brutalization, alcoholism and an increasing pleasure in killing itself also had some influence, along with an image of masculinity according to which shooting people to death was evidence of male toughness. Finally, there was the comforting knowledge that the killings had the unconditional backing of the political leaders.[29]

The statements with which SS-Einsatzgruppen, Wehrmacht units and police attempted to justify the killing of Jews, Soviet POWs or Gypsies made an instrumental connection between familiar anti-Semitic, anti-Russian and anti-Gypsy clichés and the demands of German war-making and administration of the occupied territories. Alongside the stigma of the 'unproductive consumer' and the 'alien element,' they invoked the catchwords of spy and partisan against their victims. Stereotypes such as these enabled the murderers to conjure up a balance sheet with the bogey-man of 'Jewish bolshevism,' the partisan activities of 'Russian sub-humans,' or the 'espionage' of 'Gypsy agents' on one side, and their crimes on the other, and to draw the conclusion that the killings had made a positive contribution to the war effort. Sometimes the murder itself provided legitimation for further killings. When Einsatzkommando 9 was preparing to shoot 20 Gypsies in Vitebsk in early 1942, an old Gypsy woman pleaded for her life. The commandant refused, with the comment that if she were spared the execution could not be kept secret.[30]

DIFFERENCES IN TREATMENT

Despite these common elements, significant differences can be identified between the mass deaths of Soviet POWs, Jews and Gypsies. The principal differences appear to lie in the hierarchical nature of Nazi racial policy and in the definitions of the various victim groups, arising from different patterns of hostility toward Russians, Jews and Gypsies, as well as in the intensity of persecution.

First, Nazi racial policy had a hierarchical structure. The central threat in this system came from 'Jewry,' who, unlike the Russians or Gypsies, were declared the 'universal enemy' of 'the Aryan peoples' and given the eschatological stamp of evil itself. Thus, Hitler, whose anti-Semitic tirades were legion, mentioned the Russians or other Slav peoples only in passing, and Gypsies hardly at all. Moreover, Eva Justin, a leading associate of the Race Hygiene Research Center in the Reich Health Bureau (Rassenhygienische Forschungsstelle im Reichsgesundheitsamt), which led the project of racial classification of the Gypsies, commented in 1943 that the "Gypsy problem" was not comparable to the Jewish problem insofar as the Gypsy character, unlike that of the Jewish intelligentsia, was not in a position to "undermine or endanger" the German people as a whole.[31]

Broadly, the same is true for the Nazi attitude toward the Soviet Union: Here, the vision of 'Jewish bolshevism' was unquestionably central to the construction of hate objects and negative projections, especially since reference to the Soviet Union as 'Russo-Judaea' had been part of right-wing rhetoric ever since 1917, and not only in Germany. 'Ordinary' Russophobia and anti-Slavism complemented this image since it was agreed that the Russians were 'sub-humans,' easily dominated and incapable of self-government. Only this 'inferiority'—it was argued—could explain how a tiny 'Jewish-Bolshevik' elite had been able to establish dominance. Conversely, this implied an expectation that the political system would collapse if this leadership cadre in the Red Army, state and society were to be exterminated.[32]

In contrast to the comprehensive Nazi hate-object—the 'Jewish counter-race'—that was allegedly contending with the 'Aryan peoples' for world domination, the Nazi stereotype of the 'Gypsy,' in particular, encompassed two contradictory and even mutually exclusive types. The differences between them had important consequences for the Nazi persecution of Gypsies in Germany and in the occupied territories of eastern and south-eastern Europe. Outside of the Reich, and particularly in eastern Europe, anti-Gypsy fantasies were directed primarily against traveling Gypsies, who (it was imagined) used their wanderings to disguise their activities as spies for the 'Jewish-Bolshevik enemy.' Inside the Reich, it was imagined that the 'Gypsy *Mischlinge*' were the real threat; partially or entirely sedentary, they maintained close contacts with non-Gypsies and were thereby allegedly 'penetrating' the 'body of the German nation.' Conversely, the largely endogamous Sinti who traveled around Germany were declared to be 'tribally authentic' (*stammecht*) or even—as Himmler and the SS Ancestral Heritage (*Ahnenerbe*) Office put it, in a racialist version of the traditional romantic image of the Gypsy—'pure-blooded,' and, since they originated in India, basically 'Aryan.' In the last phase of the war the Russian population, too, was combed for 'Aryan' elements. By contrast, the Nazis categorically denied that any Jew could aspire to Aryan status.

The fixation on the hate-object of the 'Gypsy *Mischling*,' which can be shown to have characterized attitudes in the Reich proper, was also linked to the special role of the concept of race hygiene in the Nazi persecution of the Gypsies. 'Race hygiene' existed alongside racial anthropology, which classified 'alien races' as inferior, and as a second variant of a form of racism that operated with the notion of 'genetic heritage' (*Erbgut*). According to this approach, certain groups within a race or a people were to be excluded on the grounds that they were inferior. In the Nazi system these included people who did not appear to conform to the norms of the 'German *Volksgemeinschaft*,' for example, homosexuals, and those classified as 'asocial.'[33]

Second, the definition of who counted as a Soviet POW from the German point of view between 1941 and 1945 was clearly a function of progress in the war effort itself. Within this group, the Wehrmacht and the Einsatzgruppen made a selection according to political and racist criteria (Communist Party functionaries in the first case, Jews or 'Asiatics' in the second). In the persecution of German Jews at least, the machinery of persecution operated uniformly with quite precise definitions. Such designations were not available for people stigmatized in the Reich as 'Gypsies' or 'Gypsy *Mischlinge*.' Who was a 'Jew' was decided by the Nuremberg Laws of 1935. This group needed to be distinguished by definition in one direction only, namely in relation to 'first-degree *Mischlinge*.' By contrast, it was the 'Gypsy *Mischlinge*' who stood at the center of the persecution of Gypsies in the Reich. No juridically precise definition of this term existed. Whatever characterization did exist was formulated vaguely with reference to genealogy and a criterion of 'social conformity.' This led to complications, since the relative importance of these two levels of definition—heredity, on the one hand, behavior in terms of degree of assimilation with the majority population, on the other—was a matter for debate. Beyond this, the concept of 'Gypsy *Mischling*' had to be defined in contradistinction to two other categories, or in two directions: against the 'pure-blooded' or 'tribally authentic' Gypsies, on the one hand, and against members of 'non-Gypsy families' with a 'trace of Gypsy blood,' on the other. If the definitions of 'Gypsies' and 'Gypsy *Mischlinge*' were vague in themselves, and complicated even more by rivalries between different institutions with competing criteria, the business of assigning real individuals to the notional categories created an additional problem. At the same time, this problem gave the persecutors on the ground an opening to apply the instructions they received from the center in accordance with their own interpretation, and that normally meant at the expense of the victims.

Third, it is difficult to understand the differences among the Nazi images and definitions of 'Jews,' 'Gypsies' and 'Russians' without knowing the history of these representations, which were similar in some respects but in others quite distinct. The ambivalence of attraction and revulsion was differently balanced, in ways that were specific to the dominant depiction of the Jew, the Gypsy and the Russian. In the social construct of the Gypsy, the dominant negative attributes associated with the cliché of the uncivilized and dangerous barbarian had a positive counterpart in the image of the noble savage. Cosmopolitanism and openness were cancelled out by the stigma of an urge for aimless and irregular wandering; simplicity of life and expectations corresponded to primitivism; innocence and lack of prejudice were related to a limited intellect, carefree sensuality, uncontrolled instincts and indecency.

In watered-down form, many of these perceptions featured in the image of Russians, although here simplicity and primitivism were most emphasized: namely, as a helot nation willing to put up with suffering and hard work, and of Russia as a 'colossus of clay' bound to collapse at the slightest prodding from outside. As applied to the Russians, these notions should be read against the background of Germanic colonization in the East and centuries-old struggles for power; in regard to the Gypsies, processes of social discipline that had been going on in western Europe since the Early Modern period provide the key background.

The equally ambivalent image of 'the Jew' was given particular shape by Christianity's deep-rooted and long-standing doubts about its own religious beliefs.[34] Even when an individual Jew abandoned the Jewish religion, he remained a symbol of the 'chosen people,' and thus an object of envy from a Christian, and then post-Christian, perspective. At the same time, the Jew personified all that, though rejected in the making of the New Testament, he nevertheless persisted in challenging by his very existence: Christianity's claim to be self-evident. This dichotomy between 'chosen one' and 'reject' was replicated in the myth of the 'Jewish plutocrat' and the 'Jewish Bolshevik,' and echoed in the contradictory images of the arch-traditional Orthodox Jew and the 'subversive' modernizer.

Fourth, while Germany's Wehrmacht and political leaders abandoned the Soviet POWs to die in millions in 1941 and early 1942, only to place greater stress on maintaining their labor force later on, the systematic murder of Jews and Gypsies continued uninterrupted from mid-1941 until shortly before the end of the war. Of course, the Jews were subject to a much more radical degree of persecution than the Gypsies, who were not threatened with murder in all the states occupied by or allied with Germany. While in the case of Germany within its 1937 borders—Austria, the Protectorate of Bohemia and Moravia, and Estonia—it is difficult to decide whether the Jews or the Gypsies suffered more extreme persecution, the German police and occupying authorities in west European countries—France, Belgium and the Netherlands—devoted more time to, and showed greater thoroughness in, the deportation of the Jews than in the registration and deportation of those classified as 'Gypsies.' Very few Roma were deported from the parts of Italy occupied by the Germans from the autumn of 1943, while the SS and the police at least attempted the systematic deportation of Jews.

In the case of Hungary, the removal of Roma to concentration camps in 1944–45, for all its horror, cannot be equated with the systematic deportation of Hungarian Jews to Auschwitz-Birkenau. The situation in Lithuania, Latvia, Slovakia, Poland, Serbia and the German-occupied part of the Soviet Union was analogous. There is no evidence of deportations or mass shootings of Gypsies in Denmark, Norway, Greece or Bulgaria. By contrast, the lives of European Jews were permanently under serious threat from northern Norway to Rhodes and from France to the German-occupied parts of the Soviet Union. This difference can be explained by the ideological dominance of anti-Semitism as well as by the way in which the image of the Jewish enemy was mobilized in German war-making and occupation policy. In German-occupied eastern Europe, for example, the murder of Jews was increasingly regarded as a tried and trusted method of dealing with supply bottlenecks, epidemics and housing shortages. In comparison to the Jews concentrated in large numbers in the Old Russian Pale of Settlement, eastern European Roma constituted a numerically insignificant group. This also explains why they were much less crucial to a policy of murder that was simultaneously racist and utilitarian.

DEFINING GENOCIDE

In 1948 the United Nations defined genocide as "any of the following acts committed with intent to destroy, in whole or in part, a national, ethnical, racial or religious group, such as: (a) killing members of the group; (b) causing serious bodily or mental harm to members of the group; (c) deliberately inflicting on the group conditions of life calculated to bring about its physical destruction in whole or in part; (d) imposing measures intended to prevent births within the group; (e) forcibly transferring children of the group to another group."[35]

There is no dispute that the murder of European Jewry fits these criteria. The mass shootings by Einsatzgruppen, police and military in eastern Europe and Serbia, their concentration in the Lodz ghetto and in Auschwitz-Birkenau, the gassing of thousands of prisoners, and the compulsory sterilizations inside and outside of the camp system mark the Nazi crimes against the Gypsies, too, as genocide. By contrast, letting the Soviet POWs die does not appear to be treated anywhere in the literature as genocide, since Nazi Germany let them die in their millions but did not link this to any project of eliminating the Soviet population as such. On the contrary, the majority of them were assigned the role of a helot population for the German 'master race' in its mission to colonize the East.

If we weigh the term 'genocide,' derived from international law, against the more open concepts of 'mass extermination' or 'mass crime,' the latter two terms have the same status from a moral point of view as well as from the perspective of historical research. In the context of Nazi policies of extermination, the phrase 'mass extermination' allows us to consider, alongside the murder of Jews and Gypsies, events such as the death of Soviet POWs, which, in terms of the numbers affected, were extraordinarily significant.

The most controversial aspect of the UN Convention on Genocide lies in the concept of intent, which must underlie a policy of extermination if it is to qualify as genocide. There are four positions on this question: The first holds that a word such as 'genocide,' essentially a legal term, cannot be usefully applied in the social sciences. A second position proposes that the term 'intent' be interpreted in such a way that the destruction of a national, ethnic, religious or racial group would count as genocide unless there was no evidence of human intention—as in the case of natural disasters, or an epidemic introduced by accident. The advocates of a third position insist that an overall plan is the necessary precondition for genocide. This is how Guenter Lewy proceeds in his book *The Nazi Persecution of the Gypsies*, taking into account the fact that there is no evidence in Nazi policy toward the Gypsies of a plan based on a long-term project of annihilation.[36]

Two objections to this position can be stated. First, it was a demand, at least of the Race Hygiene Research Center which was responsible for the racial classification of the Gypsies, that the estimated 90 percent of Gypsies whom they classified as '*Mischlinge*' should be sterilized and kept in sex-segregated camps. The aim of this policy was explicitly the 'disappearance' of the Gypsy *Mischlinge*.[37] This phrase cannot be used to support a simple intentionalist argument; the race hygienists' call for the 'disappearance of the Gypsy *Mischlinge*' cannot be equated with a politically implemented program of genocide. At the same time, however, there was a clear consensus between race hygienists and the German police authorities that 'Gypsy *Mischlinge*' should be prevented from reproducing themselves and/or should be 'eradicated' in other ways.

The second objection is of a more fundamental kind. None of the central episodes of mass murder in the 20th century can be proven to have been based on long-term planning[38] or a pre-determined program of killing. This also applies to the Nazi murder of Jews and Gypsies. This point becomes particularly clear when we consider that before the war the object of anti-Jewish policy in the Reich was to force the Jews to emigrate, notably, to Mandatory Palestine, while the deliberate killing began only three years later. Political leaders who were planning murder from the beginning would hardly have pursued a policy that drove the victims beyond their reach. As recent detailed research has demonstrated, the murder of the Jews emerged out of a series of individual decisions, which only in late 1941 and early 1942 came together to form a general policy adding up to genocide.

A situational decision-making process can also be documented for the murder of the Gypsies in Auschwitz-Birkenau. The initial impulse for the order to deport the Gypsies to Birkenau was Himmler's desire to culturally and biologically breed a 'racially pure' minority of Gypsies that would restore their 'Aryan' character. This necessarily raised the question of what was to be done with the remaining 'Gypsy-like persons' (*zigeunerische Personen*). The initiative for the Gypsy deportations in late 1942, however, lay not with Himmler but with the Reich Criminal Police Office. The police authorities used the SS-leader's romantic racist ideas for their own ends, skillfully harnessing Himmler to their purposes. Since 1942 the Kripo leadership had been trying to compensate for its loss of control over society by intensifying the use of concentration camp imprisonment. The deportation of purportedly deviant 'Gypsy *Mischlinge*' was in keeping with this line. In the process, the criminal police were prepared to countenance the large-scale death of allegedly 'inferior' Gypsy prisoners—assuming this was not actually intended. The answer to the question of how any survivors would be dealt with could await the end of the war, which they fantasized would be a German victory.[39]

A fourth position in defining 'genocide' argues that we need to take into account the intimate connection between stigmatizing a group, speculative considerations about how to get rid of its members, and the situational escalation of persecution into mass murder. Neither in the case of the murder of the Gypsies, which was not linked to an intention to kill the whole group, nor in that of European Jewry, where the intention was total destruction, was there a plan already prepared and awaiting implementation in 1933 or 1939. What happened in the form of shootings, imprisonment under murderous conditions, gassing and forced sterilization was intentional mass destruction, which in that sense amounted to genocide.

NOTES

1. Henry Friedlander, *The Origins of Nazi Genocide: From Euthanasia to the Final Solution* (Chapel Hill/London, 1995).
2. Christian Streit, *Keine Kameraden. Die Wehrmacht und die sowjetischen Kriegsgefangenen 1941-1945* (Stuttgart, 1978).
3. See Yehuda Bauer, *Rethinking the Holocaust* (New Haven/London, 2001); Christopher R Browning, *The Path to Genocide. Essays on Launching the Final Solution* (Cambridge, 1995); *Ordinary Men. Reserve Police Battalion 101 and the Final Solution in Poland* (New York, 1992); Christian Gerlach, *Kalkulierte Morde. Die deutsche Wirtschafts- und Vernichtungspolitik in Weißrussland 1941 bis 1944* (Hamburg, 1999); Christian Gerlach and Aly Götz, *Das letzte Kapitel. Der Mord an den ungarischen Juden* (Stuttgart/Munich, 2002); Ulrich Herbert (ed.), *National Socialist Extermination Policies. Contemporary German Perspectives and Controversies* (New York/Oxford, 1999); Raul Hilberg, *The Destruction of European Jews* (New York, 1985); Peter Longerich, *Politik der Vernichtung. Eine Gesamtdarstellung der nationalsozialistischen Judenverfolgung* (Munich, 1998); Hans Mommsen, *Auschwitz, 17. Juli 1942. Der Weg zur europäischen 'Endlösung der Judenfrage'* (Munich, 2002); Dieter Pohl, *Holocaust. Die Ursachen, das Geschehen, die Folgen* (Freiburg, 2000); Michael Wildt, *Generation des Unbedingten. Das Führungskorps des Reichssicherheitshauptamtes* (Hamburg, 2002); Leni Yahil, *The Holocaust. The Fate of European Jewry 1932-1945* (New York/Oxford, 1990).
4. Hans Jansen, *Der Madagaskar-Plan. Die beabsichtigte Deportation der europäischen Juden nach Madagaskar* (Munich, 1997); Magnus Brechtken, *"Madagaskar für die Juden". Antisemitische Idee und politische Praxis. 1885-1945* (Munich, 1998).

5. See footnotes 9 and 10 in this article.

6. Ulrich Herbert, "Arbeit und Vernichtung. Ökonomisches Interesse und Primat der 'Weltanschauung' im Nationalsozialismus," in Ulrich Herbert (ed.), *Europa und der 'Reichseinsatz'. Ausländische Zivilarbeiter, Kriegsgefangene und KZ-Häftlinge in Deutschland 1938-1945* (Essen, 1991), pp. 384-426, here pp. 415-18.

7. Streit, *Keine Kameraden*, p. 136.

8. Aktennotiz, 2. 5. 1941, Document 2718 PS, International Military Tribunal (IMT), Major War Criminals, Nuremberg 1947-49, Volume 31, p. 84; see also Gerlach, *Kalkulierte Morde*, pp. 46-59.

9. Wirtschaftspolitische Richtlinien für Wirtschaftsorganisation Ost, Gruppe Landwirtschaft vom 23. 5. 1941, Document EC 126, IMT, Volume 36, p. 135.

10. Streit, *Keine Kameraden*, p. 136.

11. Einsatzbefehl Nr. 8, 17 July 1941, IMT, NO - 3414, based upon the notorious Kommissarbefehl, OKH, Gen. Z.b.V. beim ObdH, Nr. 75/41 g. Kdos. Chef., 6. 5. 1941, Annex 2, Document 877 PS, International Military Tribunal [IMT], Major War Criminals, Nuremberg 1947-49.

12. Ulrich Herbert, *Fremdarbeiter. Politik und Praxis des 'Ausländer-Einsatzes' in der Kriegswirtschaft des Dritten Reiches* (Bonn, 1999), pp. 158-208.

13. Michael Zimmermann, *Rassenutopie und Genozid. Die nationalsozialistische 'Lösung der Zigeunerfrage'* (Hamburg, 1996); The National Socialist 'Solution of the Gypsy Question,' in Herbert (ed.), *National Socialist Extermination Policies*, pp. 186-209; Guenter Lewy, *The Nazi Persecution of the Gypsies* (Oxford/New York, 2000); Martin Luchterhandt, *Der Weg nach Birkenau. Entstehung und Verlauf der nationalsozialistischen Verfolgung der 'Zigeuner'* (Lübeck, 2000).

14. Examples: Staatsarchiv Detmold, M 1 JP/1611, Kommandeur der Gendarmerie Minden, 27. 2. 1937; Landesarchiv Berlin, Rep. 142 OGT 1-10-1-23, Landrat Hameln, 20. 9. 1934; Generallandesarchiv Karlsruhe, 364/Zug 1975/ 3II/Fasc. 23, Bezirksamt Mosbach, 11. 6. 1934; Staatsarchiv Marburg, Landratsamt Marburg, Bürgermeister von Neustadt, 21. 2. 1936.

15. Antoni Galinski, "Obóz dla Cyganów w Lodzi," in *Biuletyn Okregowej Komisji Badania Zbrodni Hitlerowskich w Lodzi* (Lodz, 1989), pp. 47-56, Zimmermann, *Rassenutopie*, pp. 221-9, Erika Thurner, *National Socialism and Gypsies in Austria* (Tuscaloosa/London, 1998), pp. 102-5.

16. Gerlach, *Kalkulierte Morde*, pp. 628-55, 859-84.

17. Bundesarchiv Berlin, R 58/217, EM 92, 23 Sept. 1941, p. 299; Zentrale Stelle der Landesjustizverwaltungen Ludwigsburg (Central Office of State Justice Administration, hereafter: ZS), AR 72 a/60, Verdict against Wiebens *et al.*, fol. 34-36; Institute for Contemporary History, Munich, MA 701/1, BdS, EK 3, Kauen 1 Dec 1941, Full listing of executions carried out in the area of EK 3 to Dec. 1, 1941, fol. 31; BAB, R 58/219, EM 150, 2.1. 1942, fol. 364; Bundesarchiv Berlin, R 58/218, EM 119, 20 Oct. 1941, fol. 239; for White Russia, see Gerlach, *Kalkulierte Morde*, pp. 1063-7.

18. Piotr Kaszyca, "Die Morde an Sinti und Roma im Generalgouvernement, 1939-1945," in Waclaw Dlugoborski (ed.), *Sinti und Roma im KL Auschwitz-Birkenau 1943-44* (Auschwitz, 1998), pp. 117-43. On the decision-making process, see

Dieter Pohl, *Nationalsozialistische Judenverfolgung in Ostgalizien 1941-1944. Organisation und Durchführung eines staatlichen Massenverbrechens* (Munich, 1997), p. 114.

19. Historical Archives Riga, Fonds 70, Inventory 5, file 15, p. 45; Staatsarchiv Nuremberg, ND, NOKW 2072, 281. Sdv., 23.6.42, Kommandierender General v.21.11.41. -VII 1045/41; ND, NOKW 2022, 281. Sdv., Abt. VII/I a, Tgb. Nr. 457/43 geh., 24.3.43, Bezug: O.K. 534, Br.B.Nr. 193/43 geh. v. 22.3.43, an Feld-Kdtr. 822; ZS, AR-Z 497/67, p. 143-44, SSPF Lettland - KdO, I a Nr. 800/42, 11. 3. 1942 and 3. 4. 1942.

20. Special Archives Moscow, 1323-2-292 b, p. 93, Runderlass des Befehlshabers der Ordnungspolizei im Generalgouvernement, 13 Aug. 1942.

21. Christopher Browning, *Fateful Months: Essays on the Emergence of the Final Solution* (New York, 1985); Walter Manoschek, *'Serbien ist judenfrei'. Militärische Besatzungspolitik und Judenvernichtung in Serbien 1941/42* (Munich, 1995); Zimmermann, *Rassenutopie*, pp. 248-58.

22. ZS, V 503, AR-Z 36/76, Vol. 1, Supplementary File of the State Commission Serbia on Establishing Crimes by the German Occupiers and their Auxiliaries in Serbia. See also Browning, *Fateful Months*, p. 71, and Manoschek, *'Serbien ist judenfrei,'* p. 178.

23. Staatsarchiv Nuremberg, ND, NOKW 1221, Ten-Day Report, 31 March 1942, fol. 4; NOKW 1444, Ten-Day Report, 20 April 1942, fol. 4; ibid., Ten-Day Report, 30 April 1942, fol. 4., BAB, R 70-Serbien-33, fol. 36.

24. Manoschek, *'Serbien ist judenfrei,'* p. 178; Zimmermann, *Rassenutopie*, pp. 256-7.

25. *Der Dienstkalender Heinrich Himmlers 1941/42.* Bearbeitet, kommentiert und eingeleitet von Peter Witte, Michael Wildt, Martina Voigt, Dieter Pohl, Peter Klein, Christian Gerlach, Christoph Dieckmann und Andrej Angrick (Hamburg, 1999), p. 405.

26. Zimmermann, *Rassenutopie*, pp. 297-304; Gilad Margalit, "Rassismus zwischen Romantik und Völkermord. Die 'Zigeunerfrage' im Nationalsozialismus," *In Geschichte in Wissenschaft und Unterricht* 7/8 (1998), pp. 400-20; Guenter Lewy, "Himmler and the 'Racially Pure Gypsies,'" in *Journal of Contemporary History* 34 (2), 1999, pp. 201-14.

27. There is no evidence of a fundamental discussion or of a basic decision-making process on Gypsy policy among the National Socialist leadership in spring 1942.

28. Zimmermann, *Rassenutopie*, pp. 72-5.

29. See Browning, *Ordinary Men*.

30. ZS, AR 72 a/60, Urteil gegen Wilhelm Wiebens, pp. 34-6.

31. Eva Justin, *Lebensschicksale artfremd erzogener Zigeunerkinder und ihrer Nachkommen* (Berlin, 1944), p. 120.

32. Hans-Erich Volkmann (ed.), *Das Russlandbild im Dritten Reich* (Cologne/Vienna, 1994).

33. See Burkhard Jellonnek and Rüdiger Lautmann (ed.), *Nationalsozialistischer Terror gegen Homosexuelle. Verdrängt und ungesühnt* (Paderborn, 2002) Wolfgang Ayaß, *'Asoziale' im Nationalsozialismus* (Stuttgart, 1995).

34. Lutz Niethammer, *Kollektive Identität. Heimliche Quellen einer unheimlichen Konjunktur* (Hamburg, 2000), pp. 440-1; Mordechai Breuer and Michael Graetz, *Deutsch-Jüdische Geschichte in der Neuzeit.* Vol. 1: *1600-1780* (Munich, 1996), pp. 49-60.

35. Frank Chalk and Kurt Jonassohn (eds.), *The History and Sociology of Genocide. Analyses and Case Studies* (New Haven/London, 1990), p. 10.

36. Lewy, *Nazi Persecution*, pp. 221-4.

37. Robert Ritter, "Die Zigeunerfrage und das Zigeunerbastardproblem," *Fortschritte der Erbpathologie, Rassenhygiene und ihrer Grenzgebiete* 3 (1939), pp. 2-20; "Primitivität und Kriminalität," in *Monatsschrift für Kriminalbiologie und Strafrechtsreform* 31 (1940), pp. 198-210.

38. Concerning this topic I disagree with Yehuda Bauer's point of view. See Bauer, *Rethinking the Holocaust*, p. 12.

39. Zimmermann, *Rassenutopie*, pp. 297-304; Patrick Wagner, *Hitlers Kriminalisten. Die deutsche Kriminalpolizei und der Nationalsozialismus* (Munich, 2002), pp. 129-43.

NAZI AND POSTWAR POLICY AGAINST ROMA AND SINTI IN AUSTRIA

ERIKA THURNER

INTRODUCTION

In postwar Austria there was minimal interest in the fate of the Roma.[1] Not only was research regarding the Gypsy genocide taboo, but for years attempts on the part of individuals and institutions to uncover and publish Nazi crimes against the Roma and Sinti were ignored and/or boycotted both socially and politically. The social marginality of this group and the lack of interest by the majority of society complemented each other. Even established historians showed only limited interest in the special treatment/exclusion of social outsiders. Thus, the study of the Roma/Sinti remained a minor theme. Even today awareness in Austria of the Nazi policy of genocide of the Roma and Sinti is slight.

Despite this neglect, important facts and findings have been available in published form for more than two decades.[2] Austrian Roma were affected by the racial theories and measures of the Nazi rulers similarly to the Jews. These two minorities—Jews and Roma—had little in common until the Nazi period. As a result of the National Socialist policies of persecution and extermination their destinies became interlocked. This meant that both groups were subjected to discrimination, expulsion, isolation, abrogation of rights, imprisonment, forced labor, sterilization, experimentation and extermination. The persecution of the two groups was carried out with the same radical intensity and cruelty, but the Jewish genocide received top priority in planning and execution because of the different social status and image of the Jews (as the eternal foe in Nazi ideology), as well as their larger numbers. The social position and economic situation, as well as the smaller numbers, of the Roma were not considered a threat to German culture;[3] hence, in Nazi ideology the Roma and Sinti were perceived as a 'secondary problem' and not a dangerous race like the Jews. Nevertheless, the Nazi period ended for the majority of the Austrian Roma in a 'final solution.' They were murdered in the gas chambers of Auschwitz-Birkenau or other extermination camps. The horrifying result: fewer than one-third of Austrian 'Gypsies' survived the Nazi Holocaust.[4]

The theoretical basis for this persecution was the Nuremberg racial laws, which became operative in Austria as well as in Germany as of March 1938. The "racially unworthy, criminal and anti-social Gypsies" caused classification problems for the Nazis since in theory they should have counted as Aryans because of their Indian origin. Thus the Roma were at first included in the larger circle of 'asocial' persons. This was only a temporary solution, for it has been proven beyond doubt that the Roma were already suffering discrimination for racial reasons, even if the scheme of extensive racial persecution had not yet been worked out in its final form.[5] In 1936 a permanent Eugenic and Population Biological Research Station under Dr. Robert Ritter was established in Berlin;[6] its task was to produce a scientific basis for further measures and to draft a 'Gypsy law.' This law, formulated in 1939, was never made public, but the Gypsy question and persecution continued throughout the Nazi era, under SS-Reichsführer Heinrich Himmler as overall chief of police.[7]

This chapter analyzes Nazi policy toward the Roma in Austria and discusses postwar attitudes toward Roma survivors and their descendants as a continuity of Austrian Gypsy policy.

PERSECUTION AND CONCENTRATION ON AUSTRIAN TERRITORY

At the start of World War II, 11,000 Roma and Sinti lived in the territory of present-day Austria. Nearly 8,000 Roma (Ungrika-Roma) inhabited the southeastern part, the Burgenland (part of western Hungary before 1921, with a Roma population that constituted 2.5 to 3 percent of the population). There they had lived nomadically, or in a settled or partially settled state, some of them for more than 300 years. However, giving up the nomadic way was a far cry from integration or assimilation. In Austria, as elsewhere, the dominant policy was the traditional one of trying simultaneously to make Roma settle and to drive them away. Therefore, the Roma settlements were seldom in the villages themselves but on the fringes, and often well outside the village boundaries. Until 1938, other groups, including 3,000 Sinti and Lovara, had dwelled for three to five generations in Austria, predominantly as nomads, making a living from their traditional occupations.[8]

In general, dislike and mistrust of the Roma was so strong in everyday life that when the National Socialists came to power, the Roma merely suffered a culmination of the existing policy of discrimination. All the measures that could be carried out under Nazi rule had already been formulated as ideas, especially in the two central areas of persecution, the Burgenland and Salzburg, where National Socialists soon infiltrated the local administration, rural constabulary and police. Their demands and published proposals to solve the so-called Gypsy problem included, for example, separation and internment in forced labor camps, expulsion from the country, annihilation through sterilization and reducing the 'Gypsies' to the same level as the Jews.[9]

In March 1938, near the time of the *Anschluss,* Austrian National Socialists in the Burgenland initiated the first independent measures of persecution: forbidding children to attend school, prohibiting the playing of music as a profession, banning 'Gypsies' from voting, restricting their movements, and notably, subjecting them to forced labor under the surveillance of SS- and SA-squads. These actions were taken even before the setting up of internment camps and before Himmler issued the Circular Decree of December 1938 (demanding regulation of the "Gypsy question according to racial characteristics") and the Settlement Decree of October 1939.[10]

It can thus be seen that persecution of the Roma in the Nazi Reich was a process that developed its own momentum and evolved as it went along. Although the general direction was established, the details, timetables, means and finally the degree of intensity and brutality were not planned in advance. The orders from above relating to the 'Gypsies' were carried out because ideological discrimination had become deeply embedded in the population over the centuries. From the outset the radical proposals and petitions of Austrian National Socialists (prior to March 1938, 'illegal Nazis') influenced the entire Nazi program against the 'Gypsies' in Austria, and the Burgenland in particular was ahead of Nazi Germany itself (e.g., in the early exclusion of Roma children from school attendance).[11]

Local measures and orders issuing from the center complemented each other. As of 1938–9 individuals and groups of Roma were deported to concentration camps (Dachau, Buchenwald, Mauthausen and Ravensbrück). In June 1939 only Burgenland Roma were affected by Himmler's "Preventive Measures for Fighting the Gypsy Plague in Burgenland"—the name given to the first large deportation of some 3,000 Roma to the concentration camps of Dachau and Ravensbrück. As of 1938, special forced labor camps and central collection centers were set up. These *Zigeuner-Anhaltelager* (Gypsy internment or collection camps) existed in Germany as well as in countries occupied by the Nazis. They included the harshly run camps in Austria, which existed in the two main areas of persecution, the Burgenland and Salzburg. In Salzburg the Salzburg-Maxglan camp, for about 300 inmates, was erected in 1938. A total of more than 4,000 prisoners passed through the Burgenland Lackenbach camp, which existed from fall 1940 until March 1945.

Both Austrian camps were established as family camps. Daily life there was marked by hard work and a lack of facilities, with personal freedom restricted to the bare minimum. Men, women and children suffered the same horrors and oppression as prisoners in concentration camps: beatings, standing for hours at roll call, food deprivation and slave labor under the harshest conditions.[12] They were different from the big concentration camps only in the fact that the *Zigeunerlager*—set up in preparation for the 'deportation to the East'—served as transit camps. From there the inmates were shipped to the ghettos, and to concentration and extermination camps—where the majority died in gas vans or gas chambers or as a result of the miserable conditions in the camps.

FINAL DESTINATIONS: GHETTO LODZ/AUSCHWITZ-BIRKENAU

The systematic physical extermination of Roma from Austria began with five transports to the Jewish ghetto in Lodz. Between December 1941 and March 1942 a total of 5,007 Roma and Sinti were assembled in Austria and deported to Lodz. All died in the gas vans of Chelmno or as a result of the wretched conditions in the ghetto. The next step can be seen as the final stage of the 'final solution' for the Roma from Austria: Heinrich Himmler's infamous Auschwitz Decree of December 1942. In the instructions issued in January 1943 it was noted that all 'Gypsy half-breeds' (*Mischlinge*) and *Rom-Zigeuner*, as well as Gypsies from the Balkans, were to be sent to concentration camps "regardless of the degree of mixture." (In 1939, 8,500 so-called *Rom-Zigeuner* (meaning Austrian 'Burgenland-Rom' or 'Ungrika-Roma') had been classified as *zigeunerisches Mischlingslumpenproletariat* with an extremely high degree of mixture.[13]) The destination was the Gypsy family camp in Auschwitz-Birkenau established especially to receive them.

For the majority of European Roma who were deported to Auschwitz-Birkenau, the family camp for Gypsies was in fact their final destination. As of March 1943, more than 20,000 Roma from 11 European countries streamed into this camp.[14] As part of this campaign, some 2,900 Roma and Sinti from Austria arrived at the family camp in ten transports. In addition to victims who until then had lived outside the camps (in hiding or not yet recognized as Gypsies), prisoners from the Salzburg camp as well as from the Lackenbach camp were shipped to Auschwitz.[15]

Horrific conditions in the Gypsy camp of Birkenau Section BIIe awaited those who were deported. The situation in the 32 barracks even surpassed the misery that was the general state of affairs in the rest of the camp. Several concentration camp memoirs contain accounts by members of other persecuted groups "about the peculiar people whose strange, illustrious colorfulness suddenly vivified the camp." Others, such as prisoners who performed official functions, were aghast at the miserable conditions to which human beings were being subjected, but especially those that prevailed in the grossly overcrowded barracks. It is not surprising that there was no need to use physical violence: one half of the inmates succumbed to their living conditions—of diseases, epidemics and exhaustion—thus adding to the numbers of victims.[16]

The Birkenau Gypsy complex was run as a family camp. This type of concentration camp constituted an exception in the National Socialist camp system, which also included forced labor camps for the Gypsies as a group (e.g., *Zigeuneranhalte- und Arbeitslager* Salzburg, Lackenbach). However, as a family camp it by no means represented a privilege for those confined in it. Rather, it embodied their strategic and goal-oriented considerations. In some cases, such camps also served propaganda purposes, like the section of the Theresienstadt concentration camp prettied up for use as a film set (*The Führer Gives the Jews a City*). In the case of the Roma and Sinti, this facility resulted from concrete experience—persecution that involved the separation of families and, above all, the removal of children, led to resistance and unrest.[17] Thus, this policy ceased, especially when annihilation was imminent. This causal connection, as well as bottlenecks in providing camp uniforms, serves to explain the fact that some Roma were permitted to retain their own clothing.

Actually, the term 'family camp' should be relativized in the case of the Roma as well, since most families had already been torn asunder prior to their arrival in Auschwitz-Birkenau. Nearly every family was dispersed among several concentration camps. Even during the death transports, selections on the basis of work capacity were conducted. The inmates were scanned one last time before the Gypsy camp was finally closed in early August 1944. As a result, the barracks population was reduced to 2,897. The lives of these children, women and men were terminated in the gas chamber during the night of 2–3 August 1944.[18]

AUSCHWITZ DECREE
AND EXCEPTIONS

At the end of March and beginning of April 1943, most of the *Zigeuner-Anhaltelager* were closed, following Himmler's Auschwitz decree. According to instructions from January 1943, "Gypsy half-breeds, Roma and Balkan Gypsies" were moved to the center of persecution and extermination. Special regulations for "socially assimilated and pure Gypsies" intended for the majority of Sinti and Roma were not worth the paper they were written on.[19] The Salzburg-Maxglan camp in Austria was completely cleared. Only the Lackenbach camp was kept open until the end of the war. In general, the local authorities saw Himmler's Auschwitz Decree as their chance to completely rid their respective city or region of 'Gypsies.' Only in municipalities or regions where the Roma were needed in the labor force did the camps remain in operation, though with a reduced population. Thus, the rules providing for exceptions and the regulations determining who would be selected were interpreted flexibly in order to be able to adapt them to local 'constraints.'[20]

In Burgenland the Roma were needed as workers. The case of Austria and the Lackenbach camp demonstrates that the labor element played an additional, and sometimes in certain areas, a crucial role. The Roma and Sinti who had been designated as 'unwilling to work' by the Nazis were not only to be punished by means of forced labor but also annihilated.

In persecuting Roma, Nazi officials enjoyed a degree of latitude in their administrative spheres. Lower-level bureaucrats could exert direct influence and thereby affect the outcome of life-or-death decisions. Through these decisions some 600 inmates of Lackenbach camp survived. Economic considerations and the needs of industry put a stop to the pointless policy of extermination—at least in the final years of the war. Other exceptions to keep Roma alive based, for example, on racial or social grounds, as outlined in Himmler's Decree, proved to be empty phrases and saved only a few Austrian Roma from persecution.[21]

By the spring and summer of 1943, the racial researchers had still not completed their work, though they had produced expert opinions on the racial makeup of individuals in a total of 25,000 cases.[22] Most members of Robert Ritter's staff displayed great zeal, sometimes traveling to forced labor and concentration camps to examine their subjects. These researchers were not just cogs in the machinery of persecution; rather, due to their 'expert testimony'—based on drawing up genealogies and family trees, blood samples, and measurement of facial features and body parts—they were thoroughly

deserving of the designation 'perpetrators.'[23] Nor did it end there: their findings and insights resulted in several of them pursuing impressive postwar ca-
reers in their chosen profession. Only rarely did 'Attestations of Racial Purity'
save the lives of 'pure Sinti' (Himmler's romanticized decision to spare 'pure
Sinti and Lalleri').[24] The vaguely formulated criteria of 'social adaptation'
allowed for great latitude in interpretation here as well. Behind such decisions
lay blind obedience, nationalistic zeal, hair-splitting devotion to detail and
even base resentment.

On the whole, the story of the persecution of the Gypsies provides an
excellent example of that remarkable mixture of fanaticism and opportunism
that made such an essential contribution to the functioning of the system. The
extensive apparatus was set in motion with an enormous investment of money
and effort. In the case of the Roma, the implementation of persecution measures involved the SS only to a very limited extent; rather, the job was carried
out thanks to the ignominious collaboration of government authorities, the
police and other law enforcement agencies with the assistance of health, welfare and labor bureaus—in other words, the very organizations that had always been assigned the task of dealing with 'outsiders.' They all contributed to
the final result—from 200,000 to 500,000 European Roma and Sinti, as well
as other human beings persecuted as 'Gypsies' were exterminated during the
period 1933–45. As noted, fewer than one-third of the 11,000 Austrian Roma
and Sinti lived to see the end of the war in the spring of 1945.[25] Moreover,
even after liberation, survivors and their descendants had to continue struggling for a life of human dignity.

COMMON 'PERSECUTION GOALS,'
DIVERGENT POSTWAR ATTITUDES

German and Austrian National Socialists had joined forces, but the two states
went separate ways after the war. With the exception of prominent war criminals who were tried in Nuremberg (*Nürnberger Prozess*, 1945–6), most of the
perpetrators and their accomplices—protected by the political climate and the
prevailing atmosphere in their respective homelands and places of asylum—
could escape serious charges. Brief de-Nazification followed by social integration became the norm. Although Germany as a state could not escape blame
and responsibility for National Socialism, even there convictions and sanc-
tions of perpetrators and collaborators were limited to a few cases. The others
did not have to fear severe punishment, let alone social contempt. Given this

respectability of the perpetrators, there was little shame or sympathy for the victims.[26]

Austrian perpetrators and collaborators encountered an even more favorable situation. They exploited the chance offered to the Second Republic to affirm the position of the Austrian state and society as victims. After 1945, the Austrian government proceeded on the basis of the victim status that it had been granted in the Moscow Declaration of 1943. Austrians were only too glad to overlook and hush-up "Austria's shared responsibility for National Socialism and its crimes" that was likewise formulated in the Moscow Declaration. Perpetrators and accomplices found many forms of protection in the shadow of the victim myth, which brought unpleasant consequences for surviving victims of Nazi persecution. Thus, Austria saw itself as "the first victim of Hitler's policy of aggression" and, in contrast to Germany, was not obliged to pay any indemnification to the victims. Accordingly, victims could not pursue legal claims for compensation. However, the republic provided welfare payments to those in desperate need (so-called victims' welfare measures, or *Opferfürsorge-Maßnahmen*), though this, too, was done very grudgingly. From the outset, different categories of victims—and thus hierarchies—were created and certain groups were passed over.[27]

At first, only 'political persecutees' were acknowledged so as to not endanger Austria's victim status. It was not until 1949 that those persecuted on the basis of race were accepted as being entitled to support. Payments began slowly in 1952. Some victims received payment in installments as compensation for the time they had spent in prison or concentration camps. Nevertheless, pressure from the Allies was still necessary to bring this about, and there was no one to exert it on behalf of certain groups.[28]

CONTINUITIES IN STIGMATIZATION

The Roma and Sinti, above all, came to realize that Nazi socio-cultural patterns and judgments had not been eradicated in 1945. For them, a group that had suffered discrimination and exclusion prior to 1938, the process of being recognized as victims proceeded in particularly painful fashion, and to this day has not been brought to a positive conclusion. The few survivors were denied recognition as victims of racial persecution—a status that was problematic in any event—with the same intensity and tenacity they had suffered as an 'alien race.' Further stigmatization and unchanged attitudes perpetuated persecution motifs (such as harassment due to 'asocial behavior,' 'aversion to work' and criminality), which caused them considerable hardship and put them at a distinct disadvantage in their attempts to obtain indemnification. Their persecution was justified with arguments borrowed from Nazi biology and race ideology. Declarations of Austrian officials that the Nazi policies of persecution in their manifold forms—with the common goals of genocide and ethnocide—were eugenic or intended as crime prevention measures and, in any event, were socially necessary, met with scant protest.[29]

Thus, during the postwar period the National Socialists' measures of discrimination and persecution were applied with particular brutality against the victims. Instead of granting aid to those among the Roma and Sinti who had suffered at the hands of the Nazis, the Federal Ministry of the Interior issued a warning to potential concentration camp swindlers who were out to take advantage of the situation. Instead of enacting indemnification and support measures, hatred of concentration camp survivors was stirred up among law enforcement agencies. All those who could not prove beyond a doubt their right to remain in Austria—documented in citizenship papers or evidence of previous right of permanent residence—were treated as 'stateless citizens' or 'foreigners' and deported. It was no use objecting that the Nazis had confiscated these documents and that the very process of persecution had robbed them of their status. Those who refused to be intimidated and attempted, in spite of this hate campaign, to apply for compensation or victim pensions, ran the risk that their stories of concentration camps and persecution would expose them to slander charges. Some survivors were silenced in this way and thus prevented from undertaking what was in any event usually a futile attempt to obtain financial compensation.[30]

Some tried, nonetheless, and they—perhaps 10 percent of all survivors—were subjected to inquisitorial and demeaning procedures, one of which was a possible confrontation with their former persecutors in the guise of government officials and experts (i.e., SS doctors). Not a few former Nazis—quickly rehabilitated or never found out—obtained government jobs, and some were entrusted with the task of writing expert medical opinions. But it was not only former party members who were stigmatizing these victims anew. The republic generally displayed particular toughness and resistance concerning the injuries and health impairment of concentration camp survivors. The majority of government officials with jurisdiction over such issues (whether intentionally or not) assisted the state in maintaining this stance.[31]

VICTIM STATUS REFUSED,
COMPENSATION REFUSED,
BOURGEOIS STATUS REFUSED

Thus, these Roma and Sinti victims of Nazi persecution went on to become victims of the compensation process. Their standing as victims remained controversial. Not only were they denied the status of 'racial victims' during the early postwar period—although no high court ever officially confirmed this judgment—but the position they were accorded within the social hierarchy was accompanied by Nazi charges that they were 'asocial elements.' They never lost the stigma of having been criminals and thus persecuted for good reason. This meant that other groups of victims showed no solidarity with them and long refused to have anything to do with them.[32]

In spite of limited interest by the majority culture and society, some action has been taken, on the basis of previous research results, as well as of those parallel to this research.[33] In the two central areas of persecution—Lackenbach/Burgenland and Salzburg—memorials have been erected (1984/1985). A small group of Roma and Sinti and of non-'Gypsies' (*gadje*) protested against past injustices and the concentration camp pensions denied them. Although belated, this activity resulted in reparations from 1988.[34]

Once again this was done very grudgingly and the commemorative year held in 1988 did little to change this. The limited recognition of Roma and Sinti as Nazi victims (in Austria since 1988) as well as their status as an ethnic minority ('Austrian ethnic group' since 1993) came much too late. The prejudices that had already been widespread before the Nazi era, the denigration of this group that became even more intensive and extensive as a result of National Socialism, and the absence of a correction of this situation after 1945, continue to have an impact to this day, both on the victims and on their descendants.

NOTES

1. The term 'Roma' as a self-descriptive name is used as a general term for all the various groups: Roma (Ungrika-Rom), Sinti (Lalleri), Lovara, Kalderash; nowadays generally accepted as a totality for all groups. However, the majority of German and Austrian Sinti prefer to be addressed as Sinti and insist on differentiating between Roma and Sinti (or: Roma/Sinti).
2. The first unbiased study in German was conducted by a member of the Austrian resistance movement, the historian Selma Steinmetz, "Österreichs Zigeuner im

NS-Staat" (Austria's Gypsies in the National Socialist State), *Monographien zur Zeitgeschichte* (Vienna/Frankfurt/Zürich, 1966); for the Federal Republic of Germany, see Tilman Zülch (ed.), *Im Auschwitz vergast, bis heute verfolgt* (Gassed in Auschwitz, Still Persecuted Today) (Reinbek bei Hamburg, 1979). For Austria compare: Erika Thurner, "Nationalsozialismus und Zigeuner in Österreich" (National Socialism and Gypsies in Austria), *Veröffentlichungen zur Zeitgeschichte* 2 (Vienna/Salzburg, 1983). (Since 1998 a translation of this dissertation into English has been available: *National Socialism and Gypsies in Austria* [updated and expanded edition], edited and translated by Gilya Gerda Schmidt, foreword by Michael Berenbaum (Survivors of the Shoah Visual History Foundation Washington, University of Alabama Press, Tuscaloosa and London, 1998); and: in general, the fundamental, comprehensive study by Michael Zimmermann, "Rassenutopie und Genozid. Die nationalsozialistische 'Lösung der Zigeunerfrage'" (Racial Utopia and Genocide: The National Socialist "Solution of the 'Gypsy' Question") *Hamburger Beiträge zur Sozial- und Zeitgeschichte* 33 (Hamburg, 1996).

3. "The primitive Gypsy ways will never undermine or endanger the German people as a whole like Jewish intellectuals do"; see: Eva Justin, "Lebensschicksale artfremd erzogener Zigeunerkinder und ihrer Nachkommen," in: *Veröffentlichungen aus dem Gebiete des Volksgesundheitsdienstes*, Bd. 57, H. 4, Berlin, 1944, p. 120.

4. There are no exact figures. In early research results we estimated that less than half, and later, less than one-third, of the Austrian Roma and Sinti population did not survive. According to new research findings, based on data collections, about 20 percent survived the Nazi persecution. See Historikerkommission (Florian Freund, Gerhard Baumgartner, Harald Greifeneder) (ed.), *Vermögensentzug, Restitution und Entschädigung der Roma und Sinti* (Vienna, 2002), http://www.historikerkommission.gv.at

5. See Hans Buchheim, "Die Zigeunerdeportation vom Mai 1940," in *Gutachten des Instituts für Zeitgeschichte*, Bd. I, Munich, 1956, S. 57.

6. From 1937 on, it was called Eugenic and Criminal Biological Research Station.

7. See Thurner, "Nationalsozialismus und Zigeuner in Österreich," p. 18; 1998 edition, p. 12.

8. Walter Dostal, "Die Zigeuner in Österreich," in Archiv für Völkerkunde, Bd. X (Vienna, 1955), pp. 1-5.

9. Tobias Portschy, "Die Zigeunerfrage. Denkschrift des Burgenländischen Landeshauptmannes," Eisenstadt 1938, S. 36: "Der Geschlechtsverkehr zwischen Zigeunern und Deutschblütigen muß als Verbrechen der Rassenschande den strengsten Strafbestimmungen unterworfen werden. Wer die Zigeuner ihrem Charakter nach kennt, wird sie unbedingt den Juden in jeder Beziehung gleichstellen müssen."

10. "Ordnung in der Zigeunerfrage" (Order re the Gypsy Question), Grenzmark, Burgenland, 4 Aug., 1938; see: Thurner, "Nationalsozialismus und Zigeuner in Österreich," p. 39.

11. See Thurner, "Nationalsozialismus und Zigeuner in Österreich," pp. 40-1: Portschy began a campaign to exclude Gypsy children from school attendance

in fall 1938. Efforts in the *Altreich* to follow the path of Portschy had begun: "Exclusion already begins in the classroom; in addition to the Burgenland, West German cities also adopted this measure." They had to wait until November 1941 for such a decree.

12. Ibid., pp. 42–102.

13. Robert Ritter, "Zigeuner und Landfahrer" (Gypsies and Travelers), in *Der nicht-sesshafte Mensch* (Nomadic People). *Ein Beitrag der Neugestaltung der Raum- und Menschenordnung im Großdeutschen Reich* (Munich, 1938), p. 77. ("In contrast to the Jews, the Gypsy half-breeds [are] socially more inferior... than those who are racially pure.")

14. *Hefte von Auschwitz* (*Auschwitz Journals*), Museum of Auschwitz (Krakow, 1966); compare also: "Gedenkbuch. Die Sinti und Roma im Konzentrationslager Auschwitz-Birkenau," Staatliches Museum Auschwitz-Birkenau, in *Zusammenarbeit mit dem Dokumentations- und Kulturzentrum Deutscher Sinti und Roma*, 2 Bde. (Munich/London/New York/Paris, 1993).

15. Ibid.; compare also: "Widerstand und Verfolgung im Burgenland," Dokumentationsarchiv des Österreichischen Widerstandes (Vienna, 1979), pp. 252; 288–9.

16. Testimonies of 'Gypsy' prisoners and prisoners (*Ärzte, Arztschreiber*—Ella Lingens, Hermann Langbein); compare: Steinmetz, "Österreichs Zigeuner im NS-Staat" (1966, 1979); Thurner, "Nationalsozialismus und Zigeuner in Österreich" (1983, 1998). See also testimonies of survivors, for example Karl Eberle, who was in the Gypsy camp for one week and was then sent to the main camp, describing it as a civil institution compared to the Gypsy camp. Conversation, 30 April 1981.

17. In 1940 in Salzburg prison, the police tried to separate children from their families. The protests of the parents—acts of resistance and chaos—put a stop to this trial; see: Erika Thurner, "Eine tatsächliche Befreiung hat es nicht gegeben. Konzentrationslager in der Erinnerung von Roma und Sinti," in Tomas Dvorak, *et al.* (eds.), *Festschrift für Ctibor Necas* (Brno, 2003), p. 367

18. *Auschwitz Journals* 8 (1965), p. 55; compare also: "Widerstand und Verfolgung im Burgenland," 251 f., also Documents 54 and 55, 290 ff.

19. Express letter of 29 Jan. 1943, RSHA V A 2 No.59/43g, or Decree of RSHA V A 2 No.48/43g dated 25 Jan. 1943, and V A 2 No.64/43g dated 28 Jan. 1943, for the Alps and Danube districts. Source: Hans-Joachim Döring, "Die Zigeuner im NS-Staat," Bd. 12 der Kriminologischen Schriftenreihe (Hamburg 1964), pp. 156, 214–16; compare also Michael Zimmermann, "Die nationalsozialistische Vernichtungspolitik gegen Sinti und Roma," in *Politik und Zeitgeschichte*, supplement to the daily *Das Parlament*, B16–17, (Bonn, 1987), pp. 36f.

20. A ruling that granted exemption to socially adjusted individual 'Gypsies' with a permanent residence and members of the armed forces existed only on paper. It was known that the exemption clauses were only empty words on these extermination decrees. The racially pure, who were also exempted from the decree of 13 October 1942—like the other privileged—were sucked in by the campaigns if they had not gone underground. See *Auschwitz Journals* 9, pp. 41–2; Testimonies of 'soldiers' and 'pure bred Sinti'.

21. Ibid.

22. Reimar Gilsenbach, "Wie Lolitschai zur Doktorwürde kam. Ein akademisches Kapitel aus dem Völkermord an den Sinti," in *Feinderklärung und Prävention. Kriminalbiologie, Zigeunerforschung und Asozialenpolitik. Beiträge zur national-sozialistischen Gesundheits- und Sozialpolitik*, Bd. 6 (Berlin 1988), pp. 101-35.

23. Ibid., pp. 110-16

24. In reality Himmler probably followed only one goal, namely to save a limited number of pure-bred Roma (Sinti and Lalleri) for subjects of study; compare: Thurner, "Nationalsozialismus und Zigeuner in Österreich," p. 12.

25. See Ref. 4.

26. Thurner, "Die Roma. Opfer von NS-Verfolgung und Nachkriegsentschädigungs-politik," in Eleonore Lappin & Bernhard Schneider (eds.), *Die Lebendigkeit der Geschichte* (St. Ingbert, 2001), pp. 157-70.

27. Brigitte Bailer, *Wiedergutmachung kein Thema. Österreich und die Opfer des Nationalsozialismus* (Vienna, 1993); also: Robert Knight, *"Ich bin dafür, die Sa-che in die Länge zu ziehen": Die Wortprotokolle der österreichischen Bundesregie-rung von 1945-1952 über die Entschädigung der Juden* (Frankfurt/Main, 1988).

28. Bailer, *Wiedergutmachung kein Thema*, pp. 185-97.

29. Ibid., pp. 52-62; pp. 178-84.

30. In 1948 the Austrian Republic/Ministry of Security began a campaign to get rid of 'foreign gypsies' (Document first published, in Thurner, "Nationalsozialis-mus und Zigeuner in Österreich" [1983], Appendix XXVIII).

31. Bureaucratic officials and doctors who were former SS-members, for example: Dr. Gerhart Harre, university professor and leader of the *Salzburger Nervenk-linik* (SS-number 303067) was responsible for the medical certificate of Mrs. K., who survived the concentration camps Ravensbrück, Buchenwald and Bergen-Belsen; see: Thurner, "Ein 'Zigeunerleben'? Als Sinto, Sintiza, Rom und Romni in Salzburg," in Mozes F. Heinschink and Ursula Hemetek (eds.), *Roma—das unbekannte Volk* (Vienna/Cologne/Weimar, 1994), pp. 79-83; for more exam-ples, see Barbara Rieger, "Roma and Sinti in Österreich nach 1945," *Sinti- und Roma-Studien* 29 (Frankfurt/Main/Berlin/Bern/Brussels/New York/Oxford/Vi-enna, 2003), pp. 143-201.

32. Experiences of the author gained in 20 years among groups of victims in various locations (Zeitzeugen-Tagungen, KZ-Lagergemeinschaften, a.s.o.)

33. Steinmetz, "Österreichs Zigeuner im NS-Staat"; Thurner, "Nationalsozialismus und Zigeuner in Österreich" (1983); Thurner, *Kurzgeschichte des nationalsozial-istischen Zigeunerlagers Lackenbach, Eisenstadt* (1984). Selma Steinmetz and the author were engaged in gaining restitution for Roma/Sinti—in cooperation with other concentration camp inmates (members of the KZ-Verband, or other KZ-Lagergemeinschaften) and/or institutions: Österreichische Liga für Men-schenrechte, Gesellschaft für Politische Aufklärung; and, 1989 ongoing, to-gether with Roma and Sinti organizations.

34. An amendment of the *Opferfürsorgegesetz* for 'Lackenbach-prisoners,' 1988, and symbolic acts of recognition, e.g., Chancellor of Austria Franz Vranitzky, vis-ited the Lackenbach memorial in 1988; see Rieger, "Roma and Sinti," p. 170.

STORY, HISTORY AND MEMORY: A CASE STUDY OF THE ROMA AT THE KOMAROM CAMP IN HUNGARY

KATALIN KATZ

This essay presents a central chapter of the Hungarian *Porrajmos* ('Holocaust,' in Romanes, the language of the Roma, or Gypsies): the chronicle of the Komarom camp. As part of a study concluded in 2003, it also deals with the relationship of memory, story and history of the *Porrajmos*. The research on the *Porrajmos* in Hungary was carried out from a social science perspective, using a narrative methodology. It traces the construction of memory in its historic, social and political context. From this viewpoint, the memory of what happened to the Roma during World War II, particularly in Hungary, has been neglected to a certain extent and the role of the Komarom camp barely receives a mention.

Memory includes various expressions of remembering, but also of forgetting, enforced forgetfulness and denial. Difficulties in acknowledging the *Porrajmos* stem from a number of reasons: because it is related to a detached community, which experienced exclusion; because of its traumatic character; and because of the struggle between the social center and the periphery for the writing of history. Hence, the tragedy of the Hungarian Roma has never been recorded in a comprehensive manner.

THE *PORRAJMOS* IN HUNGARY

The persecution of the Roma in Hungary neither began with the outbreak of World War II nor ceased with the end of the war. However, it reached a peak during the Nazi occupation of Hungary between 19 March 1944 and 4 April 1945. During this period, which is relatively short compared to other countries in Europe, the German Nazi persecution and extermination machine worked hand-in-hand with the Hungarian Nyilas (Arrow Cross), with its mix-ture of cruelty and efficiency.[1]

Moreover, Hungarian Roma were persecuted for racist reasons in an at-tempt to wipe them out. Their names were registered; they were confined to their homes; assigned to forced labor; led to assembly points, compelled to board trains and sent to the Komarom camp inside Hungary and to concen-tration camps beyond the border; they were also forced to take part in 'death marches' to undisclosed destinations on empty stomachs; and were massacred in their home towns.[2] In the absence of precise documentation, it is impossi-ble to know the exact number of lives taken.[3] Today the survivors and their descendants are not only struggling against attempts to disavow and erase the memory of what happened to them, but also against new persecutions.

REMEMBERING
AND FORGETTING

The theories dealing with memory studies unite various elements that merge in the process of construction: the community—its history and central events, its organization and make-up, as well as the social powers working within it and around it; psychic factors; the ways individuals coped with the experi-ences they and members of their families underwent; cultural features and 'memory techniques;' and the current circumstances of the community and its needs.[4] Memory negotiates among all these sometimes conflicting issues, in order to create a story that will serve as a basis for transmission, and to which changes can be made in the future. Constructing memory is in effect a persis-tent struggle over what will be recorded and what will be forgotten; over what will be erased after having been inscribed and what will be recalled after it has already been forgotten; over what will be written and what will be recounted; and no less importantly, over how it will be retold.

Accordingly, memory includes both remembering and forgetting. These conflicting faculties battle continuously in an attempt to negotiate for space in the memory field. The areas of remembering and forgetting there are not fixed and each 'wins' or 'loses' parts of its territory during the construction process. The memory space is also constantly reformulated when it is illuminated from a different perspective, while the dark areas of forgetting conceal details that lose their power when not articulated.

FORGETTING
THE *PORRAJMOS*

In order to understand why the *Porrajmos* has been forgotten or erased from memory, we must deal with two principal aspects of memory construction: the intra-cultural facet of the Roma community and the inter-cultural social-political dimension (which examines the place of the Roma among European nations), and the relationship between them.

One of the central characteristics of Roma culture that has influenced the construction of memory in general and that of the *Porrajmos* in particular is the community's lack of a historical collective memory.[5] This is connected in part to the fact that the Roma are steeped in an oral culture as opposed to a written one. It is also linked to the absence of a hierarchical organization among the Roma and their dispersion throughout the world without their ever having had a defined territory of their own.[6] The traumatic nature of *Porrajmos* memories has caused further difficulties in telling the stories. According to Halbwachs, the community constructs the collective memory and memory reflects the community's construction; Roma fragmentation does not allow for narrative continuity.[7] In the absence of a narrative, there is no structured memory or collective or communicative meta-narrative with other communities.

The main reason for the severed-fragmented memory of the Roma, however, is their history of continuous persecution in Europe.[8] For 500 years the Roma were slaves in eastern Europe, while in western Europe they were expelled wherever they went and even persecuted to death.[9] This situation continued until the end of the 19th century when their persecution assumed a more modern facade, but did not cease.[10] Life in the shadow of persecution and in a position of slavery breaks the continuity of collective memory; this is also what happened to the Africans who were brought to America as slaves.[11]

Forgetting the *Porrajmos* goes hand-in-hand with the position of Roma in society in general. The "postmodern condition," notes Loytard, associates knowledge with power through narrative means.[12] Knowledge combined with power also constructs the hegemonic memory formulated by the central authority. The various narratives receive 'status,' that is, expression and legitimacy, based on the social standing of the storytellers. The ruling social power grants legitimacy to narratives that it endorses. The Roma, as an excluded group in society, have not gained the legitimacy to add their unique story to the hegemonic memory of the Holocaust, which is considered largely the story of the Jews as victims, and of the Germans as persecutors.

The Roma, as a community are regarded as 'the other,' which is struggling for recognition of its culture and rights in European society. The issue of power, which participates in the mutual establishment of memory and community, is illustrated through the postcolonial theory.[13] The Roma in Europe are the eternal 'other,' whose exile is in their homeland and their homeland is in their exile—in the absence of a fatherland and their own territory. Hence, their attempts to establish a memory of their genocide and their demands to include the *Porrajmos* as part of the history of the Holocaust have had little impact.

The struggle is complex and plagued with internal contradictions and ambivalences, emanating both from the central authority and from the peripheral communities. Society in general transmits an ambiguous message to marginal groups, requiring that they assimilate and renounce their cultural identity, while at the same time rejecting their attempts at integration and insisting that they maintain their foreignness and 'otherness.' These dynamics are also characteristic of the position of memory and its mode of construction. The marginal and rejected position of the Roma in society pushed the story of the *Porrajmos* into the margins of history far away from the center due to their status as the eternal 'other' in the European social context.

Consequently, traditional Roma culture, together with the Roma's marginal social position, has led to the memory of the *Porrajmos* remaining an intra-community memory. The community constructs the memory;[14] in so doing, the shards of memory of a disintegrating community such as that of the Roma can revive and strengthen it. To some degree, the stories of the *Porrajmos* were compiled into a common narrative among the Roma communities, but it was only in the late 1980s and the 1990s that attempts were made to impart these narratives to the outside world as well.[15] Most of these efforts, however, encountered indifference or a demand to distinguish between remembrance of the Jewish Shoah and Roma memory.[16] The time that has elapsed since the war and the sparse documentation on the subject have impeded its penetration of public consciousness. Testimonies from the few remaining survivors are difficult to obtain, although their significance in the documentation process is great.

NARRATIVITY
AND TRAUMATIC MEMORY

During the construction process of traumatic memory, which has a major role in rehabilitating both the life of the individual[17] and that of the collective,[18] 'memory work' must be undertaken in order to insert the traumatic event(s) into the continuity of the personal life story or into the history of the collective. Memory work is narrative. The traumatic story or stories are recounted and edited over and over again until they crystallize into a tale of significance, which can be absorbed into the personal life story or into the historic meta-narrative of the collective, and become an integral part of the historic events of the community. Without memory work, traumatic memory is dislocated and fragmented, leaving the individual or the collective rent and wounded.

Memory work requires two interdependent conditions: narrating, on the one hand, and social recognition, on the other. Without social recognition, that is, an expression of interest in the victim of the trauma and support of him or her, narration of the story is impossible. However, telling the story itself is also a condition enabling the victim to solicit sympathy in order to undergo rehabilitation. An encouraging social environment and the ability of the victim to recount the story are important components of the rehabilitation process.[19]

A number of narrativity stages take place during the process of traumatic memory work:

1. During and immediately following the traumatic state, the memory has not yet formed itself into a story and leaves the individual as well as the collective shaken, with a fixed recollection of the scenes of the events. The pictures are replayed repeatedly. There is a sense of threat. One hears the voices and smells the odors. This is the first stage of non-narrativity.

2. With a change in the traumatic situation, the victims recount the event to themselves, to those close to them or to members of their community, an intimate tale that is told for their own benefit. This is the stage of intra-narrativity.

3. Providing there is a supportive environment, the story will be carried outside the inner circle. The wounded will relate what happened to them and solicit sympathy, enabling them to retell the story and thus work over their trauma. This is the stage of inter-narrativity.

4. Based on the previous stages, the traumatic story can then be formulated into a memory of meta-narrative, which is placed within the continuity

of the life story and history. This story receives personal and social significance as it offers meaning and connects with the past and the future without violating identity.

This ideal process of memory work is always more complex in reality, and especially so where memory of the *Porrajmos* is concerned. Firstly, the end of the traumatic event is not at all clear-cut. Persecution of the Roma continued even after the change of the Nazi regime and continues today, albeit in a less extreme manner than that of the Nazi exterminations. Secondly, the character of the traditional Roma culture also means that Roma narrativity naturally reaches the intra-narrativity stage, but has difficulty in passing to the inter-narrativity stage. The marginality of the Roma, the absence of a supportive environment, and society's lack of recognition of them and the legitimacy of their narrative intensify this problem.

In the struggle for legitimacy of the Roma narrative, the contest with the Jewish collective, some of which claims 'Jewish exclusivity,' plays a role. In addition, the move by the Roma to the inter-narrativity stage, which would strengthen their power in the struggle for legitimacy of their story, is connected to processes of change in their own social structure—and hence also their culture. The conditions for this shift are narrativity and flexible cross-cultural communication.[20]

CROSS-CULTURAL COMMUNICATION

The move to inter-narrativity is linked to the Roma's communication with outside society. Communication includes narrating and the ability to listen and to understand. Habermas raises the need for communication in the 'world of life,' which requires flexibility within the dialogue and the ability of different social groups to behave openly to those unlike them.[21] Flexibility in the various dialogues will lead to the formation of a pluralistic society, which recognizes multiple social identities and allows for their coexistence. This ideal encounters difficulties because of a reality consisting of "manipulative communication," which imposes on society a dialogue fixed to serve the interests of powerful groups.

The reality of manipulative communication reflects the struggles of humanitarian groups. Each group fights for its interests with narrative tools[22] in an attempt to canonize its own story.[23]

These confrontations are mainly power struggles associated with the community's place on the political map, whether it be in the center or on the periphery, and the place of 'the others' on this map.[24] With the move of the Roma to inter-narrativity, stories about the *Porrajmos* are being constructed, and with the re-organization of the Roma, their power is growing; nevertheless, opposition to granting legitimacy to the Roma narrative is also gaining strength. The struggle is not yet resolved; but the mere fact of its taking place has raised somewhat public awareness of the story of the *Porrajmos*.

The research conducted by the author was based largely on testimonies: 57 interviews conducted with Roma survivors all over Hungary. Interviews published over the years in various journals were also used, as well as all manner of written documentation that it was possible to extract from army, police and government records and newspaper articles from the war years.

The Komarom camp had a central role in the story of the Hungarian *Porrajmos*. It was the main gathering point for Roma in the final stages of the war—from November 1944 until Hungary's liberation by the Red Army in April 1945. As such, it plays both a concrete and a symbolic role in the memory of the *Porrajmos*. In this unique story, young children and their mothers were released from the camp after a relatively short time. Since many of these children survived and lived to be able to testify, the Komarom camp came to be chosen for this study.

KOMAROM

The story of the Roma in the Komarom camp recounted here is a summary based on the above sources. Extracts from the interviews will also be presented verbatim (in translation), in order to bring the victims' tales to life.

The city of Komarom is on the northern border of Hungary directly facing the Slovakian city of Komarno. Both cities, which are mirror images of each other, have a fortification system, built during the second half of the 19th century in order to guard the route to Vienna, the capital of the Austro-Hungarian Empire. During the Holocaust, their purpose was reversed and the fortresses were turned into assembly points and prisons for people of whom the country wanted to rid itself.

In the volume *Hungary* in the series *The History of the Shoah*, published by Yad Vashem, which recounts the history of the deportation and extermination of Hungarian Jews,[25] the Star Fortress in Komarom is mentioned as having served as a 'ghetto' for the Jews of Komarom and the surrounding villages, and as a boarding station for the trains. It is described as a place where atrocious acts were carried out prior to the deportations. Nothing is mentioned about the Roma. However, between November 1944 and April 1945, in addition to Jews, Communists and other persecuted peoples, thousands of Roma prisoners—in fact, mainly Roma—also passed through Komarom.

In his concluding article on the persecution of the Roma in Hungary during World War II, Puskás emphasizes the central role of Komarom,[26] as does Bársony, who writes that many thousands of Gypsies were crowded there. Bársony adds that many of the women and children were released while all the others were deported to Germany.[27]

Karsai's findings on the Gypsy question in Hungary (1919-45) are based purely on written documentation, for the most part compensation claims from the Hungarian State Bank archives.[28] His conclusion that the damage sustained by the Hungarian Roma during the Holocaust was negligible derived from the small number of claimants with Gypsy-sounding names. (It should be noted here that before their organization in the late 1990s most Roma did not have the social skills to claim compensation due to the demands of the paperwork). Nevertheless, as anecdotes, which in Karsai's opinion cannot be used for research data, he quotes stories by Roma who were imprisoned at Komarom. These stories join those that I heard from former Roma inmates of Komarom whom I interviewed.

Inter alia, Karsai writes:

> There had to be some sort of central directive, if most of the victims of the Gypsy deportation acts arrived at Komarom. During this period, they deported the Gypsies on racist grounds... although the Gypsies were not transferred from the Star Prison [in Komarom] to the territory of the Third Reich, but only the men and women who were of working age.[29]

He sums up the subject of Komarom thus:

> 298 Gypsies handed in compensation claims, of which 35 contained *no useful data*... After processing the data in 263 cases containing assessable data, I reached the following conclusions. *If I relate to all the data supplied by the claimants about the place of their deportation, those who were with them at the time of deportation and the number of their relatives who died as credible data*, out of 263 cases there was a total of 219 dead [and] 208 deportees. 33 people were sent home from Komarom, generally after three weeks imprisonment [emphasis by author]...[30]

Karsai's conclusions seem odd, especially in view of the testimonies he himself cites, unless he disbelieves them and does not consider them 'useful data.' He noted that Komarom was exceptionally crowded with Roma prisoners, at least in November-December 1944 and that it continued to operate until April 1945. These facts contradict the figures that Karsai states. The question of his conclusion is interesting as part of the subject of memory construction. Aside from the question of the figures, his reference to "generally three weeks of imprisonment" in light of the conditions described, as if it were an insignificant and uneventful time, warrants further discussion.

Writing about the Komarom camp in their second book, which documents the fate of the Roma during World War II, Kenrick and Puxon state that it also served as a concentration camp for Gypsies and Jews from the Hungarian-occupied areas of Slovakia. They add that the Roma were sent from Komarom to Dachau and only women with small children were released.[31]

Based on Karsai and Kenrick and Puxon, we can conclude that in December 1944 mothers with small children were sent home from Komarom, while all others aged 14 and up were sent onwards to various concentration camps. However, besides reference to this fact, it is interesting to study the different ways each writer has of interpreting the given information.

Karsai notes that *only those capable of work* were sent from Komarom to the concentration camps, and even this statement is presented dubiously, since he cites witnesses who err in the pronunciation of names and emphasizes their mistakes: for example, "Tacho... instead of Dachau."[32] Women and children, he adds, were sent home.

Kenrick, on the other hand, labels Komarom a 'concentration camp,' and recounts how the Roma were sent from there to concentration and extermination camps all over the Third Reich, with only women and small children being released.

The contradictory message that each author desires to transmit is clear from the wording: the former attempts to diminish and the latter to emphasize the importance of the role of Komarom in the history of the life of the Roma. This subject will be elaborated with the aid of the interviews I conducted.

Firstly, as far as the placing of the adjunct 'only' is concerned: Should it be placed next to those who were transferred to the concentration camps or to those who were released? Out of the 21 people interviewed by me personally and who mentioned Komarom, 11 were sent to concentration camps over the border and 10 were released. We know that most of those sent to concentration camps did not survive and therefore were unable to be interviewed. In other words, of the people in question, 11 were survivors of concentration camps outside Hungary, as opposed to 10 who were released from Komarom. Since in this instance there are neither statistics to speak of nor any ordered lists of names, one can assume that if survivors of the camps were a majority, the victims constituted an even larger majority.

Secondly, the basic nature of Komarom is at issue here: Was it a transit camp, or in view of what went on there, should it be included in the list of places with very clear connotations labeled 'concentration camps'? Even if we agree to the latter definition, might a stay of a few weeks be considered a period of separate significance and status in the narrative flow? Those interviewees who were also survivors of concentration camps outside Hungary effectively provide the answer to this question. These survivors have the authority of "those who were there," having experienced the magnitude of events in person. Although they were not asked to compare Komarom to the camps where they were placed afterwards, we find comparisons in their accounts. They dwell at length on the subject of Komarom, emphasizing that what they underwent there was no less traumatic than their suffering in the camps at Dachau, Ravensbruck and others. This is all the more significant in light of the fact that their stay there was so short, relative to their stay in the other camps.

The Roma's stories about Komarom in the interviews I collected shed light on the way they themselves remember and interpret what happened to them then and there. From a study of all the interviews that mentioned Komarom, a common narrative can be composed about the history of this group:

At the beginning of November 1944, usually before dawn, the gendarmes knocked on the doors of the Roma in those parts of Hungary that had not yet been conquered by the Red Army, which was advancing from the east. At that time most of the males had been drafted into the 'Labor Service.' According to József Balogh:[33]

> Suddenly at night there were knockings on the window... We were taken through the village as if we were murderers or robbers, on each side a gendarme, gendarme, gendarmerie! There were... at least three hundred, all of them Gypsies. We have got worn out shoes, but completely worn out, and they put a red ribbon on our arm... on it was written 'Labor Service'... What did they do? There came a command to shave everybody!... against lice. Every one of us—on every place of the body that had a little hair—out! These old Gypsies—they had these big moustaches—they cried for their moustache... We walked and walked... The hunger bothered us so much, that we hardly walked, we supported each other.

Those who had been taken far away from their homes with the labor divisions were spared in the arrests for Komarom. Those who were at home were assembled with everyone else.

> Lajos Sárközi: Before dawn on 4 November they surrounded us... We were in the Star Prison in Komárom. About 8,000 to 10,000 people were gathered there, the large majority of whom were Gypsies. They came from all over the country, even from the districts of Szolnok and Csongrád [in Eastern Hungary].[34]

The Roma from the various towns and villages were taken first to a central assembly point serving a number of villages in the surrounding area. Usually it was a brick factory, which had also been used as an assembly point for the Jews.

> Friderika Krasznai: On the night of 3 November, at dawn, the gendarmes surprised us... They placed us together... They led us to Bak. They herded us like sheep into a yard. The gendarmes guarded us... In the afternoon we had to line up... in a brick factory in Zalaegerszeg. There were Jews there before us. It was full of lice and ticks... There were lots and lots of us.[35]

From the brick factory or other assembly points the Roma were taken to the nearby railway station. They were told that they were being taken to work on farms to pick carrots. They were crowded into cattle wagons, locked up and then taken on a journey of up to two weeks to Komarom. On the way the train stopped at various stations where more and more carriages were added. The journey itself entailed much suffering. There was a shortage of water and lack of air and many people collapsed on the way. Friderika Krasznai continued:

> They took us to a station where the border guard or something like that took over... They put us onto carriages... no food, no water. My sister was already in such a state in the train that we thought we wouldn't arrive with her, that she would die in the train... We arrived at Komárom.

When the Roma arrived at Komarom, they found themselves in the freezing cold, crowded into a sort of bunker—huge hollow tunnels dug underground—or out in the open, or in the rooms of the fortress which ran off the long corridors. The guards stood above them armed with rifles, machine guns and whips. For the first day or two, members of a family were left together.

Later they were sorted into groups: males over 14, women over 14 without babies, and children under 14 and mothers with young children. When they were separated, they had no way of knowing that most of them would never see each other again. The Hungarian and German guards exercised extreme cruelty toward them, whipping them, often indiscriminately.

> Friderika Krasznai: There we were met once more by Hungarian soldiers, Nyilas. They had a club in one hand. Long... from cherry wood. They beat the people. It made no difference whether it was a boy or a woman or a man. It wasn't important... They led us there to Komarom into the bunkers. In the evening the soldiers came. They were already German soldiers. Then they... removed the men. We, the children, were left alone with my mother. I was 12. The youngest was 6 months old.

> Erzsébet Kolompár: The gendarmes came at dawn. They assembled us. They told us we would never be coming home again... They took the young men, took everyone. We never saw them again. We also never saw my father... There were Roma in the camp that weren't allowed in the whole area. There were so many of them that they swarmed like ants... There was a Gypsy woman... She had a crooked stick and she even hit us with it! They turned her into a kapo. If someone caused a row or made trouble, she would hit us. And she really did hit. May God punish her! She was evil. The guards were evil, but she was as bad as they were... We were in the bunker all day. They guarded us with weapons. Anyone who got caught, the soldiers hit... if you were noisy, they shot... All the time we were there in the mud...[36]

The guards shot at those who tried to escape and at those who tried to sneak up to any source of food they could find, including piles of garbage.

> Erzsébet Kolompár: And if we went outside to the garbage pile where they threw the leftovers, anyone who was caught, they killed. There was one poor girl who was buried alive. The poor girl saved herself and escaped to our bunker. She had a smell. She stank. 'Where were you?' I asked. 'They buried me in the garbage.' I felt sorry for the poor thing. She was a blonde girl, fat. She was always running away. They caught her and buried her again in the garbage. Afterwards I didn't see her again. What happened to her? She may have died. I don't know.

The conditions were deplorable. There were no toilets and no possible means of improvising any. The situation became worse still when various diseases broke out, including typhoid. They stood, sat and lay down in the mud, filth and excrement. The cold froze their wet clothes to their bodies. The food was thrown at them roughly and it was not uncommon for the prisoners to fight and shove among themselves to grab it. The daily menu did not vary: a slice of hard black bread, and boiled cabbage or carrots.

Consequently, large numbers of Gypsies died shortly after their arrival. Nearly all the babies died, as did the elderly. They froze to death. They died from sickness, hunger and from the beatings. Every day carts or wheelbarrows passed by to collect the corpses that had piled up. They were placed onto the wagons with pitchforks and thrown into the Danube or into a huge plaster pit.

> Erzsébet Kovács: Many adults died in the camp. The children fell down. They died like flies. Mother said that if we had stayed there another week, we might have all died. There was some sort of structure there from plaster where they collected the corpses. Every day they took them in a cart... We lay down there many times next to the corpses.

In this desperate state, hope suddenly flickered among the Komarom prisoners when a British war plane lowered its flight path above the camp and distributed leaflets beginning with the words: "Dear brothers!" The leaflet promised that their suffering would soon end, and that the Allies were very close to victory and to liberating the Nazi victims of persecution.

> Friderika Krasznai: We were there for two weeks... We lay down in the mud, in the wet, and suffered... One day lots of airplanes came, American or English. May God bless them and every step they take. The airplane flew like that and threw down leaflets. I ran outside. My mother says: 'Don't run, my child, because they'll kill you.' I went outside. I lifted up a leaflet. I came back. There were some among us who knew how to read. I will never forget. It said: "Dear brothers! Do not be afraid. You won't be here much longer." Everybody was delighted...

After a number of weeks in the fortress, the Roma were taken away. Some of them were herded onto goods trains and taken to concentration camps: first to Dachau and from there to other concentration camps of the Third Reich. These stories are well known. As of December 1944, women with small children who had managed to survive until then were taken from the bunkers or collected from the yard and released.

> Erzsébet Kolompár: They also placed me in another group. My mother looked out from the bunker. She signaled with her eyes: "Run, my little girl, come back!" I ran to her. They came after me. They searched, but didn't find me. My

mother tied a scarf around my head and there was a little baby. She pushed the baby into my hands. That way the Germans didn't take me...

The majority of people who had been separated from their families and sent to other places after Komarom never returned. All the interviewees who were liberated from Komarom lost family members who had been moved to concentration camps outside Hungary.

Almost half of the Roma survivors interviewed for this research in Hungary specifically mentioned Komarom. Other interviewees, who made their way on foot to a destination unknown to them, appear to have been led toward Komarom with further groups of Roma, accompanied by gendarmes or policemen, before they were liberated by the Red Army on the way.[37] For some of the people, Komarom was one station among several on their winding journey; for others it was the center of their experience, which classified them thereafter as survivors.

A Hungarian woman who lived in the city of Komarom and witnessed the events is quoted as saying:[38]

> They even took the poor musicians. The women and children running after them. They also took them. It made us laugh to see the poor fellows bringing their double bass and clarinets with them. As if the community was marching to the Star to the sounds of music. They were all respected musicians. Their wives wrapped in fur coats. In November it was already freezing cold. There was no place left in the prison cells. A large part of the detainees were left out in the open. Dozens of small children froze to death. They threw them into the cesspool... The poor deportees... were packed tightly together by the thousands with their belongings. But in such huge numbers that they couldn't move. They relieved themselves on themselves. Women, men, next to each other. Children in their mothers' laps. Afterwards when they went on their way, excretion dripped from their clothes, their pants. By the time they came to the railway station it had frozen on them.

The story of the Roma's stay in the bunkers and out in the open, amidst the filth, in the rain, snow and winter frost, is a unique one. Komarom was not an extermination camp, even though so many people lost their lives there. It was neither a labor camp nor a formal, recognized concentration camp, with registration, inmates standing daily for lengthy periods in the cold yard for a head-count, and numbered and orderly barracks. It was a place where the Roma lived and died under extreme conditions, even by the standards of the Holocaust. And afterwards they were bullied yet again.

THE LIBERATION FROM KOMAROM

There is a striking similarity between the stories of the journey home by people released from Komarom and by other concentration camp survivors. This strongly supports the theory that the state of Komarom survivors was comparable to that of concentration camp survivors throughout the Third Reich. For these Roma women and small children, the relatively short stay in Komarom was a horrific experience, which influenced their lives from a physical, family, social, financial and spiritual point of view, as if they had been detained for many months in a well-known concentration camp.

Their release from Komarom did not liberate them from further suffering. Friderika Krasznai recounts her story in detail:

> When they liberated us from Komárom, we went on our way... One boy lay dead here next to the ditch, a second there, and a third in another place. The people were already so weak that they were unable to keep walking. My sister was already in such a state that she couldn't fasten her clothes... Then I told my mother: "Mummy! Anyone of us who dies, or you see cannot keep on going, we won't leave him here. Even dead. We will take him home." My poor mother naturally burst out crying. She said: "No, my dear, you don't have to worry. We won't abandon each other. If we have to die, we will die together in one place."... We got to Ács where the gendarmes assembled us again... A military train arrived and there was an empty carriage. They placed us there... The children died in the train. A one-year-old boy, a six-month-old girl, and I don't know who else...
>
> Erzsébet Kovács: On the way home, my mother found some biscuits in an abandoned army car. We ate them. We might have died without them. We walked all the way home.[39]

Some of the Komarom survivors boarded trains for their villages. Others made their way home on foot, during which they encountered many difficulties. The Hungarians who met them in the trains or on the roads reacted to them with a mixture of pity, disgust, repulsion, fear and hate. Some gave them food. This sometimes did more harm than good. Many died as a result of uncontrolled and excessive eating after a period of extreme hunger. Others came down with digestive and intestinal diseases. There were those who hid themselves on the way and did not dare return home for fear of persecution.

Ferenc Horváth: We didn't need tickets. Nothing. There were also conductors who had food and who gave it to us. Then we went home and then whoever ate too much died. Who would have thought that it was forbidden to eat so much? And it was forbidden, because that's the way the stomach was. It wasn't wide enough. We came home with narrow stomachs.[40]

When the Komarom survivors came to their villages, even those who had been away only a few weeks found their houses looted. Some of the houses or huts were simply razed to the ground. Other houses had been emptied of all their contents and even the doors and windows were gone. The lucky ones—mothers with a number of young, sick, weak and hungry children—who found four walls standing, went on to live in a house without doors or windows and without men or older relatives who would share the job of running their lives and raising their children. The looters and wreckers of their houses were their neighbors.

Friderika Krasznai: Finally we reached home on foot. Can you imagine, mud up to our knees, barefoot, in December. The rain was pouring down, but we did not find anything there. Not one bed, not a window, or a teaspoon. Nothing in the world. Only the four walls. Even the attic had disappeared. Nothing... A year later, in November, my brother came back. We couldn't believe that he was still alive. He came inside. We began to cry. All of us. We cried, and then my mother asked: 'So! Your father and your brother and the others. Where are they? Where did they go?' He didn't know because he had been separated from them because he was 14 then. And he came back alone.

A folk poem sums up the Roma experience in the Komarom camp:

> The ghetto room in Komarom, oh,
> Every Roma knows it
> And relates it in tears to his family
> Oh, how the ghetto rooms stink.
>
> I am a prisoner rotting in the ghetto,
> Everyone knows that that's where I live,
> Just as all my limbs are torn.
>
> Oh, God, wonder of wonders,
> Change Hitler into a farmer's beast
> Tie a rope around his neck
> And we'll lead the ox through the main street.

I am in the ghetto
My hair has been shorn
Oh, God, where am I going?
To flee or to remain?
If I run – they'll shoot me to death,
If I stay – they'll beat me to death.

RESPONSIBILITY AND RESPONSE-ABILITY

As can be seen, memory construction is complicated and takes place on various levels, both individual and social. It is also connected to complex struggles, both open and concealed, on each level concomitantly. The participants in these struggles are the victims, the attackers, the witnesses of what happened and the audience of listeners who pass the story on—each person and each group according to his or her interpretation. Disregard and silence also play an important role in memory construction since they extend the area of forgetting and enforced forgetting of the events.

Shoshana Felman approaches this subject from the viewpoint of responsibility toward one's fellow men.[41] In distinguishing the silent witness from the witness who speaks up, she obligates reaction and speech. According to her, the witness's silence deprives society not only of the knowledge of what happened to the victim but also acknowledgement of his or her existence. The responsibility of the victim is to cry out. The responsibility of the witness is to make sure the cry is heard and to pass on this voice. The responsibility of the listener is not to be deaf to the outcry but to acknowledge what has been heard. This responsibility, which Felman terms response-ability, effectively means preclusion of the right to silence and enforced silence, "prompt[ing] historical responsibility." There is an obligation not to pursue "a strategy of deafness," which has prevented, even today, the right of the Hungarian Roma to be heard and to commemorate those events, as if their voices were perceived "as voices of no one, which come from nowhere."[42]

NOTES

1. R. L. Braham and N. Katzburg, *The History of the Shoa, Hungary* (in Hebrew) (Jerusalem, 1992), pp. 267, 389.
2. J. Bársony, "Magyarországi cigány Holocaust" (Hungarian Gypsy Holocaust) *Phralipe* (Oct. 1996), pp. 11–15; D. M. Crowe, *A History of the Gypsies of*

Eastern Europe and Russia (London/New York, 1995), pp. 89-91; B. Mezey, L. Pomogyi and I. Tauber, *A magyarországi cigánykérdés dokumentumokban, 1422-1985* (The Hungarian Gypsy Question in Documents, 1422-1985) (Budapest, 1986), p. 31.

3.   The total number of lives taken is estimated at 28,000 to 50,000. D. Kenrick. and G. Puxon, *The Destiny of Europe's Gypsies* (London, 1972), p. 183; M. Lakatos, *A cigányok sorsa 1944-ben* (The Fate of the Gypsies in 1944) (Budapest, 1984).

4.   M. Halbwachs, *On Collective Memory* (Chicago, 1992), pp. 73-4; J. K. Olick, "Collective Memory: The Two Cultures," *Sociological Theory* 17 (1999), pp. 333-48.

5.   J. Yoors, *The Gypsies* (Illinois, 1987), p. 5; A. Fraser, *The Gypsies* (Oxford, 1996).

6.   Fraser, *The Gypsies*.

7.   Halbwachs, *On Collective Memory*, p. 38.

8.   Kenrick and Puxon, *The Destiny of Europe's Gypsies*, pp. 13-17.

9.   I. Hancock, *The Pariah Syndrome* (Ann Arbor, Michigan, 1988), pp. 16-29.

10.   G. Margalit, *"The Other Germany" and the Gypsies* (in Hebrew) (Jerusalem, 1999), 32-3.

11.   N. Wachtel, "Introduction: Memory and History," *History and Anthropology* 2 (1986), pp. 207-24.

12.   J. F. Loytard, "The Postmodern Condition," in M. McQuillan (ed.), *The Narrative Reader* (London/New York, 2000), pp. 157-61.

13.   H. K. Bhahba, *Nation and Narration* (London, 1990), p. 307.

14.   Halbwachs, *On Collective Memory*, p. 38.

15.   B. Muller-Hill, *Murderous Science.* (Jerusalem, 1992; Hebrew version); Hancock, *The Pariah Syndrome*; H. R. Huttenbach, "The Romani Porrajmos: The Nazi Genocide of Europe's Gypsies," *Nationalities Papers* 19 (1991), pp. 373-94.

16.   Y. Bauer, "Gypsies and the Holocaust," *The History Teacher* 24 (1991); Y. Bauer, *Rethinking the Holocaust* (New Haven, 2001); S. Katz, "The Uniqueness of the Holocaust: The Historical Dimension," in: A. S. Rosenbaum (ed.), *Is the Holocaust Unique?* 2nd ed. (Colorado/Oxford, 2001), pp. 49-68.

17.   J. Lewis Herman, *Trauma and Recovery* (Tel Aviv, 1994; Hebrew edition), pp. 92-6.

18.   Wachtel, "Introduction: Memory and History."

19.   Herman, *Trauma and Recovery*, p. 92.

20.   J. Habermas, *Communication and the Evolution of Society* (London, 1979).

21.   Ibid.

22.   Wachtel, "Introduction: Memory and History."

23.   A. Margalit, "The Lasting Past," *Zmanim* (in Hebrew) 68-69 (1999-2000), pp. 76-86.

24.   Bhahba, *Nation and Narration*, p. 59.

25.   Braham and Katzburg, *The History of the Shoa: Hungary*, pp. 277-8.

26.   B. Puskás, "Adalékok a cigányság II. világháborús tragédiájához" (Contributions to World War II. Tragedy of the Gypsy People), *Somogyi Kultúra* (in Hungarian) 6 (1995), pp. 47-52.

27. Bársony, "Magyarországi cigány Holocaust."
28. L. Karsai, *A cigánykérdés Magyarországon 1919-1945, Út a cigány Holocausthoz* (The Gypsy Question in Hungary 1919-1945: The Way to the Gypsy Holocaust) (Budapest, 1992), p. 136.
29. Ibid., p. 127.
30. Ibid., pp. 138–39.
31. Kenrick and Puxon, *Gypsies under the Swastika.* (Hertfordshire, 1995), pp. 100–6.
32. Karsai, *A cigánykérdés Magyarországon*, p. 139.
33. From Amaro Drom, interview by Zsuzsa Bódi, Aug. 1995.
34. From Ondód, interview by K. Z., in *Vas Népe,* 13 Aug. 1990. It should be noted that by October 1944 battles were taking place near the Danube-Tisza line and the Arrow Cross were fleeing; therefore it is unlikely that Roma from Csongrád and Szolnok arrived directly from these places.
35. From Zámoly, interview by Katalin Katz, 25 June 1996.
36. From Sorokpalany, interview by Ágnes Daróczi, 1995.
37. Puskás, "Adalékok a cigányság II."
38. Karsai, *A cigánykérdés Magyarországon*, pp. 124–5.
39. From Szekszárd, interview by Katalin Katz, 10 Aug. 1995.
40. From Nagykanizsa, interview by Katalin Katz, 16 July, 1996.
41. S. Felman, "The Silence of the Witness, the Betrayal of History," *Zmanim* (in Hebrew) 45 (1993), pp. 50–75.
42. Ibid.

ROMANIAN PUBLIC REACTION TO THE DEPORTATION OF GYPSIES TO TRANSNISTRIA

VIOREL ACHIM

INTRODUCTION

During World War II thousands of Gypsies living in Romania were deported by the Antonescu government to the Soviet territories between the Dniester and the Bug rivers where many of them were killed or died of hunger, cold or disease.[1] Marshal Antonescu himself took the decision of 'evacuating' Gypsies to that region. Initially, the government's measures were intended to affect all those Gypsies registered as 'problem' elements, based on a survey conducted by police and gendarmes on 25 May 1942. The survey encompassed non-settled Gypsies and, among settled ones, those with a criminal record, recidivists, those who made a living out of theft, and those with no visible means of support. In all, 40,909, including the above categories and their families, were blacklisted. This represented 20 percent of the 208,700 Gypsies living within Romania's 1942 boundaries—as estimated by the Central Institute of Statistics. However, not all those listed as 'problem' cases were deported, because soldiers and potential recruits together with their families, although originally singled out for deportation, were eventually exempted. Apart from a small number, all of the more than 25,000 Gypsies 'evacuated' to Transnistria appeared on the list made at the end of May.

The 25,000 deported during the summer and fall of 1942 fell into two main categories: (1) 11,441 were nomads (any Gypsy that had no fixed abode was lumped into this category). They were deported during an operation that took place from 1 June to 15 August 1942. (2) Approximately 14,000 were settled Gypsies, but deemed by the authorities too "dangerous and undesirable" because they belonged to the categories registered in May 1942. The majority, 13,176, were deported in September 1942 and several hundred others later on. Families were deported in toto.

On 13 October 1942, the Council of Ministers decided to suspend the deportations of Jews and Gypsies to Transnistria, probably out of foreign policy considerations. Nevertheless, a few were deported even after that date. By the time the Romanian occupation authorities pulled out of Transnistria in March 1944 and the deportees were allowed to return, some 11,000 of the 25,000 had died. This was the total Gypsy loss in Romania during the war as an outcome of the authorities' persecutions.

Without elaborating on what the authorities expected to achieve by deporting Gypsies, it would seem that the decision derived from the government's ethnic policy, or more specifically, from its project of homogenizing the population in ethnic terms.[2] The May 1942 'selection' and the deportation that followed would appear to refer only to the Gypsies who lived in the 'gypsy way.' The rest were not targeted, probably because they were perceived as being integrated into Romanian society.

The aim of this essay is to examine the Romanian response to the deportation of Gypsies to Transnistria. More specifically, the intention is to clarify whether the Romanian majority supported the authorities' policy with respect to the Gypsies.

ROMANIAN REACTIONS
TO THE DEPORTATIONS

The following assessment of the attitude of Romanian public opinion is based on documented findings that the ordinary Romanian believed the government was deporting only 'problem' Gypsies, that is, nomads, former convicts, thieves, beggars, those who had no legal trade or occupation and those who were extremely poor. The local authorities—gendarmes, police and the mayor's office—which carried out the deportation orders also had no idea about the government's real goal, which was ethnically motivated. At the local level, all they knew was that Gypsies whose way of life or actions disturbed the 'public order,' or what was considered public order at the time, were deported. This does not mean that there were no cases of people deported who did not fit the criteria of the May 1942 survey. Among the deportees were families of soldiers, potential recruits and their families, and people with a profession, as well as some Romanians, Turks and Hungarians. These were the so-called abuses committed by the gendarmes and policemen charged with carrying out the deportations. Following an investigation in Transnistria in December 1942, 1,261 persons were repatriated.[3] Like the local authorities, the public considered the deportation of the Gypsies to be a measure of social rather than ethnic cleansing. Thus, when the public took a stand on this issue, they judged it in terms of what they thought was the authorities' objective.

It should be made clear from the outset that we are discussing the common people, ordinary Romanians living in the towns and villages, not politicians or cultural figures who voiced their opinions on Antonescu's measures. When politicians protested against deportation, indeed, they did so for moral reasons—repelled by the cruelty of the treatment—but also mainly out of concern about the consequences this policy might have on interethnic relations at home and on Romania's international status. A letter dated 16 September 1942, written by Constantin I. C. Brătianu, leader of the National Liberal Party, to Antonescu on the issue of the Gypsies' deportation illustrates this point.[4] In addition to his objection on humanitarian grounds—the deportation of the Gypsies, he said, was a barbaric act that "will throw us several centuries back in human history"—his protest was primarily of a political nature. Seeking to dissociate himself from Antonescu's decision, Brătianu emphasized that the marshal alone would be responsible for that policy, for which there had been no precedent under previous governments. "These Romanian citizens in our state had not been subjected to any special treatment until now," he said. In this context he also referred to "the persecutions and expulsion of the Jews in retaliation for the [alleged] acts of their Bukovina and Bessarabia coreligionists[5] and influenced by the treatment inflicted on them in Germany." Here again his desire to defend the image of the Romanian state and nation is evident.

As will be seen below, members of the public never bothered with political arguments. However, Brătianu's letter also contended that the deportation of the Gypsies would have a negative impact on the domestic economy, a consideration ordinary citizens cared about and often mentioned in their own appeals against the government decision.

The intercessions in favor of the Gypsies by major landowners[6] and company managers[7] are also beyond the scope of this paper. There were such interventions in support of workers of Gypsy descent who had either been deported—in which case their employers would request their repatriation—or were about to be deported, or feared they might be—in which case someone would ask for an exemption. Such petitions, however, must be taken together with those of the common people, since Gypsies played a central economic role in the lives of both. The deportation of the Gypsies led to farmhand shortages in several areas, even beyond the large southern Romania estates where they usually did most of the seasonal work. The war was increasing the economic importance of the Gypsies both in agriculture and in craftwork, and the petitions some Romanian landowners and common people filed for their repatriation cited their practical utility as a main reason.

A relatively large number of documents reflecting Romanians' views on the deportation of Gypsies have been preserved in various archives, particularly those of institutions such as the Council of Ministers, Ministry of the Interior, the General Inspectorate of the Gendarmerie, and the General Directorate of Police, all of which directly enforced the policy regarding Gypsies and organized the deportations to Transnistria.

Some of these documents expressed animosity against the deportees or the remaining Gypsies. On 22 June 1942, Captain N. Dogaru,[8] a retired officer from Târgu Jiu demanded "on behalf of the population" that steps be taken against Gypsies living in two local neighborhoods. The captain asked the General Directorate of Police to send in an inquiry commission, "to see for yourselves the filth they [the Gypsies] live in, the way they deface Târgu Jiu, the trouble and robberies to which some neighborhoods are exposed, and decide to rid our beautiful Gorj county town of them." He continued:

> We think the government's colonization measures are a good opportunity and that the Gypsies in Târgu Jiu should be among the first to go. Alternatively, the municipality of Târgu Jiu and the Prefecture of Gorj County could find a commune in our county, round them up from the entire territory of the county, and colonize them there, turn them into a village where they can be put to work under stern supervision and control.

Thus, the captain suggested as a solution that local Gypsies be either 'colonized,' i.e., deported to Transnistria—an operation that had been unfolding on a national scale since 1 June—or gathered from around the county and confined in an all-Gypsy village in some commune. To this officer, Gypsies were a public disorder, which had to be treated accordingly. The authorities did not take up his suggestions immediately, but 60 Gypsies were indeed deported from Târgu Jiu during the second operation in September 1942.[9]

A similar request for the evacuation of Gypsies can be found in a petition that residents of Buciumeni commune, Tecuci County, filed in May 1943.[10] Their reasons, as summarized by the Prefecture of the Tecuci County, were that the villagers "hate to see the Gypsies not doing any work, drinking, smoking, playing cards, and only making a living out of theft." Moreover, "the Gypsies' filthy, unsanitary houses clash with the clean, well-tended houses of the other residents, and make a grim impression on whoever visits the commune." Finally, the Gypsies "were a constant hotbed of infectious diseases which can be easily transmitted to other residents." In response to the villagers' petition, the prefecture suggested that the Interior Ministry either relocate all the Gypsies to Covrag and Tofea villages, in Brăhăşeşti commune, or spread them over several communes: Brăhăşeşti (the same two villages), Cerbasca (Baciu village), Slobozia (Panu village), and Răchitoasa (Baroana village). The proposal meant in fact their dispersal in localities with a small number of Gypsies. The ministry did not take up the suggestion.

As can be seen, both petitions referred to particular groups of Gypsies who were allegedly a source of trouble. One can assume they were recently settled, originally nomadic Gypsies and, unlike the great majority of Gypsies not yet integrated into the local communities. However, since such negative petitions seem to have been extremely rare, it may be concluded that they were unrepresentative of the Romanians' view on Gypsy deportation. Criticism against deportation was much more widespread.

A few cases were reported of people, including gendarmes and policemen, who profited from the deportation of Gypsies. Some residents grabbed the possessions of their Gypsy neighbors who had been deported.[11] When settled Gypsies were deported in September 1942, a number of policemen and gendarmes took advantage of their being given too little time to liquidate their goods and bought them at a bargain price. Such cases, while despicable, can hardly be construed as evidence of anti-Gypsy feeling. They tend more to illustrate the morals of some people than their attitude toward ethnic minorities.

Disapproval of anti-Gypsy measures voiced by people of various social ranks was much more widespread. Letters and petitions to the Council of Ministers and to Marshal Antonescu himself, to the Ministry of the Interior and to the General Staff of the Army bear witness to this attitude. Many of these protests came from rural residents, but also from citizens of towns in which agriculture was a major source of income, and where social relations differed little from rural ones. Some letters and petitions bearing tens of signatures were written on behalf of entire communities asking that 'their' Gypsies not be deported, or that they be brought back if already taken.

There are quite a few examples of such letters, from all areas of the country. Most interventions were made after the deportation of 'dangerous' sedentary Gypsies in fall 1942. By order of the central authorities, a census of the remaining Gypsies was conducted in late September. The goal was not just to keep an accurate record of this population, but also to identify new targets in the event that another deportation operation was decided upon. Although, as noted above, deportations were suspended in the following month, the 'statistic census,' as it was called, nevertheless sparked panic among the Gypsies, who perceived it as a prelude to yet another wave of deportations. They flooded both the central and local authorities with requests that they be crossed off the lists and exempted from future deportations. In many places villagers and local authorities tried to intervene in order to prevent the deportation of 'their' Gypsies.

In October 1942, a group of villagers from Popoveni, Balta Verde commune, Dolj County, together with residents from other communes and the town of Craiova, filed a petition to Marshal Antonescu, requesting that the blacksmith Ilie Dincă living in Craiova not be sent away. The peasants underscored the man's importance to the community:

> We badly need him in this town, for he is a hardworking, efficient blacksmith, and he's the one we go and see when we need to fix anything in our vehicles, build new structures, shoe our oxen and horses, repair our plows and harrows—in short, anything that has to do with iron working. Not to mention that he is also skilled at wheeling, carpentry, etc.[12]

In an appeal to Marshal Antonescu sent in early October 1942, residents of Dobriţa, Gorj County, requested that five Gypsy families in their commune not be displaced. The Gypsies were the local craftsmen, and, said the peasants, "we will be left without a single blacksmith in our commune if they are moved away." The letter cited, in addition, the fact that those Gypsies had land and houses like everybody else and had never been convicted.

> Besides their trades, they also own some land which they work on like we farmers do, and they have built their own farmhouses, which are every bit as well tended as those of other residents. None of these Gypsies has ever been convicted, and they attend to their trades honestly.

The Gypsies for whom the people of Dobriţa interceded included four blacksmiths and a well digger. Signatory to the petition were 163 male residents, that is to say, the entire community.[13]

In the same period—early October 1942—the residents of Roşia Amaradia, Gorj County, wrote to Marshal Antonescu requesting that six *rudari*[14] be allowed to remain in their commune. Those Gypsies, it was said, owned land and houses and served with their trade not only their own commune, but also neighboring communities. The schoolmaster and 30 villagers signed the petition.[15]

Many town dwellers took similar action. At the end of September 1942, several residents of Craiova wrote to the Council of Ministers in support of fellow resident Ştefan Gâdea, a tinsmith by trade, asking that he not be deported to Transnistria. Besides the important service he supplied, the letter cited his moral conduct:

[T]he said Ştefan I. Gâdea has behaved in the neighborhood in such a way that no one in the community in which he lives has ever complained about his conduct or behavior. His family, consisting of his wife and two sons to whom the said Ştefan Gâdea has taught his trade, have not behaved in our midst like Gypsies, but in fact better than many native Romanians. Members of this family have never been taken to court or other seats of judgment, or even to the police stations for any criminal or other offense.[16]

The residents of Zimnicea, people "of all social conditions, but mostly plowmen," interceded with Marshal Antonescu for 'their' Gypsies in October 1942. In a petition bearing 127 signatures, they asked that deportation not apply to their local craftsmen (carpenters and blacksmiths) who "can no longer be considered Gypsies except in their distant ancestry." The full text reads:

Dear Marshal,

We, residents of Zimnicea, of all social conditions, but mostly plowmen, respectfully inform you of the following:

A rumor has spread in town, stirring up worries and confusion among those concerned, that, in addition to the *rudari* Gypsies who have already been sent to Transnistria, the measure has been extended to other categories of residents who can no longer be considered Gypsies except in their distant ancestry.

Unlike the *rudari* who, though quiet people, had no houses of their own and lived mostly in the woods, these men for whom we are now sincerely pleading with you, sir, are artisans—carpenters and blacksmiths—of whom we are constantly in need in our plowing trade. These men mend both the wooden and iron parts of our wagons, harrows, plows, and all our farming tools. The plowmen's and the blacksmiths' trades are inextricably bound to one another. And their numbers do not exceed our demand. Far from it, during the farming season when within a population of 12,000, nearly all plowmen, there are tens of wagons to fix and hundreds of plow blades to whet daily, these diligent craftsmen, these indispensable auxiliaries to farming, have to work nights, so that field work should not be inconvenienced, and may run smoothly and on time.

But these people are not even Gypsies any longer, save as a distant memory, since they have been assimilated into the mainstream, share our religion and our customs, do military service, and have two or three sons each on the battlefield, doing their duty to the nation. They also have their own houses and spacious iron and wood working shops, and as good craftsmen, have a variety of advanced tools that might be needed in their trade.

> Please rest assured, sir, that these blacksmiths are peaceful citizens with
> fixed abodes who are absolutely necessary to us, plowmen. Therefore, we sin-
> cerely and respectfully ask you to kindly see that they be allowed to stay on and
> exercise their iron working trade.
>   With highest regard.[17]

As noted, the above examples are drawn from a period in fall 1942 when
fears were rising that the deportations would extend to yet further categories
of Gypsies. The reasons cited by the villagers referred both to the status of
those Gypsies as members of their rural communities, who shared their lives
and made no trouble, and to the economic role they played. Those Gypsies
were artisans, often the only craftsmen of their kind in a locality, the welfare
of which—as these petitions pointed out—was crucially dependent on their
work. These appeals appear to have expressed an act of solidarity between the
villagers and Gypsies, based on the traditional labor division within the Romanian rural community, in which Gypsies played the distinctive role of village craftsmen.

It should be noted that the Zimnicea residents' petition mentioned the
rudari Gypsies who had already been deported. The prospect of further deportations worried the local community, prompting them to make this request.
The *rudari* were somehow set in contrast to the Gypsies for whom the locals
intervened. While portraying them as 'quiet people,' the residents sought to
excuse the authorities' decision to deport them by the fact that the *rudari* "had
no houses of their own and lived mostly in the woods." The villagers meant
that, by comparison, there was no solid reason for deporting the craftsmen. In
fact, the Romanians got along just as well with the *rudari* as they did with the
Gypsies. When a group of *rudari* wrote to the marshal one month later, in
November 1942, requesting the repatriation of their relatives sent 'for colonization' to Transnistria,[18] a group of Romanians sent a separate petition to
Antonescu asking for the return from Transnistria of Zimnicea *rudari*:

> During all the time they have lived together with us they have proved
> to be the most peaceful and hardworking people. Their job is much con-
> nected to many things necessary both to our families and to the agricultural
> work. All the above make us regret their departure and kindly ask you to al-
> low them to return to Zimnicea.[19]

Signed by 27 locals, the petition was sent along with the one composed
by relatives of the deportees. The authorities, however, did not agree to the
repatriation of these *rudari*.

The above intercessions on behalf of the Gypsies rallied broad public support. The local administration itself intervened on behalf of the Gypsies. The mayor's offices issued good conduct certificates[20] to those who felt threatened by deportation and sought to protect themselves, and also interceded with the police[21] to exempt local Gypsies from (any further) deportations. When relatives of the deportees or other villagers sought to obtain the repatriation of Gypsies, the mayor's office usually agreed to issue documents indicating the material standing of those concerned, so that they might be brought back home.[22]

Some documents reflect the villagers' desire for the return of fellow Gypsy residents. In March 1943, several residents of Dobreni, Ilfov County, asked the mayor to intercede with the governor of Transnistria for the repatriation of 12 Gypsy families deported from the commune. Their initiative came in response to a telegram from a deported resident, or, as they put it, "one of those wretched souls." In their petition, the villagers noted that they were "not migrants, nor known for doing any mischief," but rather "innocent people" whom the local chief of gendarmes had driven away from their homes in an act of personal revenge.

> We trust that the Honorable Government of Transnistria, with whom we are kindly asking you to intercede, will find our petition justified following due inquiries at their residences where they still have relatives and property and where their homes lie deserted..."[23]

Yet, the Gypsy families concerned were not repatriated.

CONCLUSION

Based on the above petitions, it seems safe to say that most Romanians did not support the government's policy toward the Gypsies during World War II. However, it should be stressed that this attitude did not apply to all deported Gypsies. All of the above-mentioned interventions were made by common people in the towns and villages on behalf of Gypsy neighbors they knew personally, with whom they had daily contact, and who served the community by their trade. Nomadic Gypsies did not enjoy such support. As some of the above examples show, people sometimes distinguished between nomadic Gypsies whose deportation was taken for granted, and sedentary ones for whom they intervened. It is worth noting that one of the arguments used by the sedentary Gypsies to defend themselves against actual or possible deportations was that they were not nomadic but had stable homes and performed useful work. For example, the president of the General Union of Roma in Romania, Gheorghe Niculescu, demanded in September 1942 that "the execution of deportation orders must concern only nomadic Roma and exempt sedentary Roma who have a stable abode and are skilled in the practice of various professions."[24]

The lack of public reaction to the deportation of the nomads was due partly to stereotypes of those Gypsies and partly to the limited contact the Romanians had with this category. By contrast, settled Gypsies benefited not only from the Romanians' sympathy but also from their support. Interventions on behalf of the Gypsies referred to specific groups in particular communities, or even to a specific individual. Solidarity with the Gypsies occurred only at the community level; there was no solidarity of the common people with all the country's Gypsies or with a certain category of Gypsies. Politicians took a different stand, illustrated, for instance, by the protest of Liberal leader Constantin I. C. Brătianu, who referred to all Gypsy residents.

As the above examples indicate, when ordinary Romanians made their intercessions they generally cited, on the one hand, the Gypsies' status as members of their rural or urban communities, noting that they led normal lives and made no trouble, and on the other, their economic role in the communities. The Gypsies for whom they intervened were artisans, sometimes the only ones available, and—as several petitions pointed out—their services were critical for local economic performance. The petitioners did not resort to political arguments, nor did they refer to civil or human rights—not that this would have been expected, given Romania's poorly developed civil awareness at the time, particularly in the rural areas.

The peasants' image of the Gypsies and their part in rural Romanian communities corroborate the results of some sociological studies conducted by the Romanian Social Institute in the interwar period.[25] These analyses focused on the Gypsies' economic and social functions in the Romanian villages—where most Gypsies lived—and their relations with the majority population. The findings showed that Gypsies were part of the rural communities in which they played specific roles, some as craftsmen and others as farm laborers. Despite distinctions within these communities between Romanians and Gypsies, as well as social barriers and the Romanian peasants' prejudice against Gypsies—deriving from the history of slavery the Gypsies had suffered in Romania for centuries—the two populations had good mutual relations. Overall, the Gypsies continued to be the poorest social category in the villages and constituted a cheap, readily available workforce. Yet, they had made some progress, especially since the 1920 land reform, when many Gypsies acquired a social and economic status close to that of Romanian peasants. This, in turn, favored their integration into the rural communities, a process that in fact had been going on since they turned to sedentary life. The Gypsies had a somewhat special relationship with the Romanians, who perceived them largely as a social category on its way to ethnic and linguistic integration and assimilation. During the interwar period, it was the prevailing view in Romanian society, that the Gypsies would be assimilated, and that completion of this process was just a matter of time.[26]

The authorities shared this positive, or at least neutral, attitude toward the Gypsies. Romania had no specific policy toward this minority until World War II. The Gypsies were seen neither as an ethnic nor a social problem, and the racist theories concerning them, as promoted by some supporters of eugenics, aroused little interest.[27] It was the Antonescu regime with its ethnic policy that turned the Gypsies into a 'problem.'

Ordered by the authorities, the deportation of the Gypsies in the summer and early fall of 1942 occurred at a time when the common people did not perceive the Gypsies as trouble. The public's—especially the peasants'—negative reaction to their deportation was ultimately intended, beyond the local circumstantial reasons, to preserve the integrity of their communities. The rural communities were faced with a brutal external interference, which attempted to remove the Gypsies—a community segment with a definite economic and social role. People feared the authorities were planning to eventually deport all of the Gypsies, not just 'problem' cases, thus altering the composition and operation of the villages. To the communities, this was an unacceptable prospect, one that would account for the negative public reaction to their deportation.

The deportation of the Gypsies to Transnistria caught the Romanian public by surprise. Public opinion had not been 'prepared' for this action. The propaganda machine of the regime had not included anti-Gypsy slurs in its agenda. The population was quick to react. Even under the Antonescu dictatorship, Romanian society retained its reflexes of self-defense. Within the limits of that period, people still knew how to voice their disagreement with government policies.

NOTES

1. On the deportation of the Gypsies to Transnistria, see Viorel Achim, "Țiganii din România în timpul celui de-al doilea război mondial" (The Gypsies in Romania during World War II), *Revista Istorică* 1-2 (1997), pp. 53-9; id., *Țiganii în istoria României* (The Gypsies in Romanian History) (Bucharest, 1998, pp. 133-52); id., "Die Deportation der Roma nach Transnistrien," in Mariana Hausleitner, Brigitte Mihok and Juliane Wetzel (eds.), *Rumänien und der Holocaust: Zu den Massenverbrechen in Transnistrien 1941-1944* (Berlin, 2001), pp. 101-11; id., "Deportarea țiganilor în Transnistria" (The Deportation of Gypsies to Transnistria), *Anuarul Institutului Român de Istorie Recentă* I (2002), pp. 127-41; Radu Ioanid, *The Holocaust in Romania: The Destruction of Jews and Gypsies Under the Antonescu Regime, 1940-1944* (Chicago, 2000), pp. 225-37.

2. On the objectives of the government's deportation of the Gypsies, see V. Achim, "The Antonescu Government's Policy towards the Gypsies," in Mihail E. Ionescu and Liviu Rotman (eds.), *The Holocaust in Romania. History and Contemporary Significance* (Bucharest, 2003), pp. 55-60.

3. See Achim, *Țiganii în istoria României*, pp. 141-2.

4. Jean Ancel (ed.), *Documents Concerning the Fate of Romanian Jewry During the Holocaust*, Vol. IV, (Jerusalem, 1985), p. 225.

5. Refers to the alleged hostile behavior of the Jewish population during the withdrawal of the Romanian administration and troops from Bessarabia and Northern Bukovina in June 1940, when the Soviet Union occupied these territories. While here Brătianu condemns the deportation of the Jews indirectly, he did this explicitly in other documents.

6. For instance, in March 1943, Ștefan Irimescu from Bucharest wrote to the governor of Transnistria asking that 19 families of Gypsies that had been deported from Țăndărei, Ialomița County, be allowed to come and work on his estate at Buhăești, Vaslui County, and in his Odobești vineyard. The petitioner explained that those Gypsy families had been working his lands for many years. United States Holocaust Memorial Museum Archive (USHMMA), RG-31.004M, reel 6; Odessa Oblast Archiv (OA), fund 2242, opis 1, delo 1912, p. 118 r.

7. For example, in October 1942, the management of the Romanian Railroad Company (CFR) interceded with the General Directorate of Police that ethnic Gypsy workers at CFR workshops in Bucharest not be deported to Transnistria, because "most of them are highly qualified especially as blacksmiths—a trade in which they are almost irreplaceable." The memo went on to portray them as "orderly, disciplined elements who make an important contribution to the war production." Arhivele Naționale Istorice Centrale, Bucharest (ANIC), fond Direcția Generală a Poliției (DGP), dosar 190/1942, p. 72.

8. ANIC, DGP, dosar 188/1942, p. 203.

9. A list of them can be found in ANIC, fond Inspectoratul General al Jandarmeriei (IGJ), dosar 126/1942, pp. 351-2.

10. Arhivele Naţionale Direcţia Judeţeană Galaţi, fond Prefectura Judeţului Tecuci, dosar 12/1943, p. 3 (Prefecture of Galaţi County to the Ministry of the Interior, 17 May 1943).

11. For example, in the commune of Bogdăniţa, Tutova County, a Gypsy back from combat found his house looted by neighbors after the deportation of his sister to Transnistria. ANIC, fond Inspectoratul Regional de Jandarmi, dosar 59/1942, p. 447 (document of Feb. 1943).

12. ANIC, DGP, dosar 190/1942, p. 65.

13. ANIC, fond Preşedinţia Consiliului de Miniştri (PCM), dosar 202/1942, pp. 216-17.

14. One of the numerous categories of Gypsies living in Romania. They generally supplied wooden objects to peasant households.

15. Ibid., p. 219.

16. ANIC, DGP, dosar 189/1942, p. 257.

17. ANIC, PCM, dosar 202/1942, pp. 234-5.

18. ANIC, DGP, dosar 194/1942, p. 118.

19. Ibid., p. 133.

20. For example, on 6 October 1942, the mayor's office of Secătura commune, Cluj-Turda County, issued a 'communal certificate' to a local Gypsy. The document showed that Traian Mocoiu was a blacksmith and a farm laborer in his spare time, and added: "At the same time, the mayor's office hereby certifies that since no other local blacksmith can replace him, the commune and especially its residents will suffer and will miss his services if he is taken to Transnistria." ANIC, PCM, dosar 202/1942, p. 203.

21. On 11 October 1942, Mayor C. Chiriţescu of Dăeşti, Argeş County, wrote to the chief of the Gendarmes Section Goranu, asking him to intercede with his superiors so that the three Gypsy blacksmiths in the commune not be apprehended. The mayor himself initialed the men's requests for being allowed to stay: "The commune urgently needs these three blacksmiths, since it does not have any other blacksmiths and if they too are arrested, the carting, agricultural works, etc. will stagnate completely, if these craftsmen are no longer in the commune." USHMMA, RG-25.004M, reel 66; Arhiva Serviciului Român de Informaţii, Fond Documentar, dosar 18844, vol. 4, p. 357.

22. See, for example, the postscript the mayor of Iclănzel, Cluj-Turda County, added to such a repatriation petition: "We hereby acknowledge that our resident Preda Moldovan, evacuated from our commune, behaved very well, and we kindly ask you to approve his return to Iclănzel." USHMMA, RG-31.004M, reel 6, OA, fund 2242, opis 1, delo 1912, p. 42 (4 Dec. 1942).

23. USHMMA, RG-31.004M, reel 6; OA, fund 2242, opis 1, delo 1912, p. 110 (March 1943).

24. ANIC, DGP, dossier 189/1942, p. 96.

25. See among other papers on the issue: Domnica I. PĂUN, "Ţiganii în viaţa satului Cornova" (The Gypsies in Cornova Village Life), in *Sociologie Românească* 1-4 (1932), pp. 521-7; and Aurel BOIA, "Integrarea ţiganilor din Şant (Năsăud) în comunitatea românească a satului" (Integration of Şant [Năsăud

County] Gypsies in the Romanian Community of the Village), *Arhiva pentru Ști-inta și Reforma Socială* 7-9 (1938), pp. 351-65.
26.   On the Gypsies' situation in interwar Romania, see Achim, *Țiganii în istoria României*, pp. 120-32.
27.   On these opinions, see ibid., pp. 133-6.

GYPSIES IN GERMANY—GERMAN GYPSIES? IDENTITY AND POLITICS OF SINTI AND ROMA IN GERMANY

GILAD MARGALIT and YARON MATRAS

In this essay we introduce the population referred to as 'German Gypsies.' We then proceed to examine forms of organization and modern representation of identity, focusing especially on the dichotomy between two distinct self-images: the first, of a minority based in German territory and culture yet distinct from mainstream German society; the second, of a group that belongs to a transnational ethnic minority dispersed both within and outside of the German context. We will try to assess the impact of historical events and group-specific traditions on the development of a political discourse(s) among Gypsies in Germany today, and on the shaping of the political agendas pursued by their respective associations.

'GYPSIES': A CONFUSION OF TERMS

In employing the term 'Gypsy,' we are referring to an ethnic group—however ambiguous this might seem in light of the fact that this group is multi-layered and diverse in its historical origins, language, traditions and self-identification. We draw a distinction between 'Gypsies' as a common term associated with a lifestyle or socio-economic organizational form, irrespective of origin, language or traditions, and 'Gypsies' as a popular, though usually external name for a population which shares a language (albeit split into several dialect groups), traditions and beliefs, and ultimately originating in India. We will call the first 'Gypsy I,' and the second 'Gypsy II,' in order to emphasize the fact that a single term is often used to denote two distinct types of population.[1]

Gypsy II is objectively recognizable primarily through language, namely, a population that speaks Romani (or *romanes*). The dialects of Romani

originate in an Indian language; the divisions among them, which are relatively recent, can be traced back to differentiation in speech forms as a result
of dispersion throughout Europe, from the southern Balkans (formerly Byzan-
tium), from about the 14th century onwards.[2] In some communities, the Romani language has been lost as a result of partial assimilation and language
shift, quite often coinciding with intermarriage and integration into, or ab-
sorption of, local indigenous peripatetic populations (as in the case of Britain
and Scandinavia). Thus, in effect, Gypsy II (descendants who speak Romani;
ultimately of Indian origin) can overlap with Gypsy I (descendants of indigenous travelers). This has caused some confusion both in popular perception
and in academic discussions, where we encounter reluctance to acknowledge
that overlap is a local phenomenon and not a global one.[3] Some recent authors have carried this line of argument even further, claiming there is no
basis for the assumption of Indian origin or the Romani language or the Romani-speaking population, and that the motivation behind two and a half centuries of linguistic scholarship devoted to the Indian origins of Romani is pure
romanticism, or even racism.[4]

As elsewhere, both types (Gypsy I and II) may be found in the German
context. The first population group includes peripatetic musicians, peddlers,
toolmakers, and operators of mobile entertainment units such as carousels.
They are usually based in a particular region and travel for their livelihood,
but not at random. Many of these groups are currently in decline due to
changing patterns of occupation, social mobility, and lax group identity. One
of the populations that stands out among the Gypsy I in Germany are the
Jenische, who developed a distinct identity in the 18th century and who absorbed, locally at least, Romani-speaking groups, as well as indigenous travelers and in all likelihood, also members of immigrant minority and traveler
groups. The Jenische are regionally dispersed but tend to concentrate in their
own villages, as a result of settlement privileges granted to them in specific
locations from the 18th century onwards.

The focus in this essay is not on populations that constitute Gypsy I—
the diverse peripatetic populations—first, because we are unaware of any
political or nationalist movement among these groups in Germany (though
associations of Yenish are active in Switzerland); and second, unlike Gypsy II,
these populations are unable to claim in any straightforward way a shared
ethnicity or culture, manifested by a common language, beliefs, traditions,
sense of historical fate (*Schicksalsgemeinschaft*) or historical territorial origin
(however recent awareness of the latter may be among Gypsy II—see below).
Our interest is in the link between such claims that are characteristic of Gypsy

II, and the construction of ethnic-national identity and participation in a political process. We direct our attention therefore to the population of Romani
speakers, known generally as Rom but locally also under group-specific self-
appellations. It is to this population (Gypsy II) that we will apply the label
'Gypsy,' alternating with the various self-designations employed by the sub-
groups.

GYPSY GROUPS IN GERMANY

The largest sub-group of German Gypsies in the latter sense consists of the
population that now refers to itself as 'Sinti.' They are descendants of a Romani-speaking immigrant population that began leaving the Balkans around
the end of the 14th century. First attestations of Gypsies in Germany date
from the early 15th century. As a sub-division of the European Romani population, the Sinti are fairly closely related, both culturally and linguistically, to
the Romani populations of Britain and Scandinavia (Finland), who migrated
to these locations via Germany. All these groups are relatively closed and
isolated, with rather strict codes regulating family, and limiting contacts with
non-Gypsies (*gadje*). They also have a shared tendency to conceal their identity from non-Gypsies, and to prevent outsiders from learning about their customs and language. Like the Romani populations of Scandinavia, Britain, and
the Iberian Peninsula, up to the late 18th century the Sinti referred to themselves as 'Kale' (lit. 'blacks'). The term 'Sinti' or 'Sinte' (see below) may be
found in 18th and 19th century linguistic documentation alongside 'Kale,' and
appears to have been borrowed from the secret vocabulary of the Yenish travelers,[5] perhaps because of its usefulness in concealing ethnic identity. Only
toward the late 19th century does the self-appellation 'Sinti' replace 'Kale'
entirely in Germany.

While the core of the Sinti population lives in Germany, a few sub-
branches settled in surrounding areas. Some Sinti populations migrated to
former German territories in Pomerania and Silesia, and others joined ethnic German settlement areas in Bohemia, Russia, Vojvodina and South Ti-
rol. Some of the latter immigrated to Germany after World War II and tried
to claim German citizenship based upon ethnic German identity. The authorities' refusal to grant their demands figured prominently in the formation of the modern political movement of German Gypsies, as we shall see
below. There are also Sinti populations in Austria, Belgium and the Netherlands. The Manouche population in France, too, is a branch of the Sintis,

preserving another self-appellation that was commonly found among German Gypsies until the 18th century (cf. *manisch*, still used by the Yenish in some areas to refer to Gypsies). Most of these groups are conscious of their German connections, and the fact that their cultural and linguistic identity was formed in German-speaking territory. This is demonstrated principally by the attempts of Sinti survivors of World War II in Eastern Europe to 'return' to Germany and settle there. Many Sinti groups in Austria, the Netherlands and Belgium maintain close ties with Sinti families in Germany. The French Manouche and the South Tyrol Sinti are aware of German vocabulary in their dialects of Romani.

Besides the Sinti in Germany, there is also a population of Lovara, whose dialect belongs to the Northern Vlax branch of Romani dialects spoken in Transylvania. They immigrated to Germany during the late 19th century. Their migration westward during this period can be seen in connection with the gradual abolition of Romani serfdom and slavery in the Romanian principalities between 1850 and 1863. Since then they have integrated Lovara families that immigrated to Germany from Austria during the 20th century. The Lovara regard themselves as German Rom (rather than Sinti). Although they maintain some links to the Sinti, including family ties in some cities, they view themselves as distinct and are very conscious of a separate identity.

Finally, there are Roma who immigrated to Germany from the late 1950s onwards. They include Lovara from Poland who arrived in the 1950s, groups such as Arli, Xoraxane, and Dzhambazi, who settled as labor migrants from former Yugoslavia during the 1960s and 1970s, and Polska Roma who came as asylum seekers from Poland during the 1970s and early 1980s, as well as groups originating in former Yugoslavia and Poland who applied for asylum in the 1980s as the only legal way to gain temporary legal status in the country, and despite overall rejection of their claims were allowed to remain in Germany as a result of special local arrangements. Some Roma belonging to these various groups have acquired German citizenship, and individuals have established Romani associations in their towns and taken up community-related professions such as teaching or social work. But unlike the Sinti and Lovara, the more recent immigrants, who speak Romani and define themselves as Roma, do not regard themselves as German Gypsies; nor do the Sinti view them as part of their community, though attitudes toward them among the German Lovara (German Roma) vary.

THE SEPARATENESS OF THE SINTI

The German Sinti have traditionally remained a closed and isolated group, except for their contacts with Sinti in neighboring countries. Their separateness has led to attempts in Romani nationalist literature to attach a distinct origin to them. Already in 18th and 19th century scholarly discussions, the name 'Sinti' was associated occasionally with that of the Indian province of Sindh. There is, in fact, no connection at all. The word 'Sinti' has the inflection typical of a European loanword in Romani, and cannot have been part of the original Indian vocabulary of the language. The fact that it is found solely among Romani speakers in Germany and neighboring regions and only in more recent sources, suggests that it is a later borrowing into this specific dialect of Romani, and was not part of the language in pre-European times. Nonetheless, the association of the Sinti with Sindh remains part of popular folklore. Romani activist and writer Vania Kochanowski was the first to suggest that the Sinti in fact originate in a separate migration from India than that of the Roma, and that they are descendants of Kshatriyas (a warrior caste) from the province of Sindh, who left for Mesopotamia in the 8th century due to climate changes, and later moved on to Greece together with the Roman legions, where they were joined by the ancestors of the Roma. The latter, according to Kochanowski, were Rajputs (another warrior caste) from Rajasthan, who fled after they were defeated in a battle in Afghanistan four centuries later.[6] This theory is also accepted in somewhat modified form by Kenrick and by Hancock, both of whom suggest that the European Romani population derives from a mixture of Indian populations who merged outside of India, prior to their immigration to Europe.[7]

Despite Hancock's claims about the existence of linguistic findings to support this (although he has never produced them), there is no evidence, and certainly no linguistic proof, to support the theory of either a Romani melting pot outside of India or of a distinct origin of the Sinti. All dialects of Romani share a consistent pattern of derivation from late Middle Indo-Aryan/early New Indo-Aryan, dating from the Early Medieval period. The absence of a particular, identifiable ancestor language of Romani within India today is not surprising. This is due first to a time span of over 1000 years in which the language has changed substantially, and then to the probable peripatetic origin of the Rom within India (likewise, there is no clearly identifiable ancestor dialect of Yiddish in the German-speaking landscape of today, or of Ladino). Another reason, no doubt, is the paucity of sources and documentation of modern Indo-Aryan languages, apart from the relatively few that enjoy the status of standard written varieties. Rather, all differences among the dialects of Romani today are easily traceable to a series of linguistic-structural innovations that took place within the past 700–800 years,[8] from so-called Early Romani. The Sinti dialect is no exception, and although quite distinct from the Romani dialects of central Europe and the Balkans, most differences are accounted for by the influence of German, as well as by common simplification, renewal and leveling processes that occurred *in situ*. Moreover, although the Sinti now use this term as a self-appellation—both collectively and in regard to individuals (*sinto sinti man*, etc.)—the language is still referred to as Romanes (*romnes*), and the terms *rom, romni* still exist, albeit in specialized form to denote family bonds (husband, wife) rather than ethnic-national ones. (Arguably, family bonds have traditionally been more significant in the isolating Sinti culture than ethnic-national ones, hence the preservation of an old term there; but the flexibility and tendency toward vocabulary renewal in the word applies to the ethnic community as a whole.)

GERMAN GYPSIES AS A MINORITY

An investigation of German Gypsy identity today must take this history into account: on the one hand, distinctness and isolation, and on the other, awareness of bonds with Gypsy groups in neighboring countries, with other Gypsy groups that have settled in the country, and, more remotely, with Gypsy groups abroad. Thus, it is certainly somewhat problematic to apply terms such as 'diaspora' and 'transnational group' to the German Gypsies. The Zentralrat deutscher Sinti und Roma, the main organization of German Sinti and Roma, has been campaigning for years to have the Sinti officially recognized as a German ethnic minority (*Deutsche Volksgruppe*) within the German nation state. This struggle implies a self-definition of a non-diaspora minority. The Sinti certainly do not regard India, their ancient land of origin, as their national homeland, and nor do Roma organizations. Nevertheless, certain expressions of Romani nationalism among Roma who immigrated to Germany from Eastern Europe, and even some implicitly nationalist notions among German Sinti, reveal clear affinities to the concepts of diaspora and transnationalism.

The emergence of Romani nationalism in the late 1960s stimulated an attempt among Gypsy intellectuals to create a national history and to base the authenticity of all Gypsy groups on an imaginary heritage of the Indian homeland. Some of these attempts led to essentialist notions.[9] Romani nationalists have faced a great challenge, since contacts among Gypsy groups dispersed throughout Europe are rather loose due to the processes discussed above, and the emergence of various Gypsy sub-cultures. These sub-cultures have absorbed local cultural elements, such as language, religion and mentality. Gypsy migrants formally adopted the dominant religions when they arrived in Europe, while maintaining certain elements of their former beliefs. In Muslim regions such as Turkey or Bosnia they embraced Islam. The earliest sources dealing with their arrival in German-speaking territory six centuries ago report that Gypsies presented themselves as Christians.[10] However, missionaries who worked among them complained that the expression of their Christianity was fairly superficial. Most German Sinti are Catholics. They adopted certain components of Catholic folklorist ritual, including the cult of the Virgin Mary and the pilgrimage to sacred Christian locations, which were probably integrated with earlier pagan rituals. But at the same time, the Gypsies have also continued to cling to their pre-Christian beliefs and to maintain customs deriving from them. These include a system of purity and impurity, various prohibitions on eating and sexual relations, and traditions and rituals concerning birth, marriage, death and illness.[11] Traditional Sinti society has tried hard to convince their reluctant German neighbors that they truly deserve to belong to Christian Europe. An attempt of Sinti in France to provide Christian legitimation for their presence in Europe can be observed in a traditional tale told in Romani:

> All the Gypsies believed in one god. When his time came to perish on the Cross (according to missionaries, confusing Jesus with God is a quite common among Gypsies), a Sinteza was present at the site. She pitied him, and did not want his feet to be nailed. So she stole one nail, and God was crucified.[12]

In order to grant authenticity and credibility to this tale, the Gypsy authors chose to connect themselves to Jesus' Passion by theft—a typical Gypsy trait, according to the surrounding non-Gypsy majority.

These attempts have lasted until modern times. However, under the influence of modernization in 20th century Germany, the Sinti have undergone a secularization process in which German nationalism and bourgeois respectability have replaced Christianity in terms of the legitimacy of Sinti existence on German soil. In an interview conducted in the 1980s, the Sinto Hans Brown said: "We are German: we think as Germans, we live as Germans and would like also to be accepted as Germans."[13]

ROMANI NATIONALISM
AND ITS IMPACT ON GERMAN SINTI

The origins of Romani nationalism lie in 1930s' Romania and Yugoslavia, where Roma intellectuals were preoccupied with Romani culture and the Romani national movement and published Romani newspapers.[14] Certain superficial expressions of Romani nationalism appeared among Sinti activists as late as the 1970s, but did not really take root among German Sinti or their organizations. Sinti lack of enthusiasm for Romani nationalism recalls the attitude that was common among German Jewry toward Jewish nationalism (Zionism) in the last decade of the 19th century and the first decade of the 20th century. While identification with Germany among German Jewry was genuine and expressed true gratitude to German society and its institutions for enabling this minority a certain degree of integration and remarkable economic and cultural success, their reluctance to embrace their own particular identity was also an outcome of the demand of the surrounding society that these perceived foreigners prove absolute loyalty to the German nation state, and of the demonstrations of hostility toward any expressions of national feeling other than that of German nationalism by members of the German community. As most Sinti were neither fully integrated into German society nor enjoyed particular economic, social or cultural success in Germany, their reluctance was due mainly to the pressures of the surrounding society.

Sinti and Roma in Germany also began very late to found their own organizations. Each Gypsy group formed its own. The first association of Sinti was founded by Vinzenz Rose in 1956. The name of the association was Verband und Interesssengemeinschaft rassisch Verfolgter nicht-jüdischen Glaubens deutscher Staatsbürger e. V. (Association and Interests Community of Racially Persecuted German Citizens of Non-Jewish Faith). It was a rather odd name for an organization whose main mission was to represent Sinti claims, as it blurred its members' identity completely. Such a name pertained equally to 'non-Aryan Christians,' that is, people of Jewish descent (such as Christians with one Jewish parent) who were persecuted by the Nazis for racial reasons. The choice of name seems to have been deliberate. In the 1950s the self-appellation Sinti was not known in Germany. Rose was probably trying to evade the derogatory association of the term *Zigeuner* (Gypsy; see below), which prevailed among the German public. The association's title recalls the Jewish Centralverein deutscher Staatsbürger jüdischen Glaubens, which, similarly, is no coincidence. Both truly reflect the desperate quest of these German minorities to be recognized and accepted as Germans. The association, which represented a few prominent Sinti families, had no national character, and was engaged mainly in the matter of compensation to its members for their persecution by the Nazis, as well as bringing to trial certain Nazi perpetrators.

In Western Europe, Romani nationalism began to crystallize during the late 1960s; this was noted in Britain as well as in other European states.[15] The Romani national revival of the late 1960s borrowed its methods from the civil rights struggle of the American Indians and from the struggle of the 1968 student movements. It climaxed in the convening of the first *Romano Kongreso* in London in 1971. As was the case in Zionism and black nationalism,[16] in Romani nationalism, too, assimilated persons played key roles. But, in contrast to Zionism of the late 19th and the 20th century and to certain streams in black nationalism, Romani nationalism had no territorial vision and did not seek to return all the world's Gypsies to India. Gypsy nationalists wish to stay in their present—mostly European—countries as equal citizens and to be recognized collectively as a unique cultural community. Romani nationalists have never used the term 'diaspora' but it seems that they implicitly accept the concept of Gypsies as a transnational group. Romani nationalism seeks to transform the tribal consciousness and identity of the various Romani groups such as the German Sinti into a unified Romani national consciousness and national identity. It emphasizes the Gypsies' Indian origins and the Romani language. The Romani national flag resembles the Indian flag with the Ashok Chakra (the Indian wheel of destiny) at the center. Some Romani nationalists emphasize the exodus from India and the subsequent wandering as their formative national experience and have made the song "Gelem Gelem" the Gypsy national anthem. Romani nationalism expects and requires all tribal groups to show solidarity with other Romani groups, such as the German Sinti, as members of the same Romani nation. Its influence can be traced in all Romani organizations in Europe.

During the civic struggle of the early 1980s, Sinti organizations used the Romani national flag as well as rhetoric that contained certain elements borrowed from Romani nationalism, but these expressions had a rather superficial character and disappeared over the years. Most German Sinti, like the German Jews in the pre-war period, evince reluctance about Romani nationalism because they fear it will jeopardize their desperate attempts to be integrated into the majority in the German nation state. Most German Sinti, like most pre-Holocaust German Jewry, prefer the assimilation model, with certain reservations that would enable them to preserve their unique ethnic subculture. No other local Romani organization in any European country is as desperately engaged or as anxious as the Zentralrat deutscher Sinti und Roma, in an apologetic attempt to persuade the German public that German Sinti truly merit the right to live in Germany.

From the late 1970s Sinti activists in Germany, influenced by the International Romani Union, began to regard the German term *Zigeuner*, meaning Gypsy, as bearing derogatory connotations. They therefore replaced it with their own name, Sinti. Since 1973 Vinzenz Rose's son, Romani, has presided over the re-activated organization which was then called Deutscher Sinti Verband (Association of German Sinti). In 1983 it was renamed Zentralrat deutscher Sinti und Roma, recalling the main Jewish organization in the FRG (Zentralrat der Juden in Deutschland). Despite its pretensions of pursuing a national struggle in the name of all Romani groups, the Zentralrat is in fact a traditional organization of a few Sinti families with no Roma on its board.

The typical Sinti choice to include the adjective 'German' in the title of their organizations has not been observed among the Roma in Germany. When, in 1960, Walter Strauss and Wilhelm Weiss, two German Roma from Frankfurt, founded the first Roma organization in the Federal Republic, they had no qualms about calling it Zentral Komitee der Zigeuner (Central Committee of the Gypsies).[17] This trend could also be traced in the organizations of the second generation after World War II. When Rudko Kawczynski, a Rom—who was born in Poland to a Roma family of non-Polish origin and as a child immigrated to Germany—founded an organization for both groups in Hamburg in 1980, he named it Rom und Cinti Union (Romani and Sinti Union).

In sharp contrast to the German Sinti, many Roma, especially activists such as Kawczynski—who was one of the first generation among Polish immigrant families to grow up in Germany and had relatives and networks all over Europe—do not regard themselves as Germans and are not eager to be considered so despite their wish, for practical reasons, to obtain German citizenship. In an interview to the communist newspaper *Neues Deutschland* in 1993, Kawczynski was asked about the German citizenship he had recently acquired. He replied: "Naturally I am not a German. When I go along the street, no one sees that I have a German passport in my pocket."[18] Rather like the first postwar generation of immigrants in Germany of east European Jewish origin, these activists regard themselves as members of a nation (Jewish people or Roma) and not as members of a German minority group (German Jews or *Gadschkene Sinti*, meaning German Sinti in the Sinti dialect). The present generation at least would never refer to itself as *Gadschkene Roma*.

These developments have surely encouraged the emergence of a Romani national consciousness and identity. However, the different self-appellations and the specific naming of the Roma and Sinti organizations express a dissimilar collective consciousness in these two Gypsy groups. The Roma have a *national* consciousness while the Sinti have a *tribal* consciousness. Between 1979 and 1985 Sinti and Roma organizations cooperated in pursuing a public campaign for civil rights and recognition in the FRG. However, the Sinti did not embark with other groups on a public campaign to promote a political concept aimed at revising the citizenship law of 1913 (which was indeed amended in 1999). Instead they chose a strategy based on the ethnic-cultural concept of German self-understanding. They have tried to persuade the German public that they, the Sinti, constitute an integral part of the German culture and German nation.

The Zentralrat demanded that the federal government recognize "German Sinti and Roma as a German ethnic group [*deutsche Volksgruppe*] with its own 600-year German history, language and cultural identity." Rose argued that "Romani is a language which has been spoken in Germany for 600 years and therefore it forms a part of the German culture."[19] This particularistic demand has no appeal to the Roma of east European origin living today in Germany, many of whom immigrated to the Federal Republic only in the last few decades. These people neither possess German citizenship nor belong to the circle of German culture. The Roma organization, Rom und Cinti Union, by contrast, demanded that the European authorities recognize all Gypsy groups as a non-territorial European people, a definition which corresponds to the transnational concept of diaspora.[20]

A central objective of the Sinti organization is to present the Sinti to the German public as German patriots and bearers of the German culture. In some of his public statements, Zentralrat chairman Romani Rose depicted the Sinti as guardians of the German cultural heritage and emphasized their contribution to German culture:

> Sinti are among the foremost people to ensure that old cultural possessions (*Kulturgut*) would remain preserved. They went to the villages and bought or secured their antique things, things that other people would just have tossed into the garbage... Some German citizens who today possess a Baroque chest of drawers do not know that they owe it to the Sinti.[21]

The Zentralrat has also tried to impress the German public with their patriotism, even inserting photos of Sinti soldiers in Wehrmacht uniform in some of their publications,[22] and participating in the Holocaust exhibition at the Documentation Center of German Sinti and Roma in Heidelberg.

The Sinti highlight their respectability and 'Germanness,' and in parallel represent their Gypsyhood as an aspect of their identity that belongs to the private domain alone. This claim of similarity to their fellow Germans calls to mind the interpretation in liberal German-Jewish circles of 'Jewishness' and 'Germanness,' and reflects the demands of the German citizenship law of those who wish to be naturalized in Germany. Despite their declaration of pursuing a national struggle in the name of all Romani groups, during the public civil rights campaign between 1979 and 1985 the Zentralrat and most of the Sinti gave a cool reception to the East European Roma refugees who sought asylum in Germany. The Zentralrat refrained from showing solidarity and support for Roma refugees in the early 1980s, when the latter requested the help of Sinti organizations in their legal struggle for the right to stay in Germany and escape deportation to their countries of origin. The Zentralrat claimed that growing numbers of foreign Roma who "abused their guest status in our country" might harm the image of German Sinti and Roma and thus wreck many of the organization's achievements.[23] Nevertheless, when the Zentralrat refers to Nazi persecution, a contradictory note emerges, implying that Sinti and Roma share a common history and similar destiny throughout Europe. It always mentions not just the 15,000 German Sinti victims but the 500,000 Sinti and Roma victims of Nazism, although this might be more for practical considerations than an expression of Romani nationalism. Nevertheless, it denotes certain notions of solidarity that transcend the boundaries of the German nation state, and is more typical of a transnational group, although most Sinti reject the notion of a diaspora or a transnational group implied by Romani nationalism.

CONCLUSION

The German Sinti are caught between two facets of their identity, the first being their group-specific loyalty. This excludes the Roma, although it acknowledges, somewhat reluctantly perhaps, that the Roma share certain traits with the Sinti. Faced with a hostile world of outsiders (*gadje*), the Sinti trust the Roma to understand them and sympathize with them, but this negative aspect of identity, the sharing of a fate or destiny, appears to be the strongest, perhaps the only binding link between the two. The other side of the Sinti identity is their Germanness, which their leaders and representatives seek to emphasize to the *gadje* world. And it is here, in seeking to align themselves with rather than distance themselves from German society that the German Sinti regard the Roma as an interfering factor, rather than a support or object of identification. Since the presence of the Roma, with their pan-Romani and international orientation, is a constant reminder to the Sinti of their distinctness, they fear that in the eyes of the *gadje*, association with the Roma will strengthen the view that they, the Sinti, are also not an integral part of German society.

NOTES

1. Cf. Y. Matras, "The Role of Language in Mystifying and De-mystifying Gypsy Identity," in N. Saul and S. Tebbutt (eds.), *The Role of the Romanies* (Liverpool University Press, 2004).
2. See Y. Matras, *Romani: A Linguistic Introduction* (Cambridge University Press, 2002).
3. E.g., Judith Okely, *The Traveller Gypsies* (Cambridge University Press, 1983); Judith Okely, "Ethnic Identity and Place of Origin: The Traveller Gypsies in Great Britain," in Hans Vermeulen and Jeremy Boissevain (eds.), *Ethnic Challenge: The Politics of Ethnicity in Europe* (Göttingen, 1984), pp. 50–65; Judith Okely, "Some Political Consequences of Theories of Gypsy Ethnicity. The Place of the Intellectual," in Allison James, Jenny Hockey and Andrew Dawson (eds.), *After Writing Culture: Epistemology and Praxis in Contemporary Anthropology* (London, 1997), pp. 224–43.
4. E.g., Wim Willems, *In Search of the True Gypsy: From Enlightenment to Final Solution* (London, 1997).
5. See Yaron Matras, "Johann Rüdiger and the Study of Romani in Eighteenth-Century Germany," *JGLS*, fifth series, 9 (1999a), pp. 89–106.
6. Vania de Gila Kochanowski, "Black Gypsies, White Gypsies," *Diogenes* 43 (1968), pp. 27–47; Vania de Gila Kochanowski, "Parlons tsigane. Histoire, culture et langue du peuple tsigane" (Paris, 1994).
7. Ian Hancock, "The Emergence of Romani as a Koïné outside of India," in Thomas Acton (ed.), *Scholarship and the Gypsy Struggle: Commitment in Romani Studies* (University of Hertfordshire Press, 2000), pp. 1–13; Ian Hancock, *We Are the Romani People* (University of Hertfordshire Press, 2002); Donald Kenrick, *Gypsies from India to the Mediterranean* (Toulouse, 1993).
8. Cf. Matras, *Romani: A Linguistic Introduction.*
9. A typical example is Ian Hancock, *The Pariah Syndrome. An Account of Gypsy Slavery and Persecution* (Ann Arbor, 1987).
10. R. Gronemeyer, "Zigeuner im Spiegel frueher Chroniken und Abhandlungen. Quellen vom 15.bis zum 18," *Jahrhundert* (Giessen, 1987), pp. 15ff.
11. E. Wittich, "The Organisation of South German Gypsies," *Journal of Gypsy Lore Society* 4, New Series 4 (1911), pp. 287–92.

12. A BBC film, *Gypsyland—It Doesn't Exist* (1983).
13. *Lustig war's das Zigeunerleben*, a film of Hannes Karnick and Wolfgang Richter (ZDF) (1981).
14. M. Bacanu, *Ţigannii. Minoritate Nationala sau Majoritate Infracional* (Bucharest, 1996), pp. 40-1; R. Djurić, "Die Roma in der Sozialistischen Föderativen Republik Jugoslawien," *Pogrom* 6 (1987), p. 45.
15. D. Kenrick, "Die britischen Roma heute," *Pogrom* 12 (March/April 1981), p. 14.
16. P. Gilroy, *The Black Atlantic. Modernity and Double Consciousness* (Cambridge, Mass., 1993), pp. 19ff.
17. V. Hoffmann, "Sie wollen keine Bürger zweiter Klasse sein," *Frankfurter Rundschau*, 15 March 1960.
18. I. Bozic, "Der Rassismus ist eine Geisteskrankheit, die man unterdruecken muss," *Neues Deutschland* 13 (14 Feb. 1993), p. 9
19. R. Rose, *Bürgerrechte für Sinti und Roma. Das Buch zum Rassismus in Deutschland* (Heidelberg, 1987), p. 11; R. Rose, "Konkreter Minderheitenschutz fuer die Sinti und Roma, " in Zentralrat Deutscher sinti und Roma Hrsg, *Minderheitenschutz fuer Sinti und Roma in Rahmen des Europarates, der KSZE und der UNO Heidelberg* (1994), pp. 10-20.
20. Y. Matras, "The Development of the Romani Civil Rights Movement in Germany 1945-1996," in S. Tebbutt (ed.), *Sinti and Roma in German-Speaking Society and Literature* (Oxford, 1998), pp. 59ff.
21. "Bei Sinti und Roma gibt es noch viel zu tun. Ein Interview mit Romani Rose," in D. Galinski, *et al.*, *Nicht irgendwo sondern hier bei uns* (Hamburg, 1982), p. 89.
22. Rose, *Bürgerrechte für Sinti und Roma,* pp. 70, 73.
23. Matras, "The Development of the Romani Civil Rights Movement in Germany," pp. 59ff.

THE POLITICS OF MEMORY
JEWS AND ROMA COMMEMORATE THEIR PERSECUTION

RONI STAUBER and RAPHAEL VAGO

INTRODUCTION

In *The Ethnic Origins of Nations* the British historian and sociologist Anthony Smith, a leading theoretician of nationalism, defines ethnic community as "a named human population possessing a myth of common descent, common historical memories, elements of shared culture, an association with particular territory and sense of solidarity."[1] Although Smith accepts the claim espoused by 'modernist' theoreticians of nationalism, such as Ernest Gellner and Benedict Anderson, that nationalism is a modern way of thinking,[2] he argues that nationalist consciousness cannot be explained merely as a consequence of modernity but is based on primordial and perennial ethnic ties and sentiments—a pre-existent cultural unit that preceded nationalism. Ethnic heritage, he claims, is an essential background to the modern process of nation building.[3]

Theoreticians who underline the durability of ethnic communities, such as Smith and John Armstrong, emphasize the permanent cultural attributes of ethnic identity, namely: memories, values, myths and symbols, recorded and immortalized in art, language and laws. These are the "cement that has maintained group identity over a long period of time."[4]

The ethno-symbolic hypothesis creates a synthesis between the opposing theories of the perennialists and the modernists, explaining the linkage between ethnicism and the formation of modern nation-states.[5] Its significance, however, pertains to the identity of ethnic minorities, whose initial concern has been protecting their cultural identity.[6]

In the case of modern Jewish history, as demonstrated by Gideon Shimoni, Smith's theory elucidates the emergence of 'cultural nationalism,' which preceded the appearance of Zionism. Shimoni claims that, "the genesis of Jewish nationalism is traceable to their ethnically self-affirming sentiments... [It] rose to the defense of Jewish cultural distinctiveness."[7]

As a consequence of specific historical circumstances, Zionism suc-ceeded in transforming cultural nationalism, or ethnic consciousness, into political nationalism, which resulted in the establishment of the State of Is-rael. For the Roma, however, the transformation to national self-determina-tion within a defined territory has never been a political alternative. Although the Roma refer to India as their historical homeland (see below), neither a return to the land of their ancient origins nor a struggle for the creation of a national state has ever been seriously considered. Nonetheless, like Jewish intellectuals in the past, members of the Romani intelligentsia perceive the Roma as a distinct people, basing their ethnic identity on cultural features, such as language, daily customs and rituals, kinship and clan ties, values, sym-bols and myths, and the ethos of wandering.

Collective memory, albeit sketchy and fragmentary, is an essential foun-dation of ethnic identity and indispensable in the process of nation building, especially when dealing with the very complicated identity of diaspora com-munities. Against the striving for cohesion amongst these communities stands the local tradition of scattered enclaves. A unique culture has evolved in each part of the diaspora due to the influence of the dominant culture of the host society. Like the early Jewish nationalist intellectuals, Romani intelligentsia who lead the struggle for strengthening a distinctive Romani ethnic identity emphasize the importance of presenting a shared history—a 'super narra-tive'—which will serve to consolidate the scattered communities. They are opposed by those who perceive the idea of a non-territorial collective Romani identity, a single people who share the same origins and history, as an in-vented narrative.[8]

Discrimination and persecution, fuelled by a hostile society surrounding them, particularly in Europe, have characterized the history of both Jews and Roma. The Roma continue to suffer hardship and prejudice, while the Jews, despite the considerable improvement in their social and political position, are still subjected to bigotry and even violent attacks. The history of persecu-tion plays a significant role in defining symbolic ethnic boundaries of both Jews and Roma, and is well integrated into Smith's and Armstrong's ethno-symbolic theory:

> Most often symbolic boundaries are words. Such words are particularly effective as traffic lights warning the group member when he is approaching a barrier separating his group from another... stressing individuals' solidarity against the alien world.[9]

Indeed both Jews and Roma have specific words for the hostile surrounding world. The Hebrew term is *goy*, a biblical word that has acquired a
negative connotation due to the persecution of the Jews; the Romani word is
gadje. The centrality of persecution in Jewish collective memory, as a definer
of ethnic boundaries, is expressed succinctly in a line of the Haggadah, recited
by the Jews during the annual Passover Seder: "In every generation there are
people who want to destroy us, and the Lord, may his name be blessed, saves
us from them."

This essay discusses the role of collective memory of persecution in
strengthening ethnic boundaries, as well as the process of nation building
among Jews and Roma. It will relate to the benefits as well as the drawbacks
of using traumatic events and the claim of victim status, in forging group identity. In addition, it will explore the impact of commemoration of the Shoah on
Romani efforts to establish an official memory of their genocide, *Porrajmos*,
and to arouse worldwide attention to their suffering.

PERSECUTION AND ETHNIC
IDENTITY—CONFLICTING PERCEPTIONS

THE JEWS

Since the rise of Jewish nationalism at the end of the 19th century, Zionist
ideologists and political leaders have viewed the symbolic role of persecution in forming Jewish ethnic consciousness with ambivalence. On the one
hand, memories of discrimination and persecution to which the Jews were
constantly subjected while they were in exile have served to strengthen the
idea of a common Jewish fate, solidarity and ethnic boundaries: Jews suffered social discrimination in both Germany and Poland and were persecuted in Russia and Yemen. Jewish nationalist leaders and thinkers perceived anti-Semitism as a continuation of historic animosity toward the
Jews. It served as proof that the Jews, who were viewed as a foreign element
within European society, would be unable to assimilate. The only solution,
claimed the Zionists, was to strengthen Jewish ethnic identity and to strive
for a national solution in the ancient Jewish homeland. Thus, Zionist leaders, authors and scholars with a nationalist outlook have tended to portray
the 2000 years of Jewish history in exile as a chain of continual persecution
and atrocities which, according to them, was almost a natural outcome of
political powerlessness, living among other nations, and depending on their

goodwill. Eminent Israeli historian Ben-Zion Dinor, who was minister of education in the 1950s, described Jewish history in exile as a cycle of continual destruction and rebuilding of Jewish centers. In this respect he saw the Holocaust as yet another *khurban* (catastrophe)—although unprecedented in its scope—in the destruction and killing that had always been the fate of the Jewish people.[10]

Some Zionist thinkers, on the other hand, thought it was imperative to base the identity of the Jewish people on symbols and myths linked to positive elements of Jewish and Israelite life in the past, such as dignity, heroism and political independence. Overemphasis on the symbolic role of anti-Semitism and victimization could undermine efforts to create a proud new Jew, able to restore Jewish sovereignty.

Zionist ideology tried to resolve the dichotomy inherent in the use of persecution as a symbol for defining ethnic boundaries, thus justifying the Zionist solution, and fear of its possible negative educational implications. It distinguished between the political powerlessness of the Jews in exile or in the Diaspora and the political and military strength of the Israelites and Jews before their banishment from the Land of Israel. David Ben-Gurion, the first Israeli prime minister, made a clear distinction between what he termed Jewish passivity in the Diaspora and Jewish sovereignty and political activism in Israel:

> In the long dark years of our wanderings, it was moral heroism that sustained us... But the Jews lost their belief that they could determine their own destiny... With his return [to Israel], the faith of the new Jew in his ability to command his own destiny and the destiny of his people was awakened.[11]

This distinction, however, had a far-reaching impact on those who were born or grew up in the Jewish Yishuv in Palestine and later in the new Israeli state. Many of this generation disdained the history of the Jews in the Diaspora, illustrated in the story *Hadrasha* (Homily), of the Israeli author Haim Hazaz, in which the hero, Youdke, demands that educators in the Jewish Yishuv stop teaching the history of the Jews in the Diaspora since it included only stories of persecution and martyrdom, and the Jew appeared as perpetually wretched and grief-stricken or begging for mercy. "We shouldn't teach Jewish history," he said; "we shouldn't teach our children the disgrace of our ancestors."[12]

This outlook also led to ambivalence on the part of the Israeli establishment in the first decade of the State of Israel toward commemoration of the

Holocaust. While some Israeli leaders saw in the Holocaust ultimate proof and a lesson for the younger generation that people without national consciousness and political sovereignty were doomed to continual persecution and eventually destruction and annihilation, the Israeli establishment in the first years of the state was very restrained in its attitude toward commemoration of the Holocaust. No prominent Israeli minister took part in the official memorial day ceremonies, and Ben-Gurion showed little interest, to say the least, in the founding and activities of Israel's Holocaust memorial institute Yad Vashem. Life, renewal and building were the watchwords of the new state. In the formative years it was important to emphasize state-building and new hope for life over Diaspora destruction, death and martyrdom. Thus, omitting the Holocaust from the structure of symbols and national myths of Israel in the 1950s was a consequence of the view that only images connected to state building should be highlighted.[13]

In addition, one of the central aims of the nation-building process conducted by Ben-Gurion was to emphasize the nation's ancestral past, skipping the long history of exile. By creating a mythical connection with the First Temple period and the life of the Israelites during the biblical era, he tried to forge a common historical background for the people of Israel, once scattered, and now gathered in the land. The period preceding the destruction of the First Temple could thus serve as a model for renewing the Jewish people's national existence.[14]

The hesitance of the Israeli establishment toward commemoration of the Holocaust was reflected in Israel's foreign relations as well. Since the destruction of European Jewry, in which so many Europeans took part, had created a historical and moral obligation on the part of European countries, and particularly Germany, to the existence and safety of the new Jewish state, the Holocaust became a political asset. However, Zionism sought to turn the Jews into a normal nation and to develop new relationships, particularly with European countries, which would be based on the immediate interests of the State of Israel rather than on bitter memories of the past—"the eternal hatred of the eternal people." There was a clear reluctance to assume the role of victim in international relations.[15]

Even before the establishment of the State of Israel and particularly during World War II, well-known figures and educators condemned this contempt for the history of the Jews in exile, claiming that it was causing indifference on the part of the younger generation to the fate of their relations who were being persecuted and annihilated by the Nazis. Criticism increased toward the end of the 1950s because of a general sense that the younger generation was detached from Jewish tradition and from Jews living in the Diaspora and was indifferent to or even lacked understanding of the historical linkage between the Jewish people and the State of Israel. At the same time historians and teachers disapproved of the whole concept of *Leidensgeschichte* (history of suffering) and the perception of the Jews in the Diaspora as a powerless entity—a historiography which employs only external frames of reference: that of the persecutors. Thus, the new education program developed at the end of the 1950s rejected the passive image of the Jew and tried instead to emphasize achievements and resistance and the ability of the Jews to control their own lives even in the Diaspora. A new concept began to dominate research of the Holocaust in Israel: describing events through the eyes of the victims and highlighting daily resistance during the Holocaust.[16]

THE ROMA

The ambivalent stance of Jewish national thinkers and Zionist leaders toward the history of persecution can be observed today among Romani intellectuals. The history of discrimination, and particularly, persecution and annihilation during the Nazi era, has helped to define the ethnic boundaries and self-identity of a victimized people. Romani leaders, scholars and intellectuals emphasize that like the Jews the Roma were persecuted and murdered on racial grounds; that is, because they belonged to a defined group of people.[17]

While Zionism, like the European national movements, was based on various annals, particularly in regard to ancient Jewish sovereignty, the Roma have no written history or even a clear historical consciousness. Thus, historical records of persecution allow the Roma, as the Polish researcher Slawomir Kapralski explained, to create a narrative that describes events chronologically, hence contributing to the development of a historical consciousness.[18]

Moreover, unlike the Jews, whose situation today is clearly distinct from the tradition of persecution, the Roma have continued to be victims of discrimination and atrocities. By emphasizing continual persecution, Romani intellectuals strive not only to explain the recent situation of the Roma in this context, but also to delegitimize current discrimination against them. Thus, they try to use their tragedy during the war as the Jewish establishment did, as a political asset, emphasizing European, and particularly

German, moral obligation, which means among other things, compensation as well as support in their struggle for civil rights.[19]

The *Porrajmos* has become the central component of Romani national identity. It is important to note that most Romani intellectuals and activists use the word Holocaust for the mass murder of Roma and other Gypsy ethnic groups during the war. Thus, they seek to create a parallel between Nazi policy toward extermination of the Jews and destruction of the Roma, namely, the notion of annihilating a people.[20]

However, it appears that like Jewish national writers and political leaders, Romani leaders and intellectuals well understand that national identity cannot be based entirely on symbols of persecution. Overemphasis on the victim syndrome might be counterproductive to efforts to strengthen Romani self-esteem and to establish new relationships with the surrounding nations. Thus, alongside the tradition of persecution, the unique Romani culture and lifestyle is presented as the epitome of freedom and non-conformism, and the antithesis of violence, oppression and chauvinism.[21]

At the same time, as in the genesis of nationalism in general and in the history of Zionism in particular, efforts to strengthen national identity and Romani self-esteem have created legends and myths that highlight the notion of bravery. The son of the Jewish merchant who joined one of the Zionist youth movements or a Maccabi sport club could imagine that he was continuing the legend of Maccabaeus, while this national and educational role is fulfilled by the current theory claiming that the Roma are the descendents of warriors known as Rajputs, who fought against the Muslim invaders of India and whose language was Romani (or *Romanes*). According to Ian Hancock:

> Because Islam was not only making inroads into India to the east, but was also being spread westwards into Europe, this conflict carried the Indian troops—the early Roma—further and further in that direction, until they eventually crossed over into southeastern Europe about the year 1300.[22]

This relatively new theory is being added to several others regarding the origins of the Roma, and accounting for their possible exile from India.[23] Common to all these ideas, which are not the province of this article, is the vague evidence that supports them. However, when dealing with the function of ethnic and national symbols, their credibility is of minor importance. Even if most theories are mere speculation, they reveal the considerable interest of Romani intellectuals and scholars in the genesis of their people. They fulfill the same traditional role of European historians, as well as Jewish Zionist historians, in the nation-building process. The Roma, it is claimed, felt compelled, or were even forced, to leave their homeland. Thus, like the story of Jewish deportation or exile, or that of other ethnic groups such as Afro-Americans, who were driven out of their homeland, exploring life in the ancient country, as well as the creation of myths and legends, is essential to the self-identity and self-esteem of a people. They serve as a necessary counter-balance to the long history of expulsion and persecution.

In addition, the ambivalence regarding the history of the persecution and the various theories and speculation about Romani origins reflect the fierce debate among intellectuals and scholars, Romani and others, over the definition of Gypsy and Romani identity. One school makes a distinction between the Romani people, whose language is a form of Romani, and who are descendents of peripatetic groups who left or were expelled from India, and other groups of 'travelers,' indigenous Europeans who adopted nomadism as a way of life. An opposing school questions the value of descent to the ethnic definition of Gypsies. Some scholars of this approach, such as Judith Okely and Wim Willems, deny the historic credibility of theories on the Indian origins of the 'Gypsies.' They regard Romani ethnic identity as social constructionism, while the alleged Indian origins are 'an invented tradition,' —to use Eric Hobsbawm's term. Gypsies are viewed as a social cultural entity, a mosaic of different ethnic groups whose common denominator is the culture of nomadism.[24]

Both Romani speakers and other 'Gypsies' were persecuted in Europe and murdered by the Nazis. The legendary years in India and the exodus, however, are solely the province of Romani speakers. Thus, creating a balance between the history of persecution and ancient Indian roots helps to strength the boundaries of the Roma as a distinct ethnic minority. The word Gypsy, or *Zigeuner*, was given by the host societies; the term *gadjo* was coined in the Middle Ages. In other words, a distinct identity was formed as a result of negative attitudes toward a group of people who were considered pariahs by European society.[25] The word 'Roma,' on the other hand, represents the legendary years of freedom as well as bravery, and the desire to create a nation as an equal constituent of the new Europe.

The balance between the Indian era of freedom and the years of persecution creates a unique fabric of ethnic symbols. The Europeans are asked to compensate the Roma, economically and politically, for the years of abuse, but at the same time to treat them with dignity, as a nation whose history dates back hundreds of years.

THE *PORRAJMOS* AS A
COMPONENT OF NATIONAL IDENTITY

The *Porrajmos* has become the focus of an emerging discourse, especially in the former communist countries but in Germany and Austria, too. The treatment of the *Porrajmos* by Roma and Roma-oriented media, local and Western media and educational-academic forums and publications, has become a means not only to mold and build historical memory but also to be used—if not manipulated—for tasks beyond commemoration. Besides rallying the Roma around their past suffering, it serves to present a set of demands from European society for recognition of the magnitude of their suffering, from commemoration to compensation.

The construction of historical memory has at least three aspects: rallying around the *Porrajmos* and its legacy in the making; strengthening the Romani historical narrative relating to their own unique lifestyle and values; and rapidly gaining recognition of the past in order to create a better future. In this respect, the Romani process differs in some ways from the construction of Holocaust memory, for while it took the Jews and Israelis two generations to forge a discourse on the ways and means to commemorate the Holocaust, the Roma act as if 'time is running out,' 'it's now or never.' This may be compared to the way that Yishuv leaders urged the formation of a Jewish state in the wake of the Holocaust and World War II. Often, it seems to outside observers as if Romani activists are trying to condense a process that took the Jews years to digest and evaluate. Admiration as well as pragmatism dictates their readiness to utilize the Jewish experience.

Due to the difficulties of deciphering the strands of Romani narrative, scholars of the Roma argue over the exact patterns of 'memory' among the Roma and whether they add up to some known form of 'historical memory.' For example, an anthropologist and a sociologist studied patterns of memory among Roma in Hungary. Michael Stewart who, in 1984 and in later years, lived among the Roma in Hungary (as well as elsewhere), wrote:

> I abandoned attempts to probe deeply into people's sense of their recent history, let alone their distant past. There was no term in colloquial Romany for the events that we have come to call 'the Holocaust'—an American Romany intellectual had coined the term Porrajmos, the 'devouring,' but one is still more likely to find this term on the internet than on the lips of the Roma in the lands occupied by the Germans during the Second World War. Daily life was lived with barely acknowledgement of those events.[26]

Later, after analyzing fragments of memories from the wartime period, Stewart continued:

> These are certainly memories, but they do not seem to me to be part of a process of remembering which involves the possession and sharing of a narrative history.[27]

Katalin Katz lived and researched historical memory among the Roma in Hungary in the post-communist period when the dynamics of memory construction and the culture of commemoration were strengthening, and researcher-activists such as Katz perhaps contributed personally to the growing mobilization and building of memory among Roma in Hungary.[28] Her study was published in Hungary in 2005 as "Repressed Memory" and in an interview given to a leading Hungarian Jewish periodical she noted that one of the aims of the book was:

> ... to get them [the Roma] recognition. To write their history [also 'their story,' in Hungarian] as part of the Holocaust. Because if the Roma are not in this story [of the Holocaust] then this is a fake history.[29]

After a brief review of ways in which the Communists distorted and excluded the fate of the Jews in the Holocaust, she continues:

> And at last the Jews entered the schoolbooks, but the Roma were forgotten. My aim is to complete the story of history of which the Roma are also part.[30]

While one scholar emphasized the 'lack' of historical memory which would add up to something all-embracing such as the *Porrajmos*—in itself, as he wrote, an 'invented' term—the other stresses that fragments of memory exist, but were left out of the story of the Holocaust—a term which Katz uses intentionally.

There is no doubt that the Roma are being supported and helped in reconstructing their past, and that in this reconstruction—and not 'invention'—outside supporters, as well as a growing number of Roma activists, products of the boom in academic studies of the post-communist years, are gradually piecing together a huge puzzle, the uncharted territory of the *Porrajmos* of the Roma. Among some basic questions, one issue is 'how much *Porrajmos* amounts, if at all, to the 'Holocaust'?

While Roma and other Gypsy ethnic groups were persecuted and murdered, leading scholars of the Nazi extinction policy in general, and annihilation of the Roma in particular, distinguished between the selective murder of
Gypsies in different part of Europe and the Nazi plan to exterminate the entire Jewish people. This distinction is not accepted by other scholars, particularly Romani researchers, and the polemic has gone beyond historical evidence to include questions of morality, hierarchy of the 'victims' and
discrimination.[31]

The wall of the Museum of the Slovak National Uprising in Banska
Bystrica, Slovakia, can serve to illustrate the essence of this debate. Two
plaques of equal size were placed alongside each other, one with the *Yizkor*
(Remember) to Jewish victims of the Holocaust, and the other to the memory
of victims of the 'Romani Holocaust,' as it appears on the plaque. Apparently,
some voices behind the scenes demanded that the plaque to the Holocaust of
Jewish victims be more conspicuous—perhaps bigger than the one devoted to
the Roma. But then, quantity could become quality—why should the plaque
to the Roma victims be smaller in size than the Jewish one? Should it be
smaller in mathematical terms? If six million victims deserve a plaque of a
certain size, should the Roma one be proportionally smaller? Or relative to
the overall numbers of victims, or to the proportion of victims among that
particular group, Jews or Roma? Or perhaps the size of the plaques should
reflect the percentage of Jewish losses in Slovakia as compared to losses
among the Roma? And one might also ask why the inscriptions referred to
'Holocaust' in both cases and not *Porrajmos* in the Roma one? It should be
noted that the plaque unveiled in Banska Bystrica is the first among seven
erected as part of a project to commemorate the persecution of the Roma in
Slovakia.[32]

Another question refers to the commemoration of events as signified
by dates. Second of August marks the extermination of Roma and Sinti in
the Auschwitz gas chambers in 1944 (on 2–3 August 1944, 2,897 Sinti
and Romani men, women, and children were killed in the gas chambers in
Auschwitz-Birkenau). Romani intellectuals and associations have followed
Jewish and Israeli ways of commemoration by instituting an annual memorial
day for the *Porrajmos* on 2 August. Like Jews and Israelis, Romani groups
have turned Auschwitz into a pilgrimage site.[33] There is no doubt that the
choice of 2 August is meant to emphasize the most significant and well-known
atrocity committed against the Roma and Sinti, and that it implies, as in the
Jewish case, that the event was part of a 'final solution,' of which the gassing
in Auschwitz became a symbol.

The outcome of Romani activism regarding commemoration, supported by a variety of NGOs as well as the liberal media in Europe, was much in evidence in 2005 in the ceremonies marking the 60th anniversary of the liberation of the camps. It was even more visible and audible in later events, especially in August, marking the 61st anniversary of the gassings in Auschwitz, notably in the speeches of dignitaries.[34]

Some countries have instituted other dates, including or without 2 August. The case of Romania is characteristic. The International Commission of Historians on the Holocaust in Romania, chaired by Elie Wiesel, included a Romani member, as well as an expert on the fate of the Roma during the Antonescu regime. The chapter of the Commission's report devoted to the Roma notes that some 25,000 Roma were deported to Transnistria, out of which half died or were killed. Romania declared the establishment of Holocaust Day on 11 October when the first deportations of Jews to Transnistria took place in 1941, but no special day was set for commemorating the Roma; yet, the Roma are mentioned on the October Holocaust Day. It may well be that the fate of the Roma in Romania will be marked in the future on another date, but will continue to be noted on Holocaust Day, which is more specifically linked to the Jewish commemoration.

As one Romani activist, Sefedin Joniz from Germany, remarked: "memory needs a place," and one might add, not only a date. Since the early 1990s there has been a widespread attempt to link Romani memory and territory, not only a 'Romani space' in the broad context, but a more localized history of persecutions—in contrast to the stereotype of the 'nomad Gypsy.' The modern, post-1989 narrative in the former communist countries seeks to establish places—of concentration, of known atrocities and cruelties, of camp-sites. These places have become the focal points for commemoration, public events, educational activities, and monuments and plaques. Since the 'Romani Holocaust' did not take place in the wide spaces of nomadic movements of people, but in specific locations, with a name and an address, from where the Roma were taken with their families, degraded and humiliated, Romani activists realized that the romantic image of the nomad traveler was counter-productive to a narrative of martyrdom, suffering, and that of the ultimate experience, the *Porrajmos*. Central and East European localities, often the peripheries of towns and villages where they dwelt in the pre-war period, became sites with monuments dedicated to the Romani *Porrajmos*, gradually creating a 'road map' of the Romani past, their presence and their suffering. At the same time, these sites bear other, positive, messages: of current rebirth and of Romani resistance and heroism in the face of the Nazis. In a major event held in the Hungarian city of Nagykanizsa, attended by the prime minister, the chief Romani spokesman told of "attempts to resist" by Romani people when they realized that they were being led to the gas chambers. This deed "indicated that human dignity was maintained, even when the resistance was seen as useless":[35]

> We are keeping the legacy [of resistance] for the future, to be ready always to defend our freedom, our lives. Our mourning turns not only to the past, but also to the present and the future, so that racism and hatred will not raise its head again.[36]

In the Czech Republic the struggle for memory tied to the physical memory of a place went beyond symbolism with a public debate over a pig farm at Lety. The pig farm—whose imagery is much utilized by the Roma and liberal press—is on the site of what the Roma consider 'a mass graveyard' and a 'World War II concentration camp.'[37] Some 1,256 Roma were interned in the Lety camp, and over three hundred died because of the terrible conditions, including a typhus epidemic. Those who survived were sent to Treblinka, Auschwitz and other extermination camps. Since the camp was staffed by Czech guards and set up by the Czech puppet government in 1945, this sparked a debate on the issue of Czech collaboration with the Nazis, or even of local initiatives. This discourse in itself is important for Romani memory building since it tackles the sensitive issue of wartime policies and attitudes of local populations and regimes toward the Roma.

Following much debate and complaints, the European Parliament passed a resolution in April 2005 urging rapid removal of the pig farm at Lety. The issue became a divisive one in Czech politics after President Vaclav Klaus expressed the view that "the camp in Lety was a labor camp for those who refused to work, and was not just for Roma. It was not a concentration camp in that sense of the word which each of us subconsciously compares with Auschwitz and Buchenwald."[38] Romani sources conducted a well-organized campaign to prove that Lety was a concentration camp. The case of the Lety pig farm in the Czech Republic has become the center of a conflict that has all the elements of a clash between memory construction, politics and the EU.

The process of Romani memory building is closely linked to that of the search for identity. Numerous bodies have attempted to place the Romani *Porrajmos* in a clear framework. Thus, the main organization of the Roma in the Czech Republic published a report on 'Compensation to Roma Victims of the Holocaust,' which clearly states:

It is unacceptable to lump Romani Holocaust victims together with Jeho-vah Witnesses, homosexuals or disabled persons because Roma constitute a nation as well as Jews.[39]

A further equation with Jews was made by Scott Thayer, deputy chief of mission in Bratislava, who represented the US at the annual memorial cere-mony for the *Porrajmos* in Slovakia in 2003. He wrote:

Slovak Roma suffered from oppression similar to that directed against the Jewish community in the inter-war period and during World War II. They were forcibly deported to concentration camps and subjected to atrocious medical experiments. There were several programs that specifically targeted Roma children.[40]

Thus, as is evident from the public discourse during the commemora-tions, which reached a peak during the 60th anniversary of the end of the *Porrajmos*, the building of collective memory and the culture of commemo-ration were strongly enhanced both in the Romani and the non-Romani media. The Romani search for identity—a long and difficult journey of self-discovery—entails an assertive stand on the uniqueness of their people, on the one hand, and emphasis on their suffering, especially compared with that of the Jews—conveyed through commemoration of the martyrdom of the 'Romani Holocaust,' or *Porrajimos,* the principal axis of memory—on the other.

CONCLUSIONS

The discourse on the Roma as a 'nation' and their fate—like that of the Jews—as targets of extermination and a 'final solution,' has been placed, liter-ally, on firm ground. The proliferation of commemoration sites, as well as monuments at concentration and other camps, both in their native lands and in Germany and Poland, has created a dense network of locations, where the culture if not the cult of collective memory is practiced. The sites of the past have become the shrines of the present plight of the Roma—of the need for recognition, restitution, retribution and revival. No respectable politician, from heads of state down to local officials, can ignore the public events around these sites. The media covers them, and perhaps, as in the Jewish case, each country has been compelled to recognize its *mea culpa* in mistreating the Roma, as well as the murderous results of racism, xenophobia, historical stereotyping, and long-term discrimination. The outcasts have thus been transformed into the focus of research and empathy, and their narratives have become an integral part of European collective memory. They have entered not only 'history' but increasingly, the textbooks of history. Programs, based on the experience of researching and teaching the Holocaust of the Jews, are aimed not only at recreating the past, but, as emphasized at every memorial event, remembering the *Porrajmos* for the future. The line running from the search for identity through a definition of origins and historical destiny to forms of modern political activism, whether at a pig farm in Bohemia or at the European Parliament, constitutes not a theoretical discussion about an 'imagined community' but a discourse about a living one, which has combined this journey of discovery with a quest for its past, in order to reach—through present day grievances over social and economic issues—their rightful place as equals among the community of fellow Europeans.

NOTES

1. Anthony D. Smith, *The Ethnic Origins of Nations* (Oxford, 1986), p. 32.
2. Benedict Anderson, *Imagined Communities* (London/New York, 1991); Smith, *The Ethnic Origins of Nations*, p. 11.
3. Smith, *The Ethnic Origins of Nations*, pp. 13–16.
4. John A. Armstrong, *Nations before Nationalism* (University of North Carolina Press, 1982), p. 3.
5. Ibid, p. 14.
6. Gideon Shimoni, *The Zionist Ideology* (Brandeis University Press, 1995), p. 10.
7. Ibid, p. 8.
8. David Mayall, *Gipsy Identities* (London, 2004), pp. 237–45; Yaron Matras, "The Role of Language in Mystifying and Demystifying Gypsy Identity," in: N. Saul and S. Tebbutt (eds.), *The Role of the Romanies* (Liverpool University Press, 2004), pp. 53–84.
9. Amstrong, *Nations before Nationalism*, p. 8.
10. Ben Zion Dinur, *Israel in the Diaspora* (Tel Aviv, 1957; Hebrew), pp. 40–5.
11. David Ben-Gurion, *Vision and Path*, Vol. 4 (Tel Aviv, 1951; Hebrew), pp. 61–2.
12. Haim Hazaz, *Collected Works* (Tel Aviv, 1967; Hebrew), pp. 221–4.
13. Roni Stauber, *Lesson for This Generation*, (Jerusalem, 2000; Hebrew).
14. Michael Keren, *Ben-Gurion and the Intellectuals* (Beersheba, 1988; Hebrew), pp. 66–75, 102–5.
15. Eliezer Don-Yehiya, "Statism and Holocaust," in Abraham Rubenstein (ed.), *In the Paths of Renewal*, Vol. 1 (Ramat Gan, 1983; Hebrew), pp. 177–81; Roni Stauber, "Between Real Politik and the Burden of the Past: Israel's Diplomats and the 'Other Germany,'" *Israel Studies* 3 (Fall 2003), pp. 100–23.

16. Stauber, *Lesson for This Generation*, pp. 135–53.
17. See for example: Donald Kenrick and Grattan Puxon, *The Destiny of Europe's Gypsies* (London, 1972), p. 60; Ian Hancock, "Genocide of the Roma in the Holocaust," www.geocities.com/Paris/5121/genocide.htm
18. Slawomir Kapralski, "Ritual of Memory in Constructing the Modern Identity of Eastern European Romanies," in Saul and Tebbutt, *The Role of the Romanies*, pp. 210–11; see also Harold Tanner, "The Roma Persecution," www.geocities. com/Paris/5121/porraimos.htm
19. Katalin Katz, "Holocaust Stories of Gypsies from Hungary: Practice of Memory and Interpretation," (Ph.D, diss., Jerusalem, 2002), pp. 320–3.
20. Steve Lipman, "The Gypsy 'Final Solution,'" www.geocities.com/paris/5121/ othervictims2.htm; Ian Hancock, "Downplaying the Porrajmos: The Trend To Minimize the Romani Holocaust," www.geocities.com/paris/5121/lewy.htm
21. Cara Feys, "Towards a New Paradigm of the Nation: The Case of the Roma," www.geocities.com/Paris/5121/paradigm.htm.
22. Ian Hancock, "Origins of the Romani People," www.geocities.com/Paris/ 5121/history.htm
23. Donald Kenrick, *The Gypsies: From the Ganges to the Thames* (Univ. of Hertfordshire, 2004).
24. Thomas Acton, "Modernity, Culture and 'Gypsies': Is There a Meta-Scientific Method for Understanding the Representation of Gypsies? And Do the Dutch Really Exist?," in Saul and Tebbutt *The Role of the Romanies*, pp. 99–115; Matras, "The Role of Language"; Mayall, *Gipsy Identities*, pp. 237–51; Wim Willems, "Ethnicity as a Death-Trap: The History of Gypsy Studies," in L. Lucassen, W. Willens and A. Cottaar, *Gypsies and Other Itinerant Groups* (London, 1998), pp. 17–34; Judith Okely, *The Traveller Gypsies* (Cambridge University Press, 1983), pp. 1–28.
25. Thomas Acton, *Gypsy Politics and Social Change* (London/Boston, 1974), pp. 60–1.
26. See Michael Stewart, "Remembering without Commemoration: The Mnemonics and Politics of Holocaust Memories among European Roma," *Journal of the Royal Anthropological Institute* (Sept. 2004), pp. 561–81.
27. Ibid.
28. See note 19 as well as Katalin Katz, "Story, History and Memory," in this volume.
29. *Múlt es Jövő* 2 (2005), p. 82.
30. Ibid., p. 83.
31. Lipman, "The Gypsy 'Final Solution'"; Hancock, "Downplaying the Porrajmos"; Yehuda Bauer, *Rethinking the Holocaust* (Yale University Press, 2001), pp. 39–67; Steven T. Katz, *Historicism, the Holocaust and Zionism* (New York/ London, 1992), pp. 126–32, 162–92; see also Michael Zimmermann, "Jews, Gypsies and Soviet Prisoners of War: Comparing Nazi Persecutions," in this volume.
32. *Dzeno Association*, 3 Aug. 2005.
33. See Michael Shafir, "Analysis: 60 Years after Central Europe's Romany Holocaust," *RFE/RL*, 2 Aug. 2004.

34. See, for example, AP's coverage of the ceremony, in *Dzeno Association*, 3 Aug. 2005.
35. See www.meh.hu, and MTI (Hungarian News Agency), 2 Aug. 2002.
36. MTI, 2 Aug 2002.
37. See, for example, Radio Prague, 29 April 2005.
38. *Dzeno Association*, 16 May 2005.
39. Ibid., 12 Sept. 2005.
40. *Pravda* (Bratislava), 2 Aug. 2003.

HUMAN RIGHTS AND ROMA POLICY FORMATION IN THE CZECH REPUBLIC, SLOVAKIA AND POLAND

EVA SOBOTKA

Where after all, do universal human rights begin? ...
In small places, close to home—so close and so small that they cannot be seen on any map of the world. Yet they are the world of the individual person: the neighborhood he lives in; the school or college he attends; the factory, farm or office where he works. Such are the places where every man, woman and child seeks equal justice, equal opportunity, equal dignity without discrimination. Unless these rights have meaning there, they have little meaning anywhere. Without concerted citizen action to uphold them close to home, we shall look in vain for progress in the larger world.[1]

INTRODUCTION

The application of a human rights objective to the formation of Roma policy in the 1990s changed the approach of Central and East European (CEE) governments to the Roma. International organizations (IGOs), such as the Organization for Security and Cooperation in Europe (OSCE), Council of Europe (CoE) and the European Union (EU) became the main arenas for drawing the attention of international society[2] to the situation of the Roma in Europe. Initially, in the early 1990s, the OSCE and the Council of Europe classified the Romani issue as a security concern (crime prevention, population regulation, assimilation); later in the 1990s it was reformulated as a subject of human rights policy. In response, the CEE states, influenced by the principle of minority rights, non-discrimination and addressing socio-economic inequalities, adopted Roma policies as defined at the transnational level by the OSCE, CoE and EU.

Although the EU accession process has helped keep the CEE governments focused on the issue of Roma, the EU has built only on the terminology and concepts developed within the CoE and the OSCE.[3] Nevertheless, some recent initiatives have further shaped this approach within the enlarged EU. The "Decade of Roma Inclusion (2005-2015)" proposed by the Soros Foundation,[4] the World Bank and the EU, encourages states to address inequality of Roma in the sphere of education, employment, housing and health. A conference on "Roma in an Enlarged Europe," organized by the European Commission's Directorate on Enlargement and the Directorate on Employment and Social Affairs, in April 2004, demonstrated that the Roma topic has attracted the attention of executive bodies of the EU,[5] while the EU Network of Independent Experts on Fundamental Rights (CFR-CDF)[6] proposed adopting a "directive specifically aimed at encouraging the integration of Roma."[7]

This essay analyzes the development of policies toward Roma in the Czech Republic, Slovakia and Poland; it distinguishes between 'human rights policy' and 'human rights politics,' and explains the influence of international politics on change in Roma policy making at the state level.

HUMAN RIGHTS AND ROMA

Human rights are linked to a great extent to progress of human kind. Progress, as Richard Rorty remarked, is "an increase in our ability to see more and more differences among people as morally irrelevant."[8] Progress might be a contested concept, but we make progress to the degree that we act upon the moral intuition that our species is one, and that each of the individuals who composes it is entitled to equal moral consideration. Since the principle of equality has been rejected in some cultural contexts as Western and European,[9] some experts have sought a common, irrefutable denominator of equality among people, arguing that regardless of cultural differences, equality stems simply from the fact that each human being has one mother and one father.[10]

If we examine the historical records we find that minorities in the past typically justified their claims, not with an appeal to human rights or equality but to the generosity of rulers to accord 'privileges,' often in return for past loyalty and services.[11] Today, by contrast, groups have a powerful sense of entitlement to equality as a basic human right, not as a favor or act of charity, and are impatient with what they perceive as lingering manifestations of a traditional hierarchical system.[12]

Since the collapse of the communist regimes, Roma in Central and Eastern Europe have increasingly benefited from human rights advocacy and instruments.[13] Efforts to alert world public opinion, both at the national and international level,[14] to the situation of Roma in Europe date back to the 1970s.[15] However, real human rights work on behalf of the Roma began only during the 1990s and focused on lobbying transnational inter-governmental organizations such as the UN, the OSCE, the CoE and the EU.[16] Consequently, a political construct of 'Roma rights' was formed as a result of international human rights advocacy, supported since the mid-1990s by the Soros and Carnegie Foundations, and earlier by the German Marshal Fund.[17] Within international organizations, Romani activists relied on the support of influential states, for example, the US within the OSCE, Finland, Hungary and Malta within the CoE, and during the 1960s and 70s, India and former Yugoslavia within the UN.

BETWEEN HUMAN RIGHTS POLICY
AND HUMAN RIGHTS POLITICS?[18]

Two approaches to Romani affairs were employed in international politics during the 1990s: human rights policy and human rights politics. 'Human rights policy' is an approach best defined as a lens through which we examine a given social, political, cultural or other issue and provide a rights-based policy using, explicitly or implicitly, human rights law as a reference.[19] For example, a human rights policy position may be found in a variety of areas, such as school desegregation, race statistics, migration, police violence, access to justice and self-determination. This tactic may compete with policies that are not rights-based but that accord with other sets of priorities such as economic efficiency, security, conflict management or local custom. A decision to do nothing is as much a policy as a decision to do something. Thomas Dye offers a particularly succinct definition of public policy, describing it as 'anything a government chooses to do or not to do.'[20]

'Human rights policy' is the opposite of 'human rights politics'. In the latter, we analyze issues from a specific perspective from that of the role they play in the world. Human rights politics is located outside the human rights paradigm or discourse and may be conducted by states as well as by non-state actors.[21] States, for example, may step out of the human rights discourse in order to view human rights from an external security perspective. More precisely, in human rights politics actors seek to explore the political functioning of human rights—how human rights work, in whose favor or against whom, and how efficiently. Ultimately, and more precisely, human rights politics is about the relation of human rights to power.

In 1975, the US cooperated with other member states of the OSCE, using human rights politics (criticism) to achieve change in the former communist bloc. The US suggested releasing political prisoners in the Soviet Union in exchange for reducing the number of US weapons.[22] During the 1990s the US continued to address its security concerns from a human rights perspective, using the OSCE as a multilateral mechanism for instituting a change in norms.[23] The US feared a possible reversal of democratic reforms in CEE due to the social-economic demise of many communities (Roma included) and inter-ethnic violence between Hungarians and Romanians in Transylvania (used by Romani agitators to create a parallel with the situation of the one million Romani minority in Romania in order to keep US attention on the issue).[24] At an OSCE meeting in Copenhagen in the early 1990s, the US took every opportunity to shape future OSCE organizational structure and policy by inculcating a human rights point of view.[25] Hence, US foreign policy *vis-à-vis* Europe, and especially *vis-à-vis* post-communist Europe, employed human rights politics in connection with various issues (such as property restitution, citizenship issues, freedom of speech), and with Roma policy in particular. Explicit concerns on the situation of Roma were raised initially in the concluding document of the Human Dimension meeting in Copenhagen, 29 June 1990.[26] Paragraph 40 of the Copenhagen document reads:

> The participating States clearly and unequivocally condemn totalitarianism, racial and ethnic hatred, anti-Semitism, xenophobia and discrimination against anyone as well as persecution on religious and ideological grounds. In this context, they also recognize the particular problems of Roma (Gypsies).[27]

Within the framework of discussion of issues of national minorities, the OSCE member states again reaffirmed their concern with the situation of Roma in a Report of the CSCE Meeting of Experts on National Minorities in Geneva in 1991. Chapter VI, paragraphs 1 and 2 read:

> The participating States, concerned by the proliferation of acts of racial, ethnic and religious hatred, anti-Semitism, xenophobia and discrimination, stress their determination to condemn, on a continuing basis, such acts against anyone.
>
> In this context, they reaffirm their recognition of the particular problems of Roma (Gypsies). They are ready to undertake effective measures in order to achieve full equality of opportunity between persons belonging to Roma ordinarily resident in their State and the rest of the resident population. They will also encourage research and studies regarding Roma and the particular problems they face.[28]

At the next Human Dimension conference, which took place in Moscow, 3 October 1991, it was concluded that:

> [State parties] recognize that effective human rights education contributes to combating intolerance, religious, racial and ethnic prejudice and hatred, including against Roma, xenophobia and anti-Semitism.[29]

The first affirmation of programs for improving the situation of Roma came one year later, during the Summit meeting in Helsinki. The Helsinki Declaration of 10 July 1992 states:

> [The Participating States] will consider developing programs to create the conditions for promoting non-discrimination and cross-cultural understanding, which will focus on human rights education, grass-roots action, cross-cultural understanding and research. Reaffirm, in this context, the need to develop appropriate programmes addressing problems of their respective nationals belonging to Roma and other groups traditionally identified as Gypsies and to create conditions for them to have equal opportunities to participate fully in the life of society, and will consider how to co-operate to this end.[30]

At the next OSCE summit in Budapest in December 1994, a decision was made to create an office within ODIHR (OSCE'S Office for Democratic Institutions and Human Rights) that would deal with the issue of Roma and Sinti and, more importantly to bind this decision to a commitment to provide sufficient resources. The Concluding Document, dated 6 December 1994, reads:

> The participating States decide to appoint within the ODIHR a contact point for Roma and Sinti (Gypsies) issues. The ODIHR will be tasked to: act as a clearing-house for the exchange of information on the implementation of commitments pertaining to Roma and Sinti (Gypsies); facilitate contacts on Roma and Sinti (Gypsies) issues between participating States, international organizations and institutions and NGOs; maintain and develop contact on these issues between CSCE institutions and other international organizations and institutions. To fulfill this task, the ODIHR will make full use of existing resources. In this context they welcome the announcement made by some Roma and Sinti (Gypsies) organizations of their intention to make voluntary contributions. The participating States welcome the activities related to Roma and Sinti (Gypsies) issues in other international organizations and institutions, in particular those undertaken in the Council of Europe.[31]

Similarly, West European states began to view the Romani issue as a security concern in the early 1990s, due to the perceived vast Romani migration from east to west.[32] Within the CoE, the issue was first addressed in the European Committee on Migration (CDMG).

However, in contrast to the US approach to the Roma, which was more concerned with the possibility of a return of communism, especially in Romania, European states, in particular, Germany, France and the UK, feared the challenge of Romani migration to their internal security.[33] In Germany, Roma became targets of racially motivated attacks, which broke out shortly after they began arriving in east Germany in 1990, and culminated in the neo-Nazi firebombing of a hostel housing 200 Romanian Roma in Rostock, to the cheers of onlookers, on 22 August 1992.[34] Some east German political parties were actively involved in inciting hatred against asylum seekers and migrants, and called for pro-active solutions to the *Asylantenproblem* (problem of asylum seekers).[35]

Consequently, security concerns of states led to human rights politics becoming a part of their foreign policy which, de facto, took the form of calls and pressure to improve the human rights situation of Roma in CEE. It is at this point that the analysis of human rights policy toward Roma in CEE began.

To gain attention, Romani 'agitators'[36] advanced powerful arguments about their situation, using international human rights organizations and their ability to draw on international 'soft' and 'hard' law[37] to make relevant states comply with their international commitments.

A significant contribution to furthering the Romani issue in CEE has been made by transnational donors, in particular the German Marshall Fund, and the Carnegie and the Soros Foundations. These philanthropic organizations, which have taken an interest in supporting activities designed to encourage the transformation from communism to liberal democracy in the CEE states, have sought topics that would attract political attention, and understood that the situation of the Roma had the potential to become the primary civil rights issue of both the region and the decade.[38]

THE FIRST POST-COMMUNIST DECADE:
A MIXED RECORD

The fall of communism in CEE created a window of opportunity for Roma to seek representation in political life; to protect and promote their language and culture; and to resume the development of their ethnic identity following the

Nazi policy of annihilation and its suppression through assimilation policies under communism. Indeed, between 1990 and 1992, the three representative chambers in Czechoslovakia—the Federal Assembly, the Czech National Council and the Slovak National Council—saw the election of a total of eleven Romani representatives. Similarly, three Romani representatives, Tamás Peli, Aladár Horváth and Antónia Hága, were elected to the Hungarian parliament between 1990 and 1994.[39] The rise of Roma representation in the CEE national parliaments in the early 1990s, has, so far, not been repeated; as of late 2004, there were four Romani MPs in the Hungarian parliament, and none in the Slovak, Czech or Polish parliaments.

The integration of Roma and wider issues of equality and diversity became principal themes of the post-1989 transition decade in the CEE states. They have chosen different approaches to Roma policy, ranging from exclusion, through assimilation and coexistence to multiculturalism. Similarly, in regard to human rights violations, states have opted either to address domestic issues of racism and xenophobia or to deny them, despite international calls for improvement. State refutation has lasted for years rather then months. Hence, 'multiculturalism' in Roma policy making in the CEE must be understood as an ideal that most states have been approaching at a slow pace.

While creating numerous openings for representation and identity-building, the first post-communist decade also saw the flourishing of anti-Roma prejudice as well as the creation of new threats against Roma, most of which had lain entrenched in the region's communist legacy and came to light through the conflict of identity of the majority populations in the transition states.[40] In the post-communist era, Romani issues were commonly interpreted as a very recent development whose origins lay in the collapse of communism and the rise of nationalism and minority rights.[41] Yet a few detected the misconception. Isaiah Berlin wrote in 1991, "In our modern age, nationalism is not resurgent; it never died."[42] Others stressed a rosier vision of post-communism: "When the curtain rose humanity suddenly found itself face-to-face with a truly multicultural and multi-polar world."[43]

Many followers of neo-Nazi ideology emerged, some of whom formed skinhead groups and extreme nationalist parties, which targeted Roma ('Gypsies') as a scapegoat for the ills of society. Music bands performed songs whose lyrics referred to Roma in a racist manner.[44] On 17 September 1991 the daily *Los Angeles Times* published a survey, which revealed that hostility to Roma was unrelated to religion or to economic or educational status:

In Hungary, 5 out of 6 persons were hostile to Gypsies. Anti-Gypsy feeling was strongest in Czechoslovakia where it was about the only thing on which Slovaks and Czechs agreed; 13 out of 14 or 91 percent of both peoples said they disliked Gypsies. "People automatically consider a Gypsy a criminal," admitted a Czech Institute manager. He said he knew that on weekends, "skinheads" seek out Gypsies, intending to kill them. "We, the whites, are very angry at Gypsies," said a Slovak taxi dispatcher. "They are given flats, and I heard that they sold things out of them or had open fires right inside the flats... I hate them."[45]

In many CEE countries, Roma are reported to be the fastest growing ethnic group.[46] For example, the 1992 Bulgarian census indicated that 23.2 percent of the Romani minority was under the age of nine, compared to 12 percent of the ethnic Bulgarian population. This high birth rate has generated a stream of sometimes speculative and alarmist news stories focusing on national demographic trends. In Slovakia, an article published in 2000 posited that, by the year 2060, the Roma would form a majority of the national population.[47]

Roma have experienced an extraordinary wave of racially motivated violence, ranging from attacks by non-state actors such as mobs to confrontations by state organs such as the police. In Romania alone, after the fall of the Ceausescu regime, more than 30 Romani settlements were set alight during 'pogroms'. On the day Romania joined the CoE, 20 September 1993, three Roma were killed, fourteen houses set on fire, and four destroyed in the village of Hadareni.

The number of Roma in the various CEE states bears no relation to the outbreak of pogroms. Romania has the highest share of Roma in the population (11 percent) and the largest number of Roma among European countries, while Poland, with 0.1 percent of Roma in the total population, is at the other end of the spectrum. However, in Poland we know of seven major pogroms during the 1990s, resulting in deaths and emigration of Roma seeking asylum abroad. Moreover, nationalist and neo-Nazi groups in Poland glorified the attacks and expressed anger with what they perceived as "Jewish support for the filthy Gypsies." The Polish National Front, for instance, displayed a poster entitled "Poles Wake Up!" in several Polish towns during the 1990s, with derogatory references to Roma:

> ... as usual our humanitarian and tolerant government does absolutely nothing to solve the [Gypsy] problem. In Romania it is similar, but there people themselves took affairs into their own hands. In our country, only the act in

Mlawa [demolition of a few Gypsy burrows — *sic*] caused uncalled for anger in Jewish-liberal circles... Because the government does not deal with the Gypsies, the nation itself has to take affairs into its own hands. Enough of those poor bastards... Let them pack their dirty bags and get out of Poland forever. Poland belongs to Poles![48]

A new trend that followed the fall of communism and the subsequent amendment or rewriting of national legislation was the denial or revoking of Roma citizenship. This problem has occurred largely in newly independent states such as the Czech Republic, Bosnia and Herzegovina, Croatia, Macedonia and Slovenia. When the Czechoslovak Federation dissolved on 1 January 1993, the Czech Republic implemented one of the most narrowly crafted citizenship laws of any of the 21 newly independent states. Thousands of Roma who had been long-term or life-long residents of the Czech lands—former Czechoslovak citizens—were left stateless and told to go to Slovakia.

What preceded adoption of the Law on Citizenship in the Czech Republic well illustrates the perversities of Czech policy toward Roma at that time. On 22 July 1992 the daily *Mladá Fronta Dnes* published part of the government's "'catastrophic (black) scenario' concerning information on economic relations between the Czech Republic and the Slovak Republic in the event that extraordinary measures will have to be adopted in connection with the possible break up of the Czechoslovak Federal Republic."[49] Part of the scenario, which deals with social affairs, contains clear references to "citizens of Romani nationality." The government was preparing to apply the regulation concerning Czech citizenship as a tool for the transfer of Roma from the Czech Republic to Slovakia, citing their ethnicity as the selection criteria. The document reads: "This process [establishment of Czech citizenship after division of the federation] should be used... to move citizens of Romani nationality to Slovakia."[50]

In addition, many local government officials grasped the opportunity to eject Romani inhabitants from municipal flats, and came up with proposals on how to restrict the selection process for municipal flats to Czech citizens. These included the necessity of a clean criminal record, limiting child-support benefits and extending the eviction rights of municipal governments. In December 1992, in an attempt to "solve in a professional way the problem of some groups of inhabitants who are unable to behave," the prosecutor-general of the Czech Republic submitted to the Czech Parliament a draft Law on Extraordinary Measures. The bill gave the local police the right to 'monitor' who was staying in an apartment at any time of the day, except between midnight and 6 am. It stated that it "would be applied only in those municipalities defined as threatened by migration."[51]

While the press was busy reporting on the prosecutor-general's legislative proposal,[52] little attention was paid to the abovementioned Czech Citizenship Law, passed on 29 December 1992, with 155 votes for and 13 against. In 1999, the law was finally amended. Implementation of the new law, however, has been incomplete and some Roma in the Czech Republic have not yet benefited (see below).[53]

De facto segregated education is another problem dating from the communist legacy. There are two variants of this problem: segregation that results from channeling Roma into special schools for the mentally handicapped, regardless of the lack of any real defect; and segregation which results from separate housing locations for the majority and the minority. Similarly, discrimination is practiced in public places, such as restaurants and swimming pools, as well as in the workplace.[54]

No general Roma policy was formulated in Poland until 2000. However, the post-1989 Polish Ministry of Education's support for segregation of Romani children in 'Gypsy classes,' aimed at addressing the poor schooling results of Romani children in Małopolska province, was later adopted as state policy. Two experimental 'Gypsy classes' were followed by the establishment of others, after gaining the pedagogical and financial support of the Ministry of Education in Mielec, Tarnów, Czarny Dunajec, Nowy Sącz and a few other places.[55] The 'Gypsy classes' have not only instituted segregation, but have a racially prejudiced and less ambitious curriculum, which purports primarily to teach Romani children elementary manners such as how to greet people and thank them. Although the original goal of this separation was to serve as 'catch up' classes, no child taught under this curriculum has ever returned to the normal schooling system.[56]

The concept of 'Roma rights,' at first rejected by all CEE governments, began to infiltrate domestic policy on Roma only after significant efforts by transnational organizations, human rights activists, governments, donors and, later, by a mushrooming number of NGOs. In addition, in some countries such as Romania, Romani activists chose not to work with political parties, preferring to focus on cooperation with human rights organizations.[57] In Romania this was largely due to political exploitation of the Romani vote and to the indifferent reaction on the part of the mainstream political parties to the pogroms which spread throughout Romania immediately after the fall of Ceauşescu.[58]

Until 1997, all CEE governments were hostile toward the concept of Roma rights, even hiding the NGOs' human rights reports under the table at international conferences (Slovakia 1999) and putting the names of human rights activists working toward improving the situation of Roma on a 'blacklist' of people damaging the reputation of the state (Hungary 1998–2002, and to some extent the Czech Republic 1994–2002).[59] Toward the turn of the century and especially the approach of accession to the EU, some states such as Hungary adopted the language of 'Roma rights' and began to proceed with implementation of specific Roma policies. These advances were made because of the political requirements of the Copenhagen criteria[60] placed on EU accession countries by the European Commission and a wider international consensus on the need to address the grave socio-economic and human rights inequalities of Romani communities.[61]

In respect to Roma, we have witnessed a shift from governments defining the issue as 'a Gypsy problem' in the early 1990s and making an analogy with crime prevention and increasing internal security (police power, supremacy of municipalities) to 'issues of the Roma community' with implications for human rights policy and increasing considerations of diversity in state educational and employment policies. This has not been mere lip service on the part of governments but a real alteration in their understanding of who Roma are and what policies need to be developed. On a broader level, we have witnessed a change in the concept of security.[62]

ADDING LEGITIMACY:
TRANSNATIONAL AGITATION FOR ROMA RIGHTS

Consensus on what constitutes suitable Roma policy has been crystallizing internationally around the linkage between Roma and human rights politics. Consequently, policy elites in national governments and international institutions, as well as NGO activists, have increasingly recognized that efforts to promote membership in NATO and the EU are contingent on assuring some degree of human (Roma) rights protection. However, to conclude that a state becomes human rights conscious because it is worried about its reputation (e.g., membership in alliances, multilateral or bilateral relations) does not reflect the complexity of the situation.

States such as the Czech Republic, Slovakia and Poland denied violation of human rights principles, proclaiming their commitment to international treaties. In response to calls by the international community to deal with infringement of Roma rights, these states have tended to claim that no article of international law was breeched and that advocacy groups invented these 'violations' or fundamentally misunderstood the situation of Roma. Such was the case of the 1993 Czech Citizenship Law, which made many Roma living in Czech lands for generations stateless; Slovakia's firm refusal in the mid-1990s to accept international criticism of increasing police and skinhead violence against Roma; and forced sterilization of Romani women.

Similarly, in the many instances of discrimination against Roma, these states have resisted the arguments of human rights advocates who pointed out the precedence of international law over domestic legal provisions. They have argued that their own legal system has a different definition of discrimination from that presented by their critics. In addition, they reject examples from European Court of Human Rights (ECHR) case law on discrimination, although their domestic legislation does not, in most cases, provide remedies to plaintiffs.

The power of human rights discourse has proved especially important in the process of norms change. Usage of human rights language by treaty-based bodies at the level of the UN and the CoE ultimately led to a shift in state thinking about Romani issues. There is no doubt that human rights advocates played a major role in this development. By generating and crafting language about Romani issues in their submissions to treaty-established bodies and human rights reports, they conceptualized the issue in a way that caused states to slowly move the focus of their approach to Roma away from social policy and 'crime prevention' toward a more human rights oriented policy. The 'new' human rights focus included three aspects: non-discrimination, minority rights and a developmental approach.[63]

The dramatic shift in norms that took place from 1998 on ultimately led to redefinition of the problem and the object of policy. This transformation opened up possibilities for new voices by altering contexts and making new types of action possible, such as Roma rights campaigns, which seemed to emerge virtually out of nowhere. In the absence of any norms about Roma and/or discrimination, Roma claims concerning discrimination and racially motivated violence could not be heard. Once norms were developed stating that Roma had a right not to be harassed, the Romani claim could be regarded as legitimate. With norms about equality in place, marginalized actors or their advocates could harness the rhetoric of equality to make their case for different treatment and to call into question the 'naturalness' of dominant, racist and mostly unwritten norms.

In order to become human rights policy, public policy had first to break away from the pre-1990 line, when the dominant means had been assimilation of Roma, either by coercive administrative measures or by milder methods such as 'assimilation plus social integration'; and second, to firmly reject the discriminatory nature of policies immediately after the end of communism (such as the Czech Citizenship Law and segregated education), and the failure to adequately address the growing level of racially motivated violence.

Before norms could be used instrumentally in Roma rights politics, possibilities for their use had to be created by:

1. Adding actors: It is essentially governments that define agendas and actions of human rights research, monitoring, reporting and even advocacy, by having/or not having a policy.
2. Adding meaning: Understanding rapid policy development requires seeing the political importance of meanings.

Rejection of human rights politics in relation to Roma by their home countries led to development of human rights advocacy. Advocates, following the rules of the international system and reporting within the framework of treaty-based processes, have contributed to the development of new meaning(s) concerning Roma. Two leading factors caused a shift in meaning during the 1990s. First, Roma have been increasingly seen as a national minority. Some states have approached this new classification hesitantly, since they have never viewed and do not wish to view Roma as a national minority, arguing that because they lack distinctive characteristics Roma do not qualify as such. Thus, in the debates on 'the special situation of Roma' and 'their unique status,' governments tended to regard Roma as a 'social stratum' and/or an 'ethnic group.' The discussion in academic scholarship has focused on whether policies toward Roma should be drafted in reference to national/ethnic minorities or to immigrants.[64]

Second, the human rights concept, and especially the non-discrimination principle, has been increasingly applied in analyses and consequently in policy proposals on Roma. Shifts in terminology usage were first made by advocacy organizations lobbying for Roma rights and subsequently (ten years later) by CEE governments.

MECHANISMS OF NORMS CHANGE

Two types of mechanisms in policy change have been utilized: human rights treaty-based processes under the UN and European Convention system and political processes under the OSCE, CoE and EU.

The CoE's 1953 European Convention is perhaps the most highly regarded international instrument in the field of human rights. It does not protect minority rights per se, but establishes a broad framework of fundamental rights of individuals. Article 14 of the Convention further provides that:

> The enjoyment of the rights and freedoms set forth in this Convention shall be secure without discrimination on any grounds such as sex, race, color, language, religion, political or other opinion, national or social origin, association with a national minority, property, birth or other status.

In many ways the European Convention is similar to the 1966 UN International Covenant on Civil and Political Rights (ICCPR). Unlike the latter, however, the European Convention established a court whose judges are drawn from the member states. The court has the authority to receive petitions from any person, NGO or group of individuals claiming to be the victim of a violation by one of the High Contracting Parties. The court may also hear complaints brought by one state party against another. Significantly, the court is empowered to adjudicate such claims. In the event of violation of the convention, the court may issue a judgment, which may include an order to the violating party to pay damages to the plaintiff.

The European system, to which Roma rights activists familiarly refer as "the beauty of Strasbourg," has some major shortcomings. First, the European Convention is limited by the terms of its own text. Unlike the ICCPR, the European Convention prohibits discrimination only with respect to rights that are specifically included in the Convention itself. In other words, state parties to the European Convention may discriminate in regard to rights contained in their national constitutions or laws but not included in the European Convention. In an effort to close this gap, the CoE adopted Protocol 12 on 4 November 2000. This amendment to the Convention, which bears similarities to the equal protection clause of the 14th Amendment or Article 26 of the ICCPR, provides that any right set forth by national law shall be secured without discrimination. It also prohibits discrimination by public authorities. Protocol 12 will come into force after ten countries have ratified it. As of late 2004, 27 of the CoE's 43 member states had signed Protocol 12, but none had ratified it yet.

In addition, the European Convention is limited by the types of remedies it may apply. Although the court can award damages, including significant monetary compensation, it does not have the power to strike down laws that violate the Convention and it cannot force or compel governments to change practices that systematically violate it. For example, in an ongoing court case that began in early 1999, Romani plaintiffs from Ostrava, the Czech Republic, alleged that the education system in the Czech Republic practiced de facto segregation on racial grounds. If the court finds in favor of the plaintiffs, it can award them damages, but has no power to order the overall desegregation of Czech schools. While some states have been willing to change laws or practices that could otherwise form the basis for repeated suits, others (notably Turkey) have been more reluctant to do so.

Several other treaties are relevant to the protection of minorities: the ICCPR, mentioned above; the Convention against Torture and Other Cruel, Inhuman or Degrading Treatment or Punishment; the European Convention for the Prevention of Torture and Inhuman or Degrading Treatment or Punishment; and the International Convention on the Elimination of All Forms of Racial Discrimination. The two torture treaties are relevant in that minorities tend, disproportionately, to be victims of police brutality.

These four treaties function in similar ways. First, they establish a committee of experts. Second, they establish an obligation for state parties to the treaty to report, at specified time intervals, to the committee on their compliance with it. In their review of state reports, as well as in their consideration of specific cases or situations, these bodies provide authoritative interpretations of treaty law. However, they neither adjudicate cases nor have the power to censure states.

Generally speaking, the UN system does not play a very significant role in Europe, given that the enforcement machinery of the European Convention is much more effective than that established under the UN. Nevertheless, in light of the increase in human rights problems that Roma and other racial minorities have faced in Europe over the past decade, particularly in central and southern Europe, the UN Committee against Torture and the Committee on the Elimination of Racial Discrimination are viewed by some NGOs as significant forums for bringing pressure to bear on key countries. The 2001 UN World Conference against Racism, Racial Discrimination, Xenophobia and Related Intolerance in Durban (and the many preparatory events associated with it) served as a vehicle for several European non-governmental organizations to promote the Roma issue.

Minority treaties also exist—namely, the Framework Convention on the Protection of National Minorities and the European Charter for Regional and Minority Languages. Neither treaty, however, specifies remedies in the event of violation.

The Contact Point for Roma and Sinti Issues, established in 1994 and housed within the OSCE Office for Democratic Institutions and Human

Rights, and the High Commissioner for National Minorities, with a seat in The Hague established in 1992, greatly influence policy making toward Roma. The CoE embraces the European Commission against Racism and Intolerance (ECRI) and a number of policy discussion committees (such as family and social matters).

The OSCE and the CoE serve as political mechanisms for the drafting of resolutions and declarations, the language being carefully selected and used to achieve particular objectives. Political processes have had the effect of shaping cognitive maps of Romani issues, and we can observe that while in the early 1990s the CoE concentrated more on fulfillment of minority rights, especially aspects such as language and culture, in the second half of the 1990s, the focus shifted toward lobbying for anti-discrimination provisions.

ECRI, a political body for monitoring expressions of intolerance, racism, and discrimination in the member states, was established by a decision of the CoE on 9 October 1993. ECRI is mandated to consider all necessary measures to combat violence, discrimination and prejudice faced by persons or groups, on the grounds of race, color, language, religion, nationality and national or ethnic origin. ECRI issues country-by-country reports pertaining to these concerns. Prior to publication, the content is discussed confidentially with the relevant state, which has the right to block public release of the report. ECRI also draws up general policy recommendations addressed to the governments of all member states. In 1998, ECRI issued General Policy Recommendation No. 3: Combating Racism and Intolerance against Roma/Gypsies, noting that Roma/Gypsies suffer throughout Europe from persistent prejudice, are victims of a racism that is deeply-rooted in society and that these prejudices lead to discrimination against them in many fields of social and economic life, and are a major factor in their social exclusion.[65]

The process of enlargement of the EU, by conditioning membership on the fulfillment of the Copenhagen criteria, requiring stability in regard to minority and human rights, rule of law and institutions guaranteeing democracy, had a carrot and stick effect on accession states in improving Roma policy.

ROMA POLICY CHANGE IN THE CZECH REPUBLIC, SLOVAKIA AND POLAND

In CEE human rights evolved from being a utopia in the early 1990s to ideology at the end of the decade.[66] Utopia and ideology are two types of cognitive bias: utopia is a vision that does not yet correspond to social reality, while ideology never corresponds to it completely. While utopia is realizable, in principle, as a transformation project, ideology cannot be 'fulfilled,' in principle. Ideologies may be former utopias that have 'come to power,' and therefore are no longer tools of radical social change.[67] The move from utopia to ideology in Roma policy took place in two ways: a) mainstreaming of human rights—inclusion of human rights in various policies and projects, and b) mainstreaming of issues by articulating them in human rights terms.[68] We have seen both, namely, Roma policy development and mainstreaming of Romani issues under the influence of human rights. Yet, as can be seen from analyzing the policy documents, the impact of the human rights discourse has not been fully integrated into the relevant states.

The Czech government adopted two framework policy documents: 'The Report on the Situation of the Romani Community in the Czech Republic and Government Measures Assisting Its Integration into Society' (hereafter Report), in 1997, and 'The Concept of Government Policy toward Members of the Romani Community, Supporting Their Integration into Society' (hereafter Concept), in 2001.[69] While the Report has a socio-cultural perspective, the Concept specifies three approaches to Roma affairs: human rights, nationality, and the wider socio-cultural dimension. The practice of Roma policy implementation in the Czech Republic shows that the socio-cultural approach prevails. Needless to say, all activities within this approach, coordinated by the Council for Romani Community Affairs, have contributed to the overall improvement of the socio-cultural situation of Roma in the Czech Republic; however, they remain insufficient for the complete integration of Roma.

Examining the structure of Roma policy drafting, it is noteworthy that it is administered entirely by an advisory body to the government, with a limited mandate. While a member of government chairs the council, this symbolic measure has little bearing on the fact that systemic, long-term integration of Roma will probably be carried out with the objective of improving their socio-economic situation. Although two more bodies, the Council for Nationalities and the Council for Human Rights, deal with the rights discourse of Roma policy in the Czech Republic, they remain marginalized in the overall policy approach toward Roma in that country.

In the Czech Republic, additional forms of representation of Roma have been developed as a result of the Act on Rights of Members of National Minorities, reinforced by its amendment (Act No. 273/2001), which guarantees members of national minorities the right to participate in cultural, social and economic life, especially with regard to matters concerning national minorities at the communal, regional and national levels (No. 6, Art. 1). This right is to be realized through the establishment of the Council for National Minorities and Committees for National Minorities at the regional and communal/municipal levels (No. 6, Art. 2).[70]

The right to be represented in committees at the local and regional levels, however, applies only to those minorities who meet the 10 percent threshold in a given community, 5 percent threshold in a region and 5 percent threshold in statutory towns and the capital Prague.[71] The requirement that the number of national minorities in a given administrative unit be established according to the "last census result" could be particularly problematic for Roma. In the Czech Republic, 0.3 percent of the population declared Romani as their ethnic identity in 1991, compared to 0.1 percent in 2001. Estimates, however, range between 150,000 and 300,000 Roma in the Czech Republic (1.5–2.7 percent of the total population). In some areas with a high concentration of Roma, particularly, in Prague, as well as in the Moravian-Silesian, South Moravian, Ústí nad Labem and Liberec regions, the condition of representation based on census data might lead to disproportional results.[72]

In addition, the minority members of the Committees for National Minorities (if any) are nominated by minority associations and need not be elected representatives of the minority in question, while the elected local and regional representatives (in the case of Roma) are most likely to be non-Romani.[73] Nevertheless, Roma participate in some Committees for National Minorities at both the regional and city levels.

These committees deal mainly with taking decisions on funding activities of national minorities and, in the case of Roma, on coordination of programs to increase social integration of Roma.[74] However, as noted by a Roma representative on the Council for National Minorities, "the Act on the Rights of National Minorities is formal and insufficient because it does not enable access of representatives of national minorities to elected local and regional authorities."[75]

The Slovak government adopted three framework documents of policy toward Roma. In 1991, Resolution No. 153/1991, entitled 'Principles of Government Policy toward Roma,' specified areas for improving the situation of Roma. A subsequent policy paper drafted by the Ministry of Labor, Social Affairs and Family, issued in April 1996, and entitled 'Resolution of the Slovak Government Proposing Activities and Measures to Solve the Problems of Citizens in Need of Special Care' discarded the approach of the 1991 resolution and reframed policy toward Roma as an issue of social policy.[76] In 1999, the Slovak government approved a redrafted policy toward Roma, 'Strategy I of the Government of the Slovak Republic for Solving Problems of the Roma

National Minority and a Set of Measures for Its Implementation: Stage I—Outlining Areas of Action'. Updates on priorities of the Slovak government on issues of Roma community, especially action plans of the Commission for Romani Community Affairs and Council for National Minorities and Ethnic Groups, do not develop the anti-discrimination and minority rights discourse further. For example, the documents do not refer to the issue of political representation.

The Polish government, which was more or less outside the mainstream discussion of an appropriate transnational Romani policy, was eventually coerced into forming one in 2001. The UK and Sweden, alarmed by the growing number of Polish Romani asylum seekers, urged the Polish government to adopt the Małopolska program (2001–2003), an experimental project aimed at improving the life of Roma in the spheres of housing, schooling, justice, police relations, health and culture. The program itself remains under-implemented due to insufficient budget allocation by the national and local governments, and has been geographically restricted to the Małopolska province in the south of Poland, an area inhabited mostly by the Carpathian (Bergitka) Roma.[77] Implementation of the Małopolska program was completed in 2003. In contrast to the Czech Republic and Slovakia, Poland is not a participant country in the 'Decade of Roma Inclusion'. Therefore, international attention is not likely to be focused on the situation of Roma in Poland.

CONCLUSION

Roma policy in the 1990s stemmed from the security concerns of states, which addressed the situation of Roma using a strategy of human rights politics. Advocacy groups of Roma rights, taking advantage of this approach employed by powers such as Germany, the US and the UK, have succeeded in inserting a human rights objective into the human rights policy of each CEE state, using mainly transnational treaty-based and political processes. While in the case of Slovakia and the Czech Republic, the human rights objective has been successfully incorporated into national Roma policies, in that of Poland it has stagnated, and older lines toward Roma, such as 'boosting domestic security,' have prevailed. This disparity has been due to uneven international attention to the Roma in the various CEE countries. While Poland came under international scrutiny for its treatment of Roma only at the end of the 1990s, very early in the decade the Czech Republic, and especially Slovakia, had become the focus of states such as the US, Germany, the UK and France, which considered the

Romani issue vital to the successful transition of the region from communism; or of states which viewed Romani migration as a threat to their internal security (e.g., Germany, France, and later during the 1990s, the UK).[78] Thus, advocates of Roma rights facilitated a change in norms, which led to transformation in the discourse on Roma, and consequently shifts in government understanding of what constitutes suitable Roma policy.

While some domestic policies toward Roma derive from the influence of human rights politics and consequently of Roma rights advocacy, the question that troubles many advocates today is to what extent the campaigns for Roma rights will remain sustainable after accession to the EU. Here the hope lies in the 2000/43 EU Race Equality Directive and Lisbon Process: political guidelines laid down by the European Council in the area of "combating poverty and social exclusion."

For EU candidates and member states, the EU Race Equality Directive, adopted by the EC in 2000, should become a powerful means to address issues of exclusion and discrimination. Similarly, the European Council has made the promotion of social cohesion an essential element in the global strategy of the Union, whose "strategic objective for the next decade [is] becoming the most competitive and dynamic knowledge-based economy in the world, capable of sustainable economic growth with more and better jobs and greater social cohesion."[79]

NOTES

1. Eleanor Roosevelt, "Where After All, Do Universal Human Rights Begin?" quoted in Sondra Myers, *The Democracy Reader* (New York, 2002), p. 25.
2. 'International society' is a term used to describe actors in international politics. The English School of International Relations was the first forum to attribute importance to the interaction of the society of states and world society. Hedley Bull defines international society as follows: "A *society of states* (or international society) exists when a group of states, conscious of certain common interests and common values, form a society in the sense that they conceive themselves to be bound by a common set of rules in their relations with one another, and share in the working of common institutions." *The Anarchical Society: A Study of Order in World Politics* (New York, 1977), p. 13.
3. Eva Sobotka, "Mobilising International Norms: Issue-Actors, Roma and the State," unpublished Ph.D. thesis, Lancaster University, 2004, p. 3.
4. www.osi.hu
5. P. Vermeersch, "European Integration and the International Romani Movement," in E. Sobotka (ed.), *International Romani Movement after 1945* (forth-

coming, 2005). For more, see *2005-2015: The Decade of Roma Inclusion* (World Bank), at: http://lnweb18.worldbank.org/ECA/ECSHD.nsf/$$vwbyid/5ACB 3FB63019D944C1256D6A00438015?Opendocument&Start=1&Count=5.

6. The CFR-CDF was set up by the European Commission upon request of the European Parliament in September 2002. Consisting of one expert per EU member state, its aim is to assess the safeguarding of fundamental rights by EU member states. For more on the CFR-CDF, see: http://europa.eu.int/comm/justice_home/cfr_cdf/index_en.htm

7. CFR-CDF, *Report on the Situation of Fundamental Rights in the European Union in 2003* (Jan. 2004), http://europa.eu.int/comm/justice_home/cfr_cdf/doc/report_eu_ 2003_en.pdf.

8. Richard Rorty, *Truth and Moral Progress: Philosophical Papers* (Cambridge University Press, 1998), p. 11.

9. Jack Donnelly, "Human Rights, Globalizing Flows and State Power," in Alison Brysk (ed.), *Globalization and Human Rights* (University of California Press, 2002), pp. 226-41.

10. Shlomo Avineri, "The Paradox of Religion and the Universality of Human Rights," unpublished conference presentation, 10th Annual Conference on "The Individual vs. the State, Universalism in Law: Human Rights and the Rule of Law" (Budapest, 2002).

11. Michael Ignatieff, *Human Rights as Politics and Idolatry* (Princeton University Press, 2001), p. 34

12. Ibid.

13. The name Roma (pl.) (Rom, sing., Romani, adj.) is neutral and politically correct. It is an endonym, since it stems from the Romani language *Romanes* and means 'human being' or 'man'. Designations such as Gypsy, in German *Zigeuner*, in Czech *cikan*, in Slovak *cigan*, in Hungarian *cigany*, in Polish *cigan*, in Romanian *tsigan*, have pejorative connotations and have been used as synonyms for lying *cikánit/cigánit/ciganit* The name Rom/Roma was also chosen by a Romani NGO, the International Romani Union, as a self-designator at the First World Romani Congress in London in 1971. In recent years, linguist Victor Friedman recommends usage of Rom, Roms, Romani. *Linguistic Emblems and Emblematic Languages* (Columbus, Ohio, 1999), pp. 319-20. However, the combination Rom, Roma, Romani has been widely used and recognized as acceptable by Roma. We can also find designation 'the Rom' used in plural. Yaron Matras, *Romani: A Linguistic Introduction.* Cambridge University Press, 2002.

14. Five congresses of the International Romani Union (IRU), an NGO uniting mostly Lovara Roma, have taken place so far: The first world Romani congress took place in London, 8-12 April 1971; the second in Geneva, 8-11 April 1978; the third, in Göttingen, 16-20 May 1981; the fourth in Serok, 4-13 April 1990; and the fifth in Prague, 24-28 July 2001. Acton argues that the style of meetings of the IRU is modeled on organizations from other nationalist traditions, such as Zionism and third world nationalism. Thomas Acton, *Gypsy Politics and Social Change* (London, 1974), pp. 233-4. At the domestic level Roma either organized in cultural organizations (Poland, Czechoslovakia) or were

active in the anti-communist dissent movement (Czechoslovakia), preparing reports about the situation of Roma and Romani women in respect to categories of international law: health, education, housing, employment, etc.

15.   In 1961 European Roma asked the UN to sponsor a separate Romani state, to be called Romanestan, at the UNESCO conference, and several Romani leaders visited UNESCO headquarters in Paris in November to select a possible site (*New York Times*, 14 Oct. 1961). In 1971, in the town of Orpington, Kent near London, the first World Romani Congress adopted the Romani anthem and the national flag, consisting of two horizontal bars, the lower green, the upper blue, with the red, sixteen-spoked *chakra*-wheel and dropped the idea of territorial requests in favor of non-territorial recognition. They further proposed objectives that the Romani elite continue to promote today, including standardization of the Romani language and a Romani encyclopedia.

16.   While Roma focused their lobbying efforts also on the EU, and the European Commission in particular, the role of the EU in shaping transnational Romani agenda began to develop only toward the end of the 1990s. This essay does not deal with interaction between Romani agitators and the EU. However, toward the May 2004 conclusion of EU accession processes, the EU is expected to take a greater role in Roma politics.

17.   European Roma Rights Center (ERRC), a public law interest organization, advocating the human rights of Roma was established in Budapest in 1996. The Roma Participation Program of the Open Society Institute, also with a seat in Budapest, was established a year later. While the task of the ERRC is to advocate Roma rights by producing first-hand research about the situation of Roma and submissions to treaty-based bodies, the role of the RPP is to enhance the political participation of Roma in the CEE region. The ERRC is modeled on the American Civil Liberties Union (ACLU), while the inspiration for RPP was the Afro-American movement (1954–66). For more, see www.errc.org.

18.   I use the distinction between human rights politics and policy presented by Dimitrina Petrova in her unpublished paper, "Social and Economic Dimension of Universal Rights" at the 10th annual conference, "The Individual vs. the State, Universalism in Law: Human Rights and the Rule of Law," Budapest, June 2002.

19.   Ibid.

20.   Thomas R. Dye, *Understanding Public Policy* (Englewood Cliffs, 1972), p. 2.

21.   Petrova, "Social and Economic Dimension of Universal Rights," author's notes; Stanley Cohen, *Denial and Acknowledgement* (Jerusalem, 1995), pp. I–V, 1–17. Cohen distinguishes between several different human rights discourses, each with its distinct validity claims and norms of professionalism—diplomatic, legal, social, scientific, etc.

22.   Erika Schlager, "A Hard Look at Compliance with 'Soft' Law: The Case of the OSCE," in Dinah Shelton (ed.), *Commitment and Compliance: The Role of Non-Binding Norms in the International Legal System* (Oxford University Press, 2000), pp. 346–71.

23.   Sobotka, "Mobilising International Norms," p. 380.

24.   Ibid.

25. Ibid.
26. As established in the Vienna Concluding Document of 1989, the Vienna mechanism allows the participating state, through a set of procedures, to raise questions relating to the human dimension in another OSCE participating state. The Moscow mechanism, agreed to at the last meeting of CSCE in 1991, builds on this and provides for the additional possibility to establish ad hoc missions of independent experts to assist in the resolution of a specific human dimension problem. (AFP, 25 Jun. 1990).
27. OSCE Human Dimension Commitments, *A Reference Guide, OSCE/ODIHR*, 2001, p. 104
28. Ibid.
29. Ibid.
30. Ibid.
31. Ibid., p. 283
32. Eva Sobotka, "Romani Migration in the 1990s: Perspectives on Dynamic, Interpretation and Policy," *Romani Studies* 2 (2003), pp. 80–121.
33. Romani agitators admit that they have exploited US concern over the return of communism in Romania to their benefit, by utilizing the connection the US administration has made between human rights politics and foreign policy since the Carter administration. Nicolae Gheorghe, a former Romani agitator, has pointed out the connection between miners strikes in Romania in the early 1990s, participation of Roma in the miners strikes, proportion of Roma in Romania and the fact that Roma as an ethnic group reside in all post-communist European countries (personal communication, 2003).
34. *The European*, 27-29 July 1990; *Stuttgarter Zeitung*, 18 Aug. 1990; *DPA*, 9 Sept. 1992; Reuters 31 Oct. 1992; Gilad Margalit, *Antigypsyism in the Political Culture of the Federal Republic of Germany: A Parallel with Antisemitism* (SICSA: The Vidal Sassoon International Center for the Study of Antisemitism, 1996), p. 8: http://sicsa.huji.ac.il/9gilad.htm
35. Margalit, *Antigypsyism in the Political Culture of the Federal Republic of Germany*, pp. 8-9; Sobotka, "Romani Migration in the 1990s," Sobotka, "Mobilising International Norms," p. 32.
36. Romani 'agitators,' both Roma and non-Roma, agitate for human rights related issues on behalf of the Roma—civil and political rights, social and economic equality or effective bans on discrimination. The usage of the term 'agitator' is preferred to the term 'activist,' because it better reflects the fact that most of those involved are employed in this occupation on a regular basis. The term 'activist' is understood to be a person who conducts human rights work voluntarily. The word 'agitating' also better reflects the nature of the work, usually done on behalf of Roma, rather than activating Romani masses for further action.
37. In recent years, non-binding instruments have sometimes provided the necessary statement of legal obligation (*opinion juris*) to provide evidence of emergent custom and have assisted in establishing the content of the norm. The use of soft law has been also closely associated with the growth of international institutions. Resolutions, declarations, codes of conduct and guidelines articulated by global international or regional organizations have been termed 'non-legal

soft law'. In general, the international legal system turned to soft law as a means of including all relevant actors, trying out solutions that are still experimental, regulating in greater detail what hard law would allow, and regulating quickly and more flexibly. Soft law thus meets many of the needs of global governance. Not one, but two hard law alternatives existed in parallel to the CSCE/OSCE and the CoE at the time of the Cold War. the UN, which included virtually all the participating states but failed to win them over as parties to the human rights mechanism until the end of the Cold War, and the European Convention on Human Rights and Fundamental Freedoms (ECHR, were open), in principle, to membership of European parliamentary democracies.

38. Sobotka, Mobilising International Norms, p. 32.
39. While in the 2002 Hungarian national election, four Romani candidates, Flórian Farkas, József Varga, Mihály Lukács and Lászlo Teleki were elected to the Parliament, at present, there are no Romani candidates in the Czech, Polish or Slovak representative bodies. Some Romani councilors were elected in local elections in the Czech Republic and Slovakia. Poland remains without any elected Roma at local or national level. For more see Eva Sobotka, *Romani Mobilization and Political Representation at the National and Transnational Levels* (Flensburg, 2004).

Table 1
Romani MPs in Czechoslovakia (1990–92)

JuDr. Vincent Danihel	Federal Assembly, Chamber of People
PaedDr. Gejza Adam	Federal Assembly, Chamber of People
Karol Seman	Federal Assembly, Chamber of Nations
Ing. Karel Holomek	Czech National Council
Dezider Balog	Czech National Council
Ondřej Giňa	Czech National Council
Zdeněk Guži	Czech National Council
Milan Tatár	Czech National Council
Ladislav Body	Czech National Council
Anna Koptová	Slovak National Council
Vladimír Zeman	Czech National Council

40. Sobotka, *Mobilizing International Norms,* p. 55.
41. Isabel Fonseca, "Bury Me Standing," in Lidia Ostałowska, *Cygan to Cygan* (Warsaw, 2000), p. 20.
42. Isaiah Berlin, "Two Concepts of Nationalism: An Interview with Isaiah Berlin," *The New York Review of Books,* 21 Nov. 1991.
43. Address by Václav Havel, President of the Czech Republic at the Conference "Europe's New Democracies: Leadership and Responsibility," Bratislava, 11 May 2001.
44. Paul Hockenos. *Free to Hate: The Rise of the Right in Post-Communist Eastern Europe* (London/New York, 1993), p. 57.

45. "World Report—Pulse Europe—Special Report," *Los Angeles Times*, 17 Sept. 1991.
46. Today, Roma are dispersed throughout all European countries with the exception of Iceland, Malta, Luxemburg and the Vatican. Taken together, there may be 8-10 million Roma in Europe, with large concentrations in central, eastern, and southern Europe.
47. Arne Mann, *Rómsky dejepis: Doplnkový učebný text pre vyučovanie dejepisu* (Bratislava, 2000), p. 19.
48. Ostałowska, *Cygan to Cygan*, p. 186; *Limits of Solidarity: Roma in Poland since 1989* (Budapest: European Roma Rights Center, 2001), p. 36; Sobotka, "Mobilising International Norms," p. 306.
49. In the early 1990s in the former Czechoslovakia, many policy issues, including human rights, were viewed in purely economic parameters. Therefore, ethnic conflict was primarily defined in terms of a fair division of assets. Viewing Romani issues through an economic prism was the narrowest way to define the problem.
50. *Mladá Fronta Dnes*, 22 July 1992.
51. Transcript of the 19th Session of the Czech Parliament, 29 Dec. 1992, p. 24.
52. "What to Do about the Romany Migration," *Mladá Fronta Dnes*, 15 Dec. 1992; Ivana Vajnerova and John Zdenek, "Pithart Government Counted on Influx of Romanies," *Mladá Fronta Dnes*, 23 July 1992; "Using the Law against Undesirable Migration," *Mladá Fronta Dnes*, 15 Dec. 1992; *Mladá Fronta Dnes*, 31 Dec., 1992; Jiří Pehe, "Law on Romanies Caused Uproar in the Czech Republic," *RFE/ RL Research Report* 7 (12 Feb. 1993).
53. The Czech Law on citizenship saw several amendments during the 1990s. However, the 1993 Czech citizenship law has had an impact on many Romani lives. Those stripped of Czech citizenship were unable to collect social security and health benefits.
54. For more on discrimination and human rights violation of Roma, see www.errc.org.
55. *The Limits of Solidarity: Roma in Poland Since 1989* (Budapest: European Roma Rights Center, 2002).
56. Ibid.
57. Josef Kucio, "Interview with Nicolae Gheorghe," *Uncaptive Minds. Fight against Poverty and Social Exclusion—Definition of Appropriate Objectives* (Brussels, 30 Nov., 2000), pp. 13-18.
58. Ibid.
59. Sobotka, "Mobilising International Norms," p. 328.
60. Copenhagen criteria are political criteria for membership in the European Union, defined by the European Council in Copenhagen in 1993: "Membership requires that the candidate country has achieved stability of institutions guaranteeing democracy, the rule of law, human rights and respect for and protection of minorities."
61. At the OSI and World Bank conference, "Roma in an Expanding Europe," Budapest, June 2003, a number of states showed, not only understanding of the concept of Roma rights, but adopted the language of Roma rights.

62.   Havel, "Europe's New Democracies."
63.   Developmental approach refers to the World Bank strategy of advancing the socio-economic situation of threatened, impoverished communities, motivating states to fight poverty.
64.   Pavel Barša, "Ethnocultural Justice in Eastern European States and the Case of the Czech Roma," in Will Kymlicka and Magda Opalski (eds.), *Can Liberal Pluralism Be Exported?* (New York, 2001), pp. 243-58.
65.   ECRI General Policy Recommendation No. 3: Combating Racism and Intolerance against Roma/Gypsies.
66.   Petrova, "Social and Economic Dimension of Universal Rights."
67.   Ibid.
68.   Ibid.
69.   "Report on the Situation of the Romani Community in the Czech Republic and Government Measures Assisting Its Integration into Society," 686/1997; "Concept of Government Policy toward Members of the Romani Community, Supporting Their Integration into Society," 599/2000, in 2001.
70.   Act on Rights of Members of National Minorities, No. 273/2001 (Minority Act). To date, there are committees for national minorities in 39 municipalities or municipal districts, in one charter town (Brno), and in four regions. There are also National Minority Boards in Prague and Liberec, most of which did not meet the requirements for national minority committees. See the Second Report Submitted by the Czech Republic Pursuant to Article 25, Para. 1 of the Framework Convention for the Protection of National Minorities, received on 2 July 2004, Para. 5, p. 5 - http://wtd.vlada.cz/files/rvk/rnm/ zprava_mensiny_2002_ eng.pdf; see also Council of the Government of the Czech Republic for National Minorities, "Report on the Situation of National Minorities in the Czech Republic in 2002," pp. 39-60 - http://wtd.vlada.cz/files/rvk/rnm/ zprava_ mensiny_2002_eng.pdf (hereafter, 'Czech Minority Report 2002').
71.   The amendment to the Minority Act reduced these thresholds, which had been defined in earlier legislation, on communities, regions and the capital city, from 15 percent to 10 percent in communities, 10 percent to 5 percent in regions; and from 15 percent to 5 percent in Prague. By means of Act No. 320/2002 Coll. on the amendment and cancellation of some acts because of the abolition of district offices, Act No. 273/2002 Coll. on the rights of the members of national minorities was amended within the legislation of the second phase of the reform of local public administration. Article 6 was amended by paragraphs 7 and 8. Paragraph 7 gave the regional authority a duty to administer and coordinate state policy toward Roma. Paragraph 8 imposes a duty on local authorities to implement state policy on increasing integration of Roma into society and fulfilling tasks leading to implementing the rights of national minorities. For more, see Act 320/2002, Section 64 on Amendment of the Act 273/2001 on the rights of the members of national minorities. In practice, this change is crucial for implementation of state policy toward Roma in the Czech Republic and gives the central government power to demand implementation of Roma policy in regions and communities. According to the Report on the state of rights of national minorities in 2002, "the Minority Act was supplemented by § 13a,

which determines that the competencies of a regional or local authority with extended competencies according to this Act are delegated powers. In this context more than ten towns concluded at the end of 2002 and at the beginning of 2003 public agreements aimed at the assurance of the exercise of delegated powers in the field of rights of the members of national minorities. These agreements should ensure the execution of public administration, i.e. the agenda of regional Roma coordinators and their cooperation with consultants for Roma affairs in communities and towns." For more, see Czech Minority Report 2002, p. 9 - http://wtd.vlada.cz/vrk/vrk.htm.

72. No research has been conducted yet on the effectiveness of the representation of national minorities through Committees for National Minorities in the Czech Republic. The Council for National Minorities, an advisory body of the Czech Government, although expressing criticism of the present system (see Czech Minority Report 2002, p. 40), does not include information on the number of Romani representatives.

73. See Second Report Submitted by the Czech Republic Pursuant to Article 25, Paragraph 1 of the Framework Convention for the Protection of National Minorities, received on 2 July 2004, para. 5, p. 5.

74. See Czech Minority Report 2002, pp. 39-60.

75. Czech Minority Report 2002, § 6, p. 82.

76. Resolution of the Government of the Slovak Republic proposing activities and measures to solve the problems of citizens in need of special care (Uznesenie vlády SR knávrhu úloh a opatrení na rešenie problémov občanov, ktorí potrebuju osobitnů pomoc , na rok 1996) of 30 April 1996, Ministry of Labor, Social Affairs and Family, Government of the Slovak Republic. See also "Conceptual Intentions of the Government of the Slovak Republic for Solution of the Problems of the Romani Population under Current Social and Economic Conditions," Ministry of Labor, Social Affairs and Family, 1997.

77. *Monitoring the EU Accession Process: Minority Protection* (Budapest, 2002) p. 422.

78. Sobotka, "Romani Migration in the 1990s"; Eva Sobotka, *Romani Migration in the 1990s: German and British Context* (Berlin, 2004).

79. Lisbon and Santa Maria da Feira European Councils 2000, for more, see http://europe.eu.int/comm/dgs/employment_social/index_en.htm.

CENTRAL EUROPEAN ROMA POLICY: NATIONAL MINORITY ELITES, NATIONAL STATES AND THE EU

PÁL TAMÁS

INTRODUCTION

There is no clear-cut answer to the question as to whether the self-image or ethnic identity of a national minority determines its readiness for social or national mobilization, or vice versa, whether political mobilization is a prerequisite for the development of identity. It seems, in fact, that identity emerges as a consequence of the experience of some form of common history. In many cases, this can mean the myth of common resistance. Nor can it be decided for sure whether discrimination strengthens or weakens a sense of unity, or the need to demonstrate it. In some cases, in some situations and according to some concepts, discrimination indeed reinforces unity. Many believe that without anti-Semitism, Jewish identity would not exist. Or, if it did exist, it would be quite different. Thus, we do not really know what Romani identity would be like had its bearers not experienced various types of recurring discrimination.

Until recently the overwhelming majority of Roma could not really integrate without a certain degree of assimilation at least at some stage of their life. Thus, like other marginal Central European religious or ethnic groups they were ready to accept their labels of identity, usually developed by the outside world, for the following three reasons:

- rejected and discriminated against by the majority, they had no other option;
- they adhered to an ideology in which some form of community-building effort played a role;
- if they were members of an elite group, they might gain direct benefit from an ideology of identity building and from identity policies generated from above, or from the majority environment.

When differences by country are taken into consideration, three comprehensive phases can be distinguished in Central European Roma policy of the 1990s and in the concomitant Roma movements:

• The era of the struggle for human rights: The early 1990s—the years of regime change, a definition of Roma political rights, and the extension or reinforcement of human rights to each and every citizen of Central European societies, including potential Roma elites – seemed to be an acceptable starting point. It became apparent, however, that prejudice against the Romani population did not disappear with the creation of a constitutional state, and that discrimination in education, employment, health and other areas was so entrenched that merely using human rights tools alone was insufficient. In those years some forms of political alliance still existed, especially in Hungary and the Czech Republic, between the majority parties, which took over the regimes and adopted an activist position on the Roma question, and the Roma civil rights elite. Thus, the first democratic Czechoslovak federal government had almost a dozen Roma members. In the period 1990−94 the founders of SZETA (a Budapest-based anti-poverty, human rights dissident group), which as early as the 1980s had demanded a more balanced Roma policy, were present in the Hungarian parliament, too, primarily in the SZDSZ parliamentary faction. However, the majority alliance soon declined or lost power, and the champions of a basic Roma civil rights program were marginalized. Nearly all Czech and Slovak Roma MPs elected after 1989 to their national assemblies were squeezed out of their respective parliaments in the early 1990s. There was no Hungarian representation in the parliaments in those years.

• Reduction of economic-institutional discrimination. From the mid-1990s the focus shifted to human rights programs, which presented fresh options for the possible treatment and elimination of discrimination. The governmental and civic actors developing those programs were aware that the Roma had been trapped in such an intricate web of disadvantages that they could only be released through the amendment of their constitutional rights or by offering them various forms of national minority organization. Consequently, willy-nilly, they had to re-examine certain social policy packages, whose forerunners Central European administrations had been attempting to adopt—although from different starting points—prior to 1989. Naturally, the element of ethnic policy was more dominant now than it had been in previous socialist regimes. But the fact remained that various social and educational packages were revived. Still, a powerful anti-discriminatory policy especially targeting situations affecting the Roma was lacking.[1]

• The beginnings of self-organization of the ethnic elite: Although the socio-economic decline of the first years of regime changes was halted by the second half of the 1990s, the situation of large masses of the Romani population could only be stabilized close to the social bottom. The Romani masses profited little from the beginnings of upward mobility in certain groups. Privatization, which resumed from the 1990s, admitted onto the social ladder primarily lower middle class Romani groups that cooperated with the majority population. It was inherent in the process that the differences within Romani society were growing at a much faster rate than that observed in the majority population. Consequently, the first attempts at self-organiza-tion of the ethnic elite, the upgrading of debates about Romani identity and, albeit at varying speeds and in different forms in each country, adding political content to the Romani side as well—will be among the international impacts discussed below.

This essay will focus on the concepts of political mobilization and counter-mobilization and their impact on shaping the ethnic identity of the Roma in Central Europe, beginning in the late 1980s/early 1990s.[2] Although elements of human rights programs had not yet been implemented and the majority of Roma in the Czech Republic, Slovakia and Hungary were experiencing frequent economic discrimination, many among the Romani elites were clearly embarking on 'ethnic awakening' and, with varying success, had also begun to develop means of ethnic mobilization. Here, differences between countries became significant: the Romani elite in the Czech Republic, for instance, appeared to be the most combative (perhaps in response to the severe prejudice they suffered and as a result of their greater segregation and isolation in the region), while political and public associations of the Hungarian Roma enjoyed the most cooperation with the majority population and with the government.[3]

RESPONSES OF THE NATIONAL STATE

The sociological-anthropological literature on Romani ethnic mobilization includes diverse positions on this process. According to Gheorge and Mirga, the Roma are changing from a social group into an ethnically mobilized community holding common interests.[4] Puxon believes that mobility was merely a response to (physical) anti-Roma violence which was marked in many places, especially in the early years of the regime changes.[5] An entire generation of young Roma was suddenly forced to react to the discrimination launched by the majority in a manner not experienced since the establishment of the communist regimes, and to re-define themselves, since they often felt themselves partially excluded from the new national communities (primarily in the Czech Republic). Spontaneous and violent actions against the Roma had occurred sporadically in the region in the past thirty years. However, this aggression should not be viewed as unexpected after a prolonged period of ethnic peace. Besides programs and political ideologies, manifestations of prejudice, believed non-existent since 1945–46, were to appear in those years in several areas of life. Although open confrontation had been rare, the majority populations of the state socialist years accepted the ideological status quo (which meant imposing Roma programs from the top down), but did not integrate Roma into many other areas of everyday social life.[6]

Why were the Roma singled out for such hostile ethnic attacks? Vermeersch claims that the first Romani mobilization wave can be explained both by the weakening of the state and by a vacuum in public administration, as well as by the pro-Roma demonstrations of the new democratic, post-dissident organizations.[7] This was true to some extent for Czechoslovakia in those years, but not for Hungary where, in an ethnically more homogenous society, ethnic mobilization in the form of minority-majority confrontation was not on the agenda from the outset and where the national state, liberated from Soviet influences, was not weakened as in Czechoslovakia before the collapse of the federal state. Other analyses suggest that international human rights and democracy-building organizations that appeared in the new democracies of the region may have played an important role in organizing the social programs of the transition in the early 1990s. Human Rights Watch and the Ford Foundation appeared in those years in Central Europe and the Soros network expanded its scope of operation. In many respects, the style of politics and the structure of inter-group power relations in emerging Roma elites were developed under their influence and these relationships survived periods of weakening or even the partial disappearance of organizational frameworks of Roma politics from this milieu in the 1990s. Both well-structured human rights arguments and ethnically defined social policies emerged at that time. In the 1990s Czech and Slovak Roma made serious efforts to set up their own parties, but these organizations did not grow into decisive forces anywhere.[8] The self-government (local independence in decision making) solutions of the Hungarian ethnic minority formally excluded or curbed the process of party organization, although various camps did emerge.

The appearance of the term 'Roma' in Central European political language after the regime changes is an important element of the new self-definition. This collective noun first appeared in the terminology of West European (Gypsy) interest organizations at the end of the 1960s and early 1970s. In 1971, activists of several countries created the World Roma Congress (WRC), which subsequently inspired the creation of organizations such as the IRU (International Roma Union) and the RNC (Roma National Congress). Articles published as early as the 1970s held that the many negative attributes associated with the word 'Gypsy' in the majority language meant it would be simpler to substitute the term 'Roma.'[9] By the 1990s the new political label had not yet fully replaced the term 'Gypsy' in political language. Hungary adopted it least; even the Minority Local Government established by the Hungarian authorities used the appellation 'Gypsy' in 1993. However, the term 'Roma' contributed to the re-arrangement of the ethno-political language and also perhaps to the ethno-genesis and consolidation of a political ethos. It should be noted that only some Central European Gypsies were actually ready to accept becoming part of a unified Roma political community. The liberal Hungarian public and social researchers are almost unanimous in attributing this partial rejection of the 'ethnic way of thinking' to the discriminative environment and to the survival of the former state pattern of assimilation. Others hold that it follows from the pre-modern nature of the Roma who cannot define themselves in ethnic-national frameworks derived from modern concepts.[10] Still other theorists insist that many of the uncertainties about formulating concepts of belonging to a community are rooted in administrative ineptitude. In any event, for the Romani elite and Romani activists, participation in collective actions, protests and in the struggle against discrimination has had a consolidating effect and has helped to build an ethnic community. The boundaries and networks so important to ethnic definition may well emerge in just such situations and in various places.

The Central European Romani organizations of the 1990s, however, were not mass movements. They could move any sizeable Romani mass at best for protest movements connected with concrete locations and events and for a short time. Consequently, the question was how the ethnic elite could convey the experiences of a new movement and the positive sentiments of unity to others—the Romani masses whose experience of their Romani identity consisted exclusively of negative events rooted primarily in local conflicts and suffering due to various forms of exclusion. Consequently, the Romani experiences of the ethnic elite and of the Romani masses may differ fundamentally, at least in respect to a 'national' or ethnic way of thinking.

The images conveyed by the media further complicate the situation. The choreography of modern majority-minority conflicts is much influenced by the way these clashes are portrayed there. The Central European media of the 1990s conveyed an important message—insofar as it reached them—to Romani groups which, out of necessity, had experienced the limitations of life's opportunities almost exclusively through what went on around them. In fact, through the tone and presentation of the Romani conflicts they learnt that there were forces in the majority society that opposed discrimination and were trying to persuade the state to take serious action against it. Thus, between a seemingly pro-discrimination local administration and the opponents of discrimination in public life, the Roma may have had some room for maneuver. One should not paint an idealistic picture of the Central European media, but for the most part, it reported fairly in the 1990s and adopted some degree of political correctness in the presentation of minority affairs, a situation that is now the norm.

Formulation of the majority media image of the Roma has become the focus of majority enlightenment campaigns as well as of international human rights organizations. In addition to this struggle in the public arena, in Hungary this picture has been supplemented by partial modernization of the traditional Romani entertainer image. The stereotypes of the Gipsy entertainer, as an organic part of the local village community, such as that held by the Hungarians, never existed among the Czech and Slovak publics. While the market for 'Gypsy musician' communities is shrinking and the one-time Romani elite belonging to those communities is diminishing, the Romani heroes of highly popular soap operas of commercial television stations serve to eliminate prejudices—although perhaps not enough to influence the majority population. However, success in widely publicized local conflicts, with the support of human rights activists from outside, against discrimination in services or in schools, certainly adds to the growing self-esteem of the local Romani population.

In the mid-1990s, a new politically charged and internationalized manner of rhetoric emerged in various forms in the region. The Czech Romani discourse was the first to become imbued not only with ethnic, but with national ideology, too. In the 1990s only a minority of the Slovak and Hungarian minority elites adopted this new language. Integration emerged not as a personal decision synchronizing individuals and the majority represented by the state but as a deal between communities and representatives of political and economic power. Since Central Europe did not have mass immigration during this period, no integration debate measurable by West European standards existed there. But in the ongoing discussion about integration and adaptation strategies of marginal groups many actors on the majority side used immigrant integration policy arguments, substituting the local Romani population for the almost non-existent immigrants.

As a result, although legal regulations in the region stipulated equal treatment for all minorities, the dominant trend in the public discourse was to treat the Roma somewhere between 'minority' and 'immigrant' issues, in Hungary, closer to the former and in Czechoslovakia, to the latter. Only in the second half of the 1990s were there specialized social and educational programs for the Roma. The concept of a 'non-territorial European people' began to appear among groups of Roma elite actively concerned with identity matters, although the notion never really became popular in Central Europe, except among the Czech Romani elite. International networks of Romani activists discovered and actively shaped this image for themselves relatively early. In fact, this concept is well represented in the articles of US-based Romani linguist Ian Hancock. According to him, it is, or could be, some sort of national liberation movement.[11]

However, since in contrast to the archetypes of such movements, national liberation would not really make sense in the Romani context (who would be the foreign oppressors and what political unit would be established if the movement were successful?), even a symbolic 'external homeland' has become important. Stressing 'common Indian roots' may serve this purpose, and transnational aspirations using 'Europe' as a symbolic reference are also used to this end.

The activities that led to the first Roma documents of the Council of Europe and the OSCE tried the 'transnational' option of a symbolic external homeland in the middle of the 1990s. These first specialized European Romani programs used human rights language as a kind of international moral standard and gradually reached a transnational community approach, which could be called 'post-national citizenship.'[12] In the eyes of some groups this special status of the Roma seems to have been reinforced by Decision No. 1203 of the Council of Europe, which refers to Roma as 'a true European minority'.

In contrast to this approach, or rather paradoxically mixed with it, is a debate in many places about authenticity, namely: Who is a true Roma? And consequently, who is authorized to represent the Roma *vis-à-vis* the outside world? Would it be the new Romani 'national intelligentsia,' which has emerged as a partner in international philanthropy and human rights activism? Or, are the 'authentic leaders' those that live and suffer together with the oppressed masses? For example, local Romani activists often participated in pickets and others protest actions against the European Roma Rights Centre (ERRC) in Budapest in the late 1990s claiming that it was not working with 'real Roma,' that is, those fighting exclusion via integration of the Romani masses.[13] In any event, the debate among Romani community builders about whether the nation or any other community-building principle could and should be used as a mobilizing vision has by no means ended.

In contrast to the concept of the 'post-national citizen,' Romani government policy makers and movements determine the conduct of Romani communities in relation to the national states that surround them. Foreign writers often present the Hungarian national minority self-government of the 1990s as a successful paradigm.[14] Interestingly, international recognition of this model, which has since been accused of corruption, political disintegration and lameness, has greatly increased and it is cited in many places as possibly worth replicating. Central European communities are not launching joint projects for influencing the majority population. Moreover, since no lasting and visible alliances of larger minorities wielding influence are perceptible anywhere, no such Romani or other minority groupings have appeared which could trigger breakthroughs on some important points. Nor have attempts been made on the part of the Hungarian elite of Slovakia or Romania to help the Roma build their own minority institutions on the lines of already existing Hungarian networks. Rather, some kind of latent competitive situation is apparent. Increasing self-consciousness of Hungarian-speaking Romani groups may lead to new identities. In many regions of Slovakia, Roma who previously pronounced themselves to be Hungarian are now publicly declaring their Romani identity. Consequently, the decrease of official Hungarian and Slovakian minority numbers is narrowing the political base of Hungarian minority elites. In Slovakia due to past political dominance but also actual population numbers, Hungarians are still the most significant minority in the country and are broadly represented in the political system. However, consolidation of the political consciousness of Romani communities and demographic processes may, within a short time, make the Roma the largest minority in the countries in question, one that would require special treatment and political recognition.

The possible impact of such a development on the political elites of other minorities cannot be underestimated. In Hungary, in the realm of symbolic politics, certain forms of Romani-Jewish relations also exist, primarily in association with Holocaust memory, but also in the context of liberal human rights programs. In the Czech Republic and Slovakia, a sufficiently large and influential Jewish community for such an alliance is lacking. However, arguments over cooperation may be superficial and asymmetric. While some Romani elite groups may consider the Jewish community a real ally in their fight against exclusion, others, albeit less numerous, regard them as competitors who were able to demonstrate their historical suffering to the majority, and received moral, cultural and even financial compensation, while the Roma were less successful. At the same time the Romani masses, as the marginalized poor, are not really interested in differences within the upper-middle classes, whom they view as monolithically affluent and culturally alien.

EUROPEAN IMPACT

In the 1990s the emergence of various international human rights organizations, and later the Council of Europe and the Organization for Security and Cooperation in Europe (OSCE), and from 1997–98 perhaps the EU, fundamentally redrew the language used by governments, public administration and the regional media in Central European Roma policy. Various European institutions triggered the actual turnabout since the majority political elites that sought membership in them depended greatly on the degree to which others considered them 'democratic,' and were consequently also willing to adopt a major change of style.

For years the EU considered minority issues the internal affairs of member states. Later, although not as obligatory laws but rather as a kind of 'common European standard,' there appeared various desirable minority policy principles (European Convention on Human Rights, Copenhagen Document – 1990, Framework Convention for the Protection of National Minorities – 1995, Article 13 of the Amsterdam Treaty – 1997, EU Charter on Fundamental Rights – 2000). In June 2000 a general anti-discrimination program was adopted under the name 'EU Race and Employment Directives'. The deadline for implementation of the directives in the member states was July 2004. However, according to ENAR (European Network Against Racism) few member states have complied.[15]

Prior to 1990 the EU did not concern itself with West European Roma. Although in the years 1986–89 it commissioned research on the schooling of Roma children,[16] this remained an isolated attempt. Undoubtedly the most important Roma policy documents of the 1990s originated in the OSCE and the Council of Europe (in 1993 and in 2000 the reports of the OSCE High Commissioner on National Minorities [HCNM] and the Verspaget Report in the Council of Europe in 1995). These texts reflect the views of predominantly non-Romani experts, which for some time also become 'official,' and 'European'. The first OSCE HCNM report, which appeared under the auspices of the office and the high commissioner personally, linked the difficulties of the Roma to regime change and transition. These problems are viewed as serious as discrimination, and the majority of Roma find it hard to overcome them. The second report was prepared by an American expert on autonomy, who was not especially interested in the specificities of the East European post-socialist transition. For him the Roma issue was one of discrimination and could be treated as a cultural problem. His conclusions were also based on that understanding: if the Roma were allowed more active involvement in political decisions, the problem would become more manageable.[17]

In the Council of Europe, a great deal of analytic work grew out of the ambitions of Dutch representative Geraldine Verspaget. It was also she who headed the work committee that prepared the report under her name. There is nothing wrong with this in itself (such individual political profile-building efforts can also be observed among some Hungarian European Parliament members, for example, Katalin Lévai). However, Verspaget's starting point was an old-fashioned 'ethnographic' Romani image, which was not entirely free of certain 'good savage' stereotypes, and surprisingly, she devoted much space to the study of 'nomadism' as a positive tradition. In fact, she concluded that it was precisely the 'communist coercion to settle' that destroyed the traditionally happy communities.[18]

At the beginning, despite these studies, officials involved in the eastern enlargement of the EU did not consider the Roma problem a matter of importance, and although when established, the Directorate General for Enlargement regularly put the question on its agenda, even by late 2005 no official had been put in charge of this problem in Brussels. In fact, the EU and the West in general began to take the Roma conflict seriously only after large numbers of Roma immigrants from Central and Eastern Europe began seeking political asylum, or at least protection, within their borders. From then on they included the Roma problem among the tasks they mapped out for candidate countries as urgently requiring a solution. The annual Brussels country reports regularly recorded any progress made, or lack of it, as well as an assessment of any new solutions. EU enlargement politicians consider social policy adjustment in the region—not necessarily in Romani matters alone— potentially the most important outcome of their work.[19]

As a result of this special Brussels attention, Roma policies of the regional governments are more consistent and more similar to one another than is customary for other sectored or area policies at times of transfer of power between conservative and social democratic governments. The programs promoting preparation of the countries for accession had elements expressly designed to aid the integration of the Roma. In most cases the PHARE program was used for this purpose.[20]

Between 1993 and 1999 the six candidate states directly affected received via this channel 20 million Euro for various Roma projects. With the approach of accession this amount increased to 11.7 million in 1999 and to 31.5 million by 2001. Although the 66.5 million Euro allocated to this area between 1993 and 2001 is dwarfed by the overall amount of assistance received by these countries (large local government contributions were made to these aid amounts and the programs were separated—as stipulated by the EU—from other projects), the role of this assistance is considered rather significant.

CENTRAL EUROPEAN PHARE ROMA PROGRAM FUNDING

	1993–1997	1999	2000	2001	Total
Bulgaria	1,565	500	3,500	6,350	11,915
Czech Republic	1,778	500	2,850	3,000	8,128
Hungary	1,919	6,900	2,500	5,000	16,319
Romania	2,661	0	1,000	7,000	10,661
Slovakia	1,935	3,800	3,800	10,000	19,535
Total	9,858	11,700	13,650	31,350	66,558

Source: European Commission, Directorate General for Enlargement, 2002

CONCLUSION

Since the accession, it is no longer clear who exactly is continuing and in what form the philosophy of Brussels Roma policy. Naturally, the divisions responsible for the enlargement no longer exist, the relevant Brussels programs having been dismantled, and the political staff of the Community only reacts to domestic conflicts in member states if they become international scandals. Satisfactory Roma programs could be developed from structural funds. However, local Roma programs must compete with all other local economy-building and social policy projects; therefore for the time being it cannot be foreseen how far the Romani elites, and those who call them their allies, will be capable of doing this. Perhaps the program based on the Open Method of Coordination adopted in March 2000 might be suitable for monitoring the situation at the European level. This program stipulates among its objectives social integration in general and the inclusion of minorities, in particular. Since its development, indicators (18 so-called Laeken indicators) have also been defined to monitor their fulfillment. The member states must develop action programs for the implementation of the program objectives and make regular reports on progress. In principle, this could amount to some sort of coordinated program for fighting Roma poverty, but the procession of social inequalities—even if they are ethnically tainted—is returned or even pushed back to national competencies. Romani elites are losing their transnational sources for movement organization and the existing common legal guarantees within the EU focus more on individual freedoms and spaces of action and much less on collective cultural or other sorts of autonomy. Romani political identity building in Central Europe in the coming years will be negotiated primarily not with Brussels or Strasbourg but with the national governments and with local public opinion dominated by non-Romani media and leaders. Most of the Romani intelligentsia is badly prepared for this political round. The space for EU action is there; however it is not really clear through which channels and tools it could be exercised even with that intensity of pressure observed in the debates prior to accession. On the transnational level Romani identity building has a much weaker umbrella now than prior to 2004.

NOTES

1.   Mária Neményi and Júlia Szalai (eds.), *A kisebbség kisebbsége* (Minority of the Minorities) (Budapest, 2005).
2.   Yasemin Soysal, "Changing Citizenship in Europe," in D. Cesarini and M. Fulbrook (eds.), *Citizenship, Nationality and Migration in Europe* (London, 1996), pp. 17–29.
3.   Gabor Kertesi, *Megalazottak és megszomotitottak* (Budapest, 1998); Agnes Diosi, *Kívül, vagy belül? A cigányság és a Magyar társadalom* (Beszélő, 2000), pp. 4, 29-38.
4.   Nicolae Gheorghe and Andrzej Mirga, *The Roma in the 21st Century: A Policy Paper* (Princeton, 1998).
5.   Grattan Puxon, "The Romani Movement: Rebirth and the First World Romani Congress," in Thomas Acton Thomas (ed.), *Scholarship and the Gypsy Struggle* (University of Hertfordshire Press, 2000), pp. 94-113.
6.   Zdenek Uherek, "Roma in the Council of Europe," in B. Müller (ed.), *The Council of Europe after Enlargement. An Anthropological Enquiry* (Praha, 1999), pp. 38–45.
7.   Peter Vermeersch, "Minority Policy in Central Europe: Exploring the Impact of the EU's Enlargement Strategy," *Global Review of Ethnopolitics* 2 (Jan. 2004), pp. 3-19.
8.   In June 1990 five Roma on the OF list of the new anti-communist bloc were elected to the Czech National Council, but the Communists also managed to

get Roma into the Council on their own list. A Roma representative was elected to the Slovak National Council, too. In 1999 there were already five registered Roma parties in the Czech Republic; at the same time, 14 Roma parties could be found on the list of registered parties of the Slovak Ministry of Interior. However, the political power of these parties is not even worth mentioning. Even the most successful of them, the ROI (Roma Civil Initiative), only managed to get 0.67 percent of the vote in 1994.

9. Peter Vermeersch, "Roma Identity and Ethnic Mobilization in Central European Politics," ECPR joint sessions, Grenoble, 6-11 April 2001.
10. Jana Plichtova, "Czechoslovakia as a Multicultural State in the Context of the Region," in: *Minorities in Central and Eastern Europe* (London, 1998), pp. 11-19.
11. E.g., I. Hancock, "The Struggle for the Control of Identity," *Transitions* 4. (1997), pp. 35-44.
12. See Soysal, "Changing Citizenship in Europe," pp. 17-29.
13. On Council of Europe policies, see MG-S-ROM 2000 [17], "Activities of the Council of Europe concerning Roma/Gypsies and Travellers," Strasbourg, 2000.
14. Neményi and Szalai, *A kisebbség kisebbsége.*
15. Boris Tsilevich, "EU Enlargement and the Protection of National Minorities – Opportunities, Myths and Prospects," 2001, www.eumap.org; Andre Liebich, "Ethnic Minorities and Long-Term Implications of EU Enlargement," 1998, www.iue.it/rsc/WP-texts/98_49t.html
16. Martin Kováts, "Problems of Intellectual and Political Accountability in Respect of Emerging European Roma Policy," Paper presented at the Romani Studies Seminar, University of Greenwich, 11 Jan., 2001.
17. Günther Verheugen, "Entering the Final Stage," speech at the *Economist* conference, Vienna, 2 June 2002.
18. Uherek, "Roma in the Council of Europe," pp. 38-45.
19. Verheugen, "Entering the Final Stage"; Michal Vasecka (ed.), *Ca Cipen Pal o Roma. Suhrnna sprava o Romoch na Slovensku* (Bratislava, 2002).
20. 2003 Activity Report. "Activities Relating to Roma, Gypsies and Travellers," Brussels, Directorate General III Migration Department, Nov. 2003.

LIST OF CONTRIBUTORS

VIOREL ACHIM is a Senior Researcher at the Nicolae Iorga Institute of History, Bucharest, Romania. His research interests include political and confessional history of southeast Europe in the 13th–15th centuries, ethnic minorities in Romania in the 1930s and 1940s, population policy in Romania during World War II, and history of the Gypsies (Roma) in southeast Europe. He edited (and provided an introductory study to) *Documente privind deportarea ţiganilor în Transnistria* (Documents Concerning the Deportation of Gypsies to Transnistria), 2 vols. (2004), and co-edited with Constantin Iordachi, *România şi Transnistria: Problema Holocaustului. Perspective istorice şi comparative* (Romania and Transnistria: The Holocaust Issue. Historical and Comparative Perspectives) (2004).

KATALIN KATZ is a Lecturer at the School of Social Work, the Hebrew University of Jerusalem, and Head of the Field Work Training Department. Her academic interests include individual and collective memory; practice, theory and training in social work; minorities-majorities, center-periphery and intercultural relations; and researching the Holocaust memories of the Roma (Gypsies). She works with and for the Roma people in Hungary. Her work "The Porrajmos in Hungary," in K. Fings (ed.), *The Gypsies during the Second World War*, Vol. 3, is forthcoming.

GILAD MARGALIT is a Senior Lecturer in the General History Department of the University of Haifa. His main field of research interest is postwar German coping with the Nazi past. Among his publications is the book, *Germany and Its Gypsies. A Post-Auschwitz Ordeal*, published in 2002.

YARON MATRAS is Professor of Linguistics at the University of Manchester, England, and editor of the interdisciplinary journal *Romani Studies*.

His main research interests include sociolinguistics and linguistic typology, language minorities, and dialects, and he specializes in Romani, German, and various languages of the Near East. *Romani: A Linguistic Introduction* (2002) is one of his more recent publications.

PÁL TAMÁS is Professor of Sociology, Director of the Institute of Sociology of the Hungarian Academy of Sciences and a well-known media commentator. He specializes in societal conflicts, especially in post-communist societies, ethnic issues, EU enlargement, and social science research. He has served as Visiting Professor and Research Fellow at US and European universities.

SHULAMITH SHAHAR is Professor Emeritus in the Department of History, Tel Aviv University. Laureate of the Israel Prize, she is a world-renown expert on Early Modern European history. Among her numerous publications are *The Fourth Estate: A History of Women in the Middle Ages* (1983), *Childhood in the Middle Ages* (1990), and *The Gypsies: The Nomads of Europe* (2006; in Hebrew).

EVA SOBOTKA is an Administrator for Communication and External Relations at the European Monitoring Centre on Racism and Xenophobia (EUMC) in Vienna. Her research interests include EU enlargement, contemporary issues of racism, anti-Semitism and xenophobia in Europe, and formation of policy towards ethnic minorities in Europe. She regularly publishes in the journals *Politologicky casopis*, *Journal for Ethnic and Minority Issues*, and *Roma Rights and Romani Studies*, and in 2004 contributed the chapter "Roma in Hungary; Minorities in Hungary," in Karl and Stefan Wolf, *Ethnopolitical Encyclopedia* (2004).

RONI STAUBER is a Senior Research Fellow at the Stephen Roth Institute and the Department of Jewish History, Tel Aviv University. His main areas of teaching and research include modern anti-Semitism, and the Holocaust and its impact on Israeli society and on Israeli–German relations. He is the author of *Lesson for This Generation—Holocaust and Heroism in Israeli Public Discourse in the 1950s* (2000; won the 2002 Eish Shalom Prize), and *Ideology and Memory* (forthcoming). He is co-editor of the annual survey *Antisemitism Worldwide*, as well as of the volume *Antisemitism and Terror* (2003).

ERIKA THURNER is Professor of Political Science and Modern History at Leopold Franzens University in Innsbruck. She has also taught at the Universities of Innsbruck, Salzburg, Linz and Vienna. The main topics of her research are Nazi policy and persecution of Roma and Sinti, as well as ethnicity and nationalism, migration and minority problems, the women's question, and gender studies. She has received several Austrian and US awards for her research work.

RAPHAEL VAGO is a Senior Lecturer in the Department of History, and Senior Research Fellow at the Stephen Roth Institute and the Cummings Center for Russian and East European Studies, at Tel Aviv University. His main areas of teaching and research include modern history of central and Eastern Europe, anti-Semitism, Holocaust and Holocaust denial, nationalism, minorities and ethnicity, post-communist systems and European integration. He was a member of the International Commission of Historians on the Holocaust in Romania and general editor of the four-volume English edition of *The History of Jews in Romania*.

PETER WIDMANN is a political scientist at the Center for Research on Antisemitism at the Technical University Berlin. He has published works on Sinti and Roma and on minority policies, and his current research focuses on the history of German criminal biology, 1890–1960. Among his recent publications are: "Fortwirkende Zerrbilder. Sinti und Roma im Nationalsozialismus und im Nachkriegsdeutschland," in: Sibylle Quack (ed.), *Dimensionen der Verfolgung. Opfer und Opfergruppen im Nationalsozialismus* (2003), and "Das Erbe des Ausschlusses. Sinti und Jenische in der kommunalen Minderheitenpolitik Nachkriegsdeutschlands," in: Yaron Matras, Hans Winterberg and Michael Zimmermann (eds.), *Sinti, Roma, Gypsies. Sprache— Geschichte—Gegenwart* (2003).

MICHAEL ZIMMERMANN (1951–2007) worked as a historian with the city of Essen (directing an exhibition project on Essen under National Socialist rule), and was an assistant professor at Bochum University; he was also a visiting professor at the Institute for Contemporary History at the University of Vienna. He published many works on the history of Gypsies in Germany and Central Europe, and on the history of German Jewry, as well as on the subjects of National Socialism and racism in general. He co-edited the volume with Yaron Matras and Hangs Winterberg, *Sinti, Roma, Gypsies. Sprache—Geschichte—Gegenwart* (2003).

INDEX